LESSON PLANS MANUAL TO ACCOMPANY

MOVING & LEARNING

The Elementary School Physical Education Experience

THIRD EDITION

BEVERLY NICHOLS, Ph.D.
Revised by Eddie G. Bedford

Mosby

Dedicated to Publishing Excellence

 Mosby

Dedicated to Publishing Excellence

Copyright © 1994 by Mosby–Year Book, Inc.

11830 Westline Industrial Drive
St. Louis, Missouri 63146

Printed in the United States of America

INTRODUCTION

This lesson plans manual has been developed for use with <u>Moving and Learning, The Elementary School Physical Education Experience"</u>. It is designed to demonstrate how the concepts, skills, and activities in the text may be used in a variety of teaching situations. The manual gives examples of lessons for elementary school children in a variety of activities and at varying developmental levels. Each lesson includes a statement of the day's objectives, and the development of fitness, motor skills, and movement concept activities. Where appropriate, a culminating activity for the lesson is included which brings together the various parts of the lesson. Material is referenced to the pages in the text where the information needed by the teacher may be found. While a variety of teaching strategies are suggested, each lesson maximizes the activity time for each child in the class. Rather than a cookbook format, selected lessons are provided for various stages of activity development enabling you to see a progression in learning, and to develop your own lesson plans for each developmental level. Additionally, the manual is perforated and three-hole punched for convenience of use.

It is imperative to understand that the single most critical factor in the lesson or unit is the teacher. Your creativity, selection of equipment, creative utilization of facilities and equipment, understanding and awareness of students' abilities, and ability to observe, evaluate and reteach during a given lesson or unit will determine the success of your physical education program. Rather than a yearly plan of lessons, this manual provides general, rather than specific, guidelines because of the vast differences in teaching situations, facilities, equipment, class size, and teaching styles.

Using the manual:
I. UNITS
   The units follow those in the text both in topics and levels.

II. LEVELS
   Because they assist in identifying the developmental needs of individuals for motor, cognitive, and social skills, the manual is organized by the four developmental levels used in your text. Using these four levels provides a wider range for skill and concept teaching. Each teacher must look at a given class and determine what level is best for that class.

III. LESSONS
   Children need time in developing the unit content if meaningful learning is to take place. Most

units are developed for ten lessons at each level which represents a minimum number of lessons for developing the skills and knowledge. Each plan represents one lesson in the unit. Three or four plans are provided: one early in the unit, one near the middle, and one late in the unit. From this progression, a teacher can see the progress, format, skills, concepts, activities and culmination of each unit. This format allows for the variety of differences described above, and allows teachers to create their own lessons adapted to the needs of the children in the class.

IV. SPECIFIC OBJECTIVES/EVALUATIVE CRITERIA

This section outlines the objectives of each lesson, and the criteria by which a teacher will evaluate the student achievement. Learning process is considered in the development of lesson objectives and progression from one lesson to the next.

V. EQUIPMENT

These lessons are developed with the assumption that a teacher strives to have one piece of small equipment for each child and as much larger equipment as possible. The more equipment that is available, the greater the participation and learning which can occur.

VI. OPENING ACTIVITY

This portion of the lesson may last from two to eight minutes and will usually involve a vigorous warmup activity, fun, review of previously taught skills, and some fitness activities. It generally brings the children quickly into movement, as well as preparing them for the lesson activities.

VII. MOTOR SKILLS/MOVEMENT CONCEPTS

This is the focus, or core, of the lesson in which new material is introduced and taught, and old material is reviewed and retaught.

In levels III and IV, "Group discussion/demonstration" is indicated often. This does not indicate a "lecture" style! It will always involve a questioning approach. a student demonstration, student experimentation (on their own) or guided discovery. It may involve a teacher demonstration and/or explanation.

Learning a new skill or concept will always be followed by the opportunity to utilize or practice it in an active (and usually fun) situation.

VIII. CULMINATING ACTIVITY

This is the climax of a lesson. It will utilize the skills and concepts taught during the lesson and bring the lesson to a meaningful ending. If the lesson is particularly active, the culminating activity should include some type of relaxation or cool down activity.

IX. FITNESS

Physical fitness should be an integral part of every lesson. It is most readily accepted by students if it is built into the lesson activities rather than used as a specific exercise warm up. For this reason, we have included fitness development in the regular class activities. It takes creativity, organization, and time, but will result in an appreciation of fitness by the students, rather than a "dread of calisthenics". Occasionally, the fitness activities may include some exercises integrated enjoyably as well.

Throughout the plans, fitness activities are designated into one of three categories: *FC for cardiorespiratory fitness activities; *FF for flexibility fitness activities; and *FS for muscular strength fitness activities. It is extremely important to discuss fitness with the children when a fitness activity is being done. Discussions should include: the muscle groups used, how strength and flexibility are developed, why cardiorespiratory fitness is so important to long-term health, how each of these components relates to a specific activity being taught, and how to perform and measure the fitness skills correctly. Fitness can be fun!

X. CONSCIOUS RELAXATION

Conscious relaxation activities are indicated as *FR in the lessons. It is important to introduce these activities into the lessons especially where the activity has been vigorous and the children need need a calming down activity before proceeding to the next part of the lesson or returning back to the classroom.

XI. SOCIAL SKILLS

The development of social skills should be an important part of the physical education experience. Children should be encouraged to share ideas as well as work cooperative in accomplishing movement tasks. Activities have been added as warm-ups, as well as motor skill and concept activities to enhance the social skills needed in partner and group physical education experiences.

XII. REFERENCES

Whenever further clarification from the text can be helpful, it is cited in the far right-hand column. However, a close working relationship between the text and the lesson plans manual is the best method for thorough teacher preparation.

Just as students need the opportunity to express their creativity within certain learning boundaries, so do teachers. Between the text and the lesson plans, I have given the basic material that should be presented to elementary school children, and a format to assist you in implementing that material. Use this manual to help focus your creativity, teaching style, and individual educational setting to provide an organized and enjoyable movement experience for your students.

I would like to thank Murray Banks for the work he contributed to the first edition of this lesson manual which formed the foundation for this edition.

Teach your students well...

Beverly Nichols

TABLE OF CONTENTS

LEVEL I

SPECIFIC OBJECTIVES/EVALUATIVE CRITERIA   EQUIPMENT

To name and move body parts on self and others.   Carpet squares
 To work cooperatively by moving body parts named by a partner.   Music

----

ACTIVITY	PROCEDURES/ORGANIZATION	POINTS OF EMPHASIS	REFERENCES

I. Opening activity
   a. Jog, skip, or gallop
   to music. (*FC)
	a. In general space. When the music stops sit on a carpet square.	a. Move with flow and speed. Are you breathing hard?	

II. Movement Concepts a. Wiggle your arms, legs, knees, feet, toes, fingers.	a. Seated on carpet square.	a. Correct identification of body parts.	p. 164
b. Touch these body parts to the carpet square: wrist, elbow, ankle, back, heel, chest.	b. Seated beside carpet square.	b. Correct identification of body parts.	
c. Balance the carpet square on your: legs, hands, shoulders, arms, stomach, and back.	c. In self space.	c. Correct identification of body parts. Strength in supporting weight of carpet.	· p. 164
d. Touch these body parts together: toes and fingers, fingers and back, hands out in front of you, hand to	d. Self space on carpet.	d. Correct identification of body parts. Hold body parts in position for 10 seconds. Where to do feel the stretching?	p. 164

opposite foot, elbow to knee. (*FF)

e. Leader selects a body part to move. Partner moves the same part.

e. Choose a partner on the nearest carpet square. Change leaders after one minute. Repeat twice.

e. Correct imitation of body parts. Move body parts in the same manner.

p. 165

III. Culminating Activity

a. How fast can you find your shoulder, knee, elbow, heel, etc

a. Self space on carpet. Teacher gives verbal cues.

a. Quick, but accurate identification of each each body part. Children work together in naming and moving body parts.

b. Carrying carpet on a body part other than the hands.

b. Children carry carpet squares to designated area.

b. Creative selection of a body part. Moving carefully to put carpet away.

3

SPECIFIC OBJECTIVES/EVALUATIVE CRITERIA	EQUIPMENT

To name and move body parts on self and others.
To identify large and small body parts.
To help a partner in achieving movement tasks.

Carpet squares
Beanbags

ACTIVITY	PROCEDURES/ORGANIZATION	POINTS OF EMPHASIS	REFERENCES

I. Opening Activity			
a. Move to music varying locomotor movements used. (*FC)	a. Randomly in general space.	a. Creative movement. How many different ways can you move?	
b. Stretch body parts. (*FF)	b. When music stops, stop on a carpet square. Imitate teacher's stretch. Repeat: move-stretch, move-stretch.	b. "Feel" that body part stretch. Breathe comfortably when stretching.	
II. Movement Concepts			
a. Review lesson #2. Wiggle toes, fingers, nose; twist leg and neck; bend wrist, knee, ankle; curve back, arms, legs; straighten legs, straighten all body parts.	a. Seated on a carpet, facing the teacher.	a. Correct identification of selected body parts. Creative thought in movement. Isolate parts to be moved.	p. 133
b. Your leg is considered a large body part. Move your leg. Can you move another large body part? Another, etc?	b. Self space on a carpet.	b. Correct identification of large body parts.	p. 134

c. The fingers are small body parts. Move your fingers. What are some other small body parts? Move your....	c. Self space on a carpet.	c. Correct identification of small body parts.
		p. 134

d. Balance a bean bag on a large body part. Another. On a small body part.	d. Self space. Bring bean bag from box to self space balancing it on your elbow.	d. Correct identification of large and small body parts.
		p. 133

e. Toss the bean bag to the carpet using several different body parts.	e. Self space on a carpet.	e. Use a variety of body parts. What were some of the body parts used?

f. One person tosses the bean bag and the other catches it on different body parts - large and small, called by the tosser.	f. With a partner, on the nearest carpet.	f. Use a variety of body parts. Toss the beanbag gently so it can be easily received.
		p. 133

g. Hold the beanbag 2-3 inches off the floor with your feet. (*FS)	g. Sitting on a carpet, legs straight.	g. Where do you feel muscles working?

h. Hold the bean bag 2-3 inches above the floor on the back of your hands. (*FS)	h. Lying on a carpet in a prone position.	h. What body parts are working? What muscles are working?

III. Culminating Activity

a. "The body machine". Begin moving one body part, then add another, then another, until the entire body is moving.	a. In self space on a carpet.	a. Can you isolate body parts for particular movements?	p. 165
b. Repeat with a partner, each adding a body part, one moves a large part, and the other adds a small body part.	b. On carpet in self space.	b. Can you isolate body parts for particular movement. Can you work together in moving large and small body parts?	p. 165

6

| SPECIFIC OBJECTIVES/EVALUATIVE CRITERIA | EQUIPMENT |

To move body parts in a variety of ways.   Music
To follow the cues given by a partner.

ACTIVITY	PROCEDURES/ORGANIZATION	POINTS OF EMPHASIS	REFERENCES
I. Opening Activity a. Move to the music, bend, stretch, twist, curl, shake, etc. (*FF)	a. Self space. Verbal cues or demonstration by teacher.	a. Movements go with speed and flow of music.	
II. Movement Concepts a. Move various body parts. Begin with one and gradually add other moving parts.	a. Self space.	a. Review previous lesson, checking for recognition and proper movement of various body parts.	p. 167
b. Move body parts that help you to move in general space. (*FC)	b. General space avoiding others	b. Use a variety of body parts for locomotor movements. Create unusual ways to move in general space.	
c. Flexion-extension How many body parts can you bend? Straighten?	c. Self space.	c. Which body parts can you bend? Straighten? Which muscles make that part bend? Straighten? Which muscles relax when you bend and extend?	p. 167
d. Balance on flexed and extended body parts. (*FS)	d. Self space.	d. Which is easier? Which body parts support weight easier?	p. 168

III. Culminating Activity
a. Partner-leader
Leader uses a variety
verbal cues -extend,
flex, bend, straighten
etc. for various body
parts.

a. In self space with a
partner. One partner is the
leader, the other must follow
the leader's movement instruc-
tions.

a. Can you follow the cues given?
What is another word for bend?
Straighten? Can you work together
in suggesting body parts and
possible movements?

p. 168

         SPECIFIC OBJECTIVES/EVALUATIVE CRITERIA   EQUIPMENT

To identify body parts used.
To assume a variety of body shapes.
To move body parts in a variety of ways.
To work with a partner in moving body parts in different ways.

   ACTIVITY   PROCEDURES/ORGANIZATION   POINTS OF EMPHASIS   REFERENCES

I. Open Activity
   a. "Statue". When music   a. Moving in general space   a. Encourage a variety of shapes
   stops, students "freeze"   to music.   during the activity. Do you
   into statues.   Hold.   feel stretching in any body parts?
   (*FC) (*FF)

   b. "Melting Statue"   b. Self space during final   b. Body parts go from "stiff"   p. 169
   During last statue,   statue, "freeze"melting into statue to "melting" mush.
   begin melting with the   a "heap" on the floor.   Melt very slowly.
   smallest body parts.

II. Movement Concepts
   a. Making body shapes.   a. Self space
      1. Make the shape of   1. Visualize the letter or
      letters, first letter   number and make it. Can you
      of your name, numbers,   describe the shape made?
      your age, etc.

      2. Make a shape sup-   2. Can you keep the same   p. 170
      ported on one body   shape and change the number of
      part, curved and sup-   body parts supporting you?
      ported on three body
      parts, etc.

3. Make large shapes, shrink them to small shapes, maintaining the same shape.

3. "Shrink" slowly while maintaining the shape.

b. Balance on body parts other than your feet. (*FS)_

b. Self space

b. Strong static balance. What body parts did you use? "Feel" muscles working to hold you.

c. Leader moves a body part. Partner moves the same part in a different way.

c. With a partner, someone nearest you, each in own self space. Choose a leader, change leaders after one minute.

c. Describe movements used How many ways could you move the body parts selected? Did you help each other in deciding what body parts to use and how to move them?

p. 170

III. Culminating Activity
   a. "Simon Says". When students miss "Simon's" direction, they must stretch body part for ten seconds, then return to game. (*FS)

a. Class group, facing the teacher.

a. Can you move body parts exactly as "Simon" does?

b . Relax your body. Teacher gives relaxation directions in soft voice, describing how each limb should feel.   (*FR)

b. Self space. Students lying on their backs, eyes closed. When the teacher touches toes, students slowly rise to leave the room.

b. Can you melt, be soft, be heavy, float, and breathe slowly and deeply?

p. 172

SPECIFIC OBJECTIVES/EVALUATIVE CRITERIA	EQUIPMENT

To define self space as the space one occupies within
  normal body extensions.   Bean bags
To move in a variety of ways in self-space.

ACTIVITY	PROCEDURES/ORGANIZATION	POINTS OF EMPHASIS	REFERENCES

I. Opening Activity
  a. Move through space.   a. General and self space.
    1. Jog, run, walk,   1. Anticipate and avoid
    throughout gym.   collision.

    2. Move in one place.   2. Explore variety of move-   p. 175
    (*FC)   ments in one place. Move
                                                            many body parts, many ways.

II. Movement Concepts
  a. Exploring self space.   a. Self space throughout gym,
                                but close to teacher.
    1. Define and describe   1. How far self space extends.   p. 173
    self space. Explore
    all dimensions.

    2. Select a self   2. What are the advantages
    space site.   and disadvantages of close,
                                                            near, spread out and far
                                                            away sites?

  b. Moving in self space.   b. Self space.
    1. Move body parts in   1. Utilize body awareness   p. 174
    and around self space.   activities previously taught,
                                                            but in relation to self space.

2. Move body parts
over, through, beyond,
etc. self space. (*FS)

III. Culminating Activity
a. Explore possible bean
bag activities in self
space.

a. Self space, each with a
bean bag.

2. Same as above, but add
jumping, hopping, leaping, etc.   p. 174

a. Can you control the bean   p. 174
bag in self space? How many
different activities could
you do?

SPECIFIC OBJECTIVES/EVALUATIVE CRITERIA	EQUIPMENT

To move in general space, varying relationships with others.
To identify and define three levels in space.   Bean Bags
To move body parts and the body through space at each level.

ACTIVITY	PROCEDURES/ORGANIZATION	POINTS OF EMPHASIS	REFERENCES

I. Opening Activity
   a. "Follow the Leader". | a. General space, moving | a. Move carefully and under
   Move through general | throughout the gym, in groups | control, avoiding the self
   space. (*FC) | of three. | space of others in your group
   | | and the other groups.

II. Movement Concepts
   a. Move body parts found | a. Self space | a. Creatively vary the body | p. 177
   in the three levels. | | parts moved in each level.

   b. Move body parts from | b. Self space | b. Move body parts from one | p. 177
   one level to another. | | level to another.

   c. Change levels while | c. General space | c. Move with as much of the | p. 177
   moving. (*FC) | | body as possible at the
   | | directed level. Are they
   | | accurately in each level?

   d. Jump at various levels; | d. Self space | d. How far can you jump at | p. 200
   use the standing long | | each level? At which level
   jump. (*FS) | | can you jump the farthest?

2. Move body parts over, through, beyond, etc. self space. (*FS)

2. Same as above, but add jumping, hopping, leaping, etc.

p. 202 - 204

III. Culminating Activity
a. Statues at various levels. Students "melt" or "grow" into various statues at each level. (*FS) (*FF)

a. Self space

a. This is a relaxing activity to finish with. Smooth movements used to form each statue. Balance and hold for several seconds at each level. Stretch body parts (arms and legs) as far out from the center as possible.

SPECIFIC OBJECTIVES/EVALUATIVE CRITERIA   EQUIPMENT

To move through general space changing level.
To define pathways as the line of movement in space.
To identify straight, curved and combination lines as pathways.
To work with a another child in creating and moving along pathways.

ACTIVITY   PROCEDURES/ORGANIZATION   POINTS OF EMPHASIS   REFERENCES

I. Opening Activity
  a. Move at various levels.
    1. Jog, walk, run or   1. General space   1. Change smoothly from one
    gallop at the various   level to another and from one
    levels.   locomotor movement to another.

    2. Stretch arms, then   2. Self space.   2. How high can you raise one
    legs at the various   leg? Raise one arm very high
    levels. (*FC) (*FF)   and the other very low. Stu-
                                                            dents should feel muscles
                                                            stretch as they reach far
                                                            into each level.

II. Movement Concepts
  a. Move from point to   a. General space   a. Select pathways that help   p. 180
  point.   avoid collisions. Make path-
                                                            ways "clean and clear".
    1. How many pathways
    can you use?

    2. Can you use one
    type of pathway up
    and another coming
    back?

b. Move around objects with different pathways. (*FC)

b. General space

b. Move among the cones and people with curved, straight or zigzag pathways identifying which is easiest, most challenging and most fun. p. 181

III. Culminating Activity
  a. Making rope pathways
    1. Draw a pathway with a rope on the floor. How many different ways can you move along your pathway?

1. In partners, in general space, one long rope for each set of partners.

1-2. Define your path (straight, curved lines). Move in a variety of ways. Which did you like best? Can you work with another child in creating a pathway and suggesting ways to move? p. 290

2. Move along someone else's pathway in a way suggested by the creator.

2. One partner stays while the other to other pathways. The remaining child suggests ways to move along the pathway

2. Can you move in the suggested way? How many different ways can you suggest to move?

3. Move along someone else's pathway.

3. In general space, children try rope pathways on the floor.

3. Describe the pathway. What ways did you move? Which were the most challenging?

b. Moving body parts through the air in various pathways.

b. Self space

b. Relaxing activity. Explore ways the hand, foot, head, etc. can move in the air.

| SPECIFIC OBJECTIVES/EVALUATIVE CRITERIA | EQUIPMENT |

To develop an awareness of dynamic and static balance.

To maintain balance in a variety of dynamic and static situations
and/or positions.

To develop the concept of base of support in assisting balance.

To work with a partner in selecting and performing various balance
positions.

| ACTIVITY | PROCEDURES/ORGANIZATION | POINTS OF EMPHASIS | REFERENCES |

| I. Opening Activity
a. "People Dodge" - running throughout general space, dodging all other people. If a collision or contact occurs, both people "take a break" and hold a balanced position for 20 seconds. Gradually narrow the game area. (*FC) (*FF) | a. General space | a. Look for and move into open spaces. As play area narrows, adjust speed and control. Feel the muscles stretch as you balance. | |
| II. Movement Concept
a. Exploring static balance.
　　1. Balance on two body parts, now one, three body parts, four body parts, etc. | a. Self space | 1. Which base of support made balance easier, wide or narrow? Did one body part or several make balance easier? | p. 184 |

2. Repeat, but during
each position lose
your balance, then re-
gain it.

3. Repeat those behav-
iors on a line.

4. How many different
ways can you balance?
(*FS)

III. Culminating Activity
    a. Partner balances -
one partner describes a
balance position (parts
to balance on) and the
other must hold that
balance for 5 seconds.

a. Self space with partner

2. How is balance regained?   p. 184
Is it helpful to use other
body parts to regain
balance?

3. Involve arms and trunk   p. 184
in the balancing process.

4. Unusual ways of balancing - for example, on knees,
buttocks, stomach, heels,
hands, etc. Use muscle
strength to hold the position.

a. Begin with easier balances,   p. 184
progress to combinations of
body parts. Discuss which
were most difficult. Did you
give good suggestions to your
partner? Could they do the
balance?

SPECIFIC OBJECTIVES/EVALUATIVE CRITERIA   EQUIPMENT

To use the concept and skills of static balance.   Hoops or Ropes
To develop the concept and skills of dynamic balance.
To develop an awareness of the use of a variety of positions
    and body parts in balance.
To use a lower center of gravity to maintain balance.
To work with a partner in solving balance challenges.

ACTIVITY	PROCEDURES/ORGANIZATION	POINTS OF EMPHASIS	REFERENCES
I. Opening Activity			
a. "Statues". Students skip, gallop or jog to music. When music stops, each assumes a statue position, balancing on a designated number of body parts. (*FC)	a. General space	a. Hold statue as motionless as possible. "Feel" how the muscles work to balance the body. Are some stretching?	p. 183
II. Movement Concept			
a. Balance while moving.	a. Self space. Each student with a hoop.		
1. With a hoop, balance in a variety of positions (various body parts in and out of the hoop).		1. What body parts did you use to balance? How did you use them?	

2. Same as above, but partner must be "attached".

3. Same as above, but partners are balancing while moving (hopping and holding hands, etc.)

4. Partners hold a position of balance, stretching the various large muscle groups. (*FF)

4. Self space with a partner. Teacher-directed or demonstration.

2. Using each other to assist in establishing and maintaining balance. How did you help each other to maintain your balance?

3. Small, well-timed movements. Attempts at this will be difficult but fun. Emphasis is on holding balance through smaller movements.

4. Slow static stretching, while balancing. Partners using each other to stretch.

p. 185

2. Balance on the hoop on a variety of body parts and positions.

2. Keep center of gravity low. Try to keep body parts off the floor and on the hoop.   p. 184

3. Walk on the hoop, balancing as you go around it.

3. Travel slowly. Use other body parts to help balance (hands or arms).   p. 185

4. Jump into the hoop, maintaining balance on landing. Explore the number of ways this can be done. (*FS)

4. Hold position upon landing. Flex knees, use arms to help hold balance.

III. Culminating Activity
  a. Partner balances.

  a. Self space with a partner.

    1. Partners are given a number. They must balance on that number of body parts together. EXAMPLE: The number four is given. One partner balances on one foot, while the other balances on two hands and one knee for a total of four body parts as base of support.

    1. Center of gravity low, wide base of support for each of the variety of positions.   p. 184

21

SPECIFIC OBJECTIVES/EVALUATIVE CRITERIA	EQUIPMENT

To walk with head up, toes pointing straight ahead and a comfortable stride.

To walk correctly in a variety of directions, pathways, speeds and levels.

To share ideas with a partner for walking in different ways.

24 cones or plastic jars

ACTIVITY	PROCEDURES/ORGANIZATION	POINTS OF EMPHASIS	REFERENCES

ACTIVITY	PROCEDURES/ORGANIZATION	POINTS OF EMPHASIS	REFERENCES
I. Opening Activity a. Walk throughout the gym, moving into every open space. Cover all areas of the gym.	a. General space, walking freely.	a. Head up, toes pointing straight ahead, with a comfortable stride. Avoid contact with other people. Move into open spaces.	p. 197
b. Fitness Activity 1. Crab walk	b. General space	1. Development of arm and shoulder strength. Keep buttocks off the floor.	p. 308
2. Seal crawl (*FS)		2. Use arms for propulsion, keep legs straight.	p. 308
II. Motor Skills/Movement Concepts a. Walking variations	a. General space and self space with teacher providing verbal cues.		
1 . Change directions while walking. In what directions can		1. Change from forward to backward to sideward with little or no hesita-	p. 199

you walk? Can you
change direction
smoothly on the signal?

2. Change pathways while
walking. In what path-
ways can you walk? Can
you walk to a spot using
one pathway and back
using another?

3. Change speed while
walking. How does your
walk change as you in-
crease speed? How did you (*FC)
keep from running? (*FC)

4. Vary the length of
the stride: How small
a step? How long a
step?

III. Culminating Activity
a. 1. Walk pretending you
   are a clown, an old
   person, a soldier, etc.

2. Walk pretending you
are on ice, eggs, mar-
bles, hot pavement, etc.

b. 1. Walk with a partner
   in different ways. Take
    turns suggesting ways to
   walk.

tion. Maintain erect posture and comfortable gait.
Lead with the correct body
surface.

2. Change pathways   p. 199
smoothly. Did your walking
change as you moved in
different pathways?

3. Maintain proper mechan-   p. 199
ics as speed increases.
As speed increases, maintain
walking, avoid running.

4. Maintain proper mechanics
as you change stride.

a. How many ways can you use p. 199
body parts to walk in different ways?

b. With a partner in general   b. How many different ways   p. 199
space.   can you walk with a partner?
                                Did you share ideas?

2. Repeat, walking in
different relationships
- side by side, facing,
one behind the other.

| SPECIFIC OBJECTIVES/EVALUATIVE CRITERIA | EQUIPMENT |

To walk with head up, toes pointing straight ahead and with a
comfortable stride.
To run with head up, arms swinging forward and backward, with
a comfortable stride, lifting knees and landing softly.
To run in a variety of directions, pathways, speeds and levels.
To share ideas with others in creating a 3 part run sequence.

| ACTIVITY | PROCEDURES/ORGANIZATION | POINTS OF EMPHASIS | REFERENCES |

I. Opening Activity			

a. Fitness builders
  1. Wall pushups
  2. Crab walk
  3. Situps
  4. V sit
  (*FS)
	a. Self space. Teacher demonstration in an enjoyable "can you" fashion.	a. Encourage enjoyment in building muscle strength. Perform each activity smoothly, mechanically correct.	p. 258 -262

b. Review walking in general space. Teacher calls or asks for suggestions of variations from lesson 1.	b. General space	b. Head up, toes pointing straight ahead, and with a comfortable stride.	p. 199
II. Motor Skills/Movement Concepts			
a. Running mechanics and variations. (*FC)	a. General space with questioning verbal cues from teacher.	a. Cues should encourage exploration of running mechanics and variations.	

1. Run in general space.

1. Avoid contact with   p. 200
others. Run with control.
Are your arms swinging forward and back? Are your feet
landing softly? Is your head
up? Are you lifting your knees?

2. Change directions
while running. Can you
change direction
smoothly? Have you
tried all directions?

2. How did you adjust your   p. 200
run for different direc-
tions? Be sure to bend forward while running backward.

3. Change pathways while
running. How did your
run differ while moving
in straight lines? Curves?

3. How did you adjust your run   p. 200
to the pathway used?

4. Change the length of
the stride while running.

4. Can you maintain good form   p. 200
with various stride lengths?.

5. Change the speed while
running. How did your
run change moving slowly?
With greater speed?

5. Can you show good run-   p. 200
ning form in slow motion?

b. Stretching the running
muscles with the sit and
reach - hamstring stretch.
(*FF)

b. Self space, demonstration
of the sit and reach - hamstring stretch.

b. Slow, steady stretching.   p. 263
Feel the muscle stretch.

III. Culminating Activity
   a. Running with others.

     1. Groups combine 3 variations of the run (one from each member)

     2. Group changes relationship - side by side, in front of or behind each other.

a. In groups of three. Change groups after each activity.

a. Maintain good running form.   p. 200

     1. Change run smoothly with little hesitation.   p. 200

     2. Adjust run to maintain relationship.   p. 200

SPECIFIC OBJECTIVES/EVALUATIVE CRITERIA	EQUIPMENT
To hop in a rhythmic manner using arms to propel the body and to maintain balance and land softly. To hop in a variety of pathways, directions, speeds and levels recognizing changes needed to vary the skill.	24 hoops

----

ACTIVITY	PROCEDURES/ORGANIZATION	POINTS OF EMPHASIS	REFERENCES

I. Opening Activity
   a. Fitness builders
     1. Inch worm (*FF)
     2. Bear walk
     3. Arm circling (*FS)
	a. Self space. Teacher demonstration in an enjoyable "can you" fashion.	a. As in past lessons, emphasize the enjoyment of activities that can build body strength and flexibility.	p. 309

II. Motor Skills Movement Concepts a. Hopping mechanics and variations. (*FC)	a. General and self space with teacher providing verbal cues. Creative and exploratory cues work best. Frequent rest breaks will be needed. During that time, discussion may take place, as well as flexibility exercises. (*FF)		
1. Hop in self and general space.		1. Maintain proper mechanics; land softly by bending knees; use arms for propulsion and balance; hop in an established rhythm.	p. 203

2. Hop in different directions.

2. How did your hop change as you moved in different directions? p. 206

3. Hop in different pathways.

3. How did your hop change as you moved in different pathways? p. 206

4. Hop at different levels.

4. How did your hop change as you moved at different levels? p. 206

5. Hop at different speeds.

5. How did your hop change as you moved at different speeds? p. 206

6. Hop over the lines.

6. How did your hop change as you moved over the lines? p. 206

III. Culminating Activity

a. "Hoop-Scotch" - hoops are placed in a line, two, then one, etc. Where there are two hoops side by side, place one foot in each. Where there is one hoop, land in that hoop on one foot. Students travel from one and to the other alternating two feet, then one, two feet, then one, very similar to hopscotch, varying their pathways as they move through each formation.

a. Alignment of hoops is as follows:

```
        O O O O
        O O O O O     A
        O O O O

        O O O
        O O O O        B
        O O O

         O O
        O O O          C
         O O
```

Students can begin at C. When they are able to get through game C, they progress to game B. If they are able to make it through game B, they may progress to game A.

a. Maintain proper hopping mechanics, particularly rhythmic hopping from hoop to hoop. Moving at an even, controllable speed. Changing smoothly from two feet to one (jump from hoop). In what pathways can you move? p. 476

| SPECIFIC OBJECTIVES/EVALUATIVE CRITERIA | EQUIPMENT |

To run with control lifting knees, swinging arms forward and
  backward and looking ahead.

To gallop (slide) by leading with one leg and drawing the rear
  leg to close in uneven rhythm.

To gallop in a variety of pathways, directions, speeds and levels
  recognizing changes needed to vary galloping.

4 t0 5 mats
24 cones or plastic jugs

| ACTIVITY | PROCEDURES/ORGANIZATION | POINTS OF EMPHASIS | REFERENCES |

I. Opening Activity
   a. "Race Track"
   A race track with
   curves and turns both
   left and right is
   marked off. Stu-
   dents run as fast as
   they want around the
   race track. When
   tired, they may rest
   in the "pit area".
   When they recover,
   they may race again.

II. Motor Skills/Movement
    Concepts
    a. Galloping (sliding)
    skills and variations.
    (*FC)

a. The race track is essen-
tially an oval with inward
and outward curves on the
sides. Mark the course with
cones, plastic jars, bean
bags, etc. The "pit area"
is a group of mats in the
center.

a. This is a wonderful opportunity for the children to
run their fastest - just for
the joy of it! Encourage pac-
ing for those who tire
quickly. Encourage good running form and mechanics: Lifting knees, looking ahead to see
where they are going and swinging
arms forward and backward.

1. Discussion, demonstration and practice of the uneven rhythm and mechanics of a gallop (slide).

1. Seated in a group and then moving in general space.

1. Galloping has an uneven rhythm. Step and close with the same foot always leading.

p. 205

2. Gallop in different directions.

2. General space with teacher providing verbal cues. Creative and exploratory cues work best.

2. Maintain good gallop (slide) mechanics. Legs relaxed. Rhythm uneven but constant. How did your gallop change as you moved in different directions?

p. 206

3. Gallop in different pathways.

3. General space

3. Maintain good pathways . How did the gallop change as you moved in different pathways?

p. 206

4. Gallop at different speeds.

4. General space

4. Maintain good speed. How did you gallop change as you moved at different speeds?

p. 206

5. Gallop at different levels.

5. General space

5. Maintain good levels. How did your gallop change as you moved at different levels?

p. 206

III. Culminating Activity
   a. "Sharks and Barracudas"

a. Students divided equally into two groups of sharks or barracudas, one group on each end line. Leader calls for galloping or running skills.

a. Assume a position for a quick reverse of pathway to give chase. Tag softly. Can you keep your gallop going as you move in the game?

p. 476

   b. Stretching/Relaxing (*FF)

b. Self space

b. Breathe comfortably while stretching. Stretch thigh and hamstring muscle groups.

SPECIFIC OBJECTIVES/EVALUATIVE CRITERIA	EQUIPMENT

To skip in uneven rhythm, lifting lead leg and swinging arms for height.

To skip in a variety of pathways, directions and speeds recognizing changes neede to vary skipping.

To move in rhythm with a partner and to an underlying beat.

Record: "Did You Ever See A Lassie"

ACTIVITY	PROCEDURES/ORGANIZATION	POINTS OF EMPHASIS	REFERENCES

ACTIVITY	PROCEDURES/ORGANIZATION	POINTS OF EMPHASIS	REFERENCES
I. Opening Activity			

a. Fitness builders
  1. Modified situps
  2. Wall pushups
  3. Crab walk
  4. Bear walk (*FS)
	a. Self space. Teacher demonstration in an enjoyable "can you" fashion.	a. Feel the muscle groups working. Perform each activity in a smooth, controlled movement.	p. 258-62

II. Motor Skills/Movement Concepts a. Skipping skills and variations (*FC)			
1. Discussion/demonstration of the mechanics and rhythm of skipping.	1. Seated in a group	1. Compare uneven rhythm to that of galloping. Legs loose and relaxed.	p. 206
2. Skip in different pathways.	2. General space with teacher providing verbal cues. Creative and explorative cues work best.	2. Maintain proper skipping mechanics and rhythm. Legs relaxed. Arm swing relaxed but strong. How did skip change as you moved in different pathways?	p. 206

3. Skip in different directions.	3. General space.	3. How did skip change as you moved in different directions? p. 200
4. Skip at different speeds.	4. General space.	4. How did skip change as you moved at different speeds? p. 200
5. Skip with a partner.	5. General Space. Help children find a partner close by.	5. How did your skip change as you moved with a partner? p. 200

III. Culminating Activity

a. Lobby Lou. If time, do this dance two times, with stretching and discussion between the two.	a. Large single circle. See explanation in text.	a. Skip in rhythm with the music. Take small skips to help stay with the music. p. 396
b. Stretch upper legs, shoulders and arms. (*FF)	b. Large single circle. Teacher demonstration and lead.	b. Static stretching of the skipping muscles. Discussion of skipping mechanics in the dance "Lobby Lou".

SPECIFIC OBJECTIVES/EVALUATIVE CRITERIA	EQUIPMENT

To start using body parts in different ways.
To start with feet in forward stride position, knees
  bent, body leaning forward and arms ready to drive.
To start various locomotor movements in different directions.
To stop with feet in a forward stride position, knees bent
  and body weight over the base of support.
	Variety of music

ACTIVITY	PROCEDURES/ORGANIZATION	POINTS OF EMPHASIS	REFERENCES
I. Opening Activity			
a. Move to music, stop- ping when music stops. (*FC)	a. General space	a. Locomotor movements must vary to suit the tempo and rhythm of music. Stop when music stops and hold position.	
b. Discussion of move- ment to music, stopping techniques.	b. Group with teacher-led questioning.	b. Flexion of knees and ankles. Absorb force with legs, feet, toes and arms.	p. 208
c. Stretching during discussion., (*FF)	c. Group with teacher-led flexibility exercise.	c. Stretching hamstrings, lower back and abdominal muscles.	
II. Motor Skills/Movement Concepts			

a. Starting activities
  1. Start with feet in
  a variety of positions.
  Which works best?
	a. Self and general space.	1. Feet comfortably apart,
		knees and ankles flexed.
			p. 208

2. Start with upper body
in a variety of posi-
tions. Which works best?

2. Slight bend at waist.

3. Start with arms in
various positions. Which
works best?

3. Arm action adds momentum
to the start.

4. Start running, hopping.
galloping, etc. to move foreward, backward and sideways.

4. Blending use of above body
part positions for a well-
balanced start. How did your
start change as you moved in
different directions?

III. Culminating Activity
    a. "Jet Pilot"

a. Children in a single
line at one boundary line
of playing area.

a. Proper starting technique
provides quicker start and
greater speed; distance can be
covered more quickly . Stop in
control on the line.

p. 467

SPECIFIC OBJECTIVES/EVALUATIVE CRITERIA	EQUIPMENT

To start using body parts in different ways.
To start with feet in forward stride position, knees
  bent, body leaning forward and arms ready to drive.
To start various locomotor movements in different directions.
To stop with feet in a forward stride position, knees bent
  and body weight over the base of support.

Variety of music

ACTIVITY	PROCEDURES/ORGANIZATION	POINTS OF EMPHASIS	REFERENCES

ACTIVITY	PROCEDURES/ORGANIZATION	POINTS OF EMPHASIS	REFERENCES
I. Opening Activity			
a. Move to music, stopping when music stops. (*FC)	a. General space	a. Locomotor movements must vary to suit the tempo and rhythm of music. Stop when music stops and hold position.	
b. Discussion of movement to music, stopping techniques.	b. Group with teacher-led questioning.	b. Flexion of knees and ankles. Absorb force with legs, feet, toes and arms.	p. 208
c. Stretching during discussion., (*FF)	c. Group with teacher-led flexibility exercise.	c. Stretching hamstrings, lower back and abdominal muscles.	
II. Motor Skills/Movement Concepts			
a. Starting activities 1. Start with feet in a variety of positions. Which works best?	a. Self and general space.	1. Feet comfortably apart, knees and ankles flexed.	p. 208

2. Start with upper body in a variety of positions. Which works best?

3. Start with arms in various positions. Which works best?

4. Start running, hopping. galloping, etc. to move foreward, backward and sideways.

III. Culminating Activity
    a. "Jet Pilot"

2. Slight bend at waist.

3. Arm action adds momentum to the start.

4. Blending use of above body part positions for a well-balanced start. How did your start change as you moved in different directions?

a. Children in a single line at one boundary line of playing area.

a. Proper starting technique provides quicker start and greater speed; distance can be covered more quickly . Stop in control on the line.

p. 467

SPECIFIC OBJECTIVES/EVALUATIVE CRITERIA	EQUIPMENT

To start with one foot in front, knees bent, body leaning and arms ready to drive.	Variety of music
To stop with one foot in front, knees bent and weight over base of support.	
To stop using body parts in different ways to absorb force.	
To stop while moving in a variety of directions.	
To start and stop on a signal.	

ACTIVITY	PROCEDURES/ORGANIZATION	POINTS OF EMPHASIS	REFERENCES

ACTIVITY	PROCEDURES/ORGANIZATION	POINTS OF EMPHASIS	REFERENCES
I. Opening Activity			
a. Starting on teacher's voice command, use a variety of locomotor movements. (*FC)	a. General space. Teacher varies timing of start commands.	a. Can you start with one foot in front, knees bent, body leaning and arms ready to drive? Vary locomotor movements.	p. 207
b. Review skills taught in previous lesson through discussion and demonstration.	b. Group with teacher-led discussion.	b. What did students remember to do for a good start? Were knees, ankles flexed? Did arm swing help?	
c. Stretching during discussion. (*FF)	c. Group with teacher-led discussion.	c. Static stretching of quadriceps, shoulders, arms and torso.	
II. Motor Skills/Movement Concepts			
a. Stopping activities	a. General space, students moving and stopping on signal.	a. Correct stop mechanics.	p. 208

1. Stop with feet in a variety of positions		1. Which position seemed best? Feet in a forward/ backward position, ankles, knees flexed.	
2. Stop leaning forward, backward or upright.		2. Hips slightly flexed, body weight pulled back.	p. 208
3. Stop with arms in a variety of positions.		3. Arms slightly extended.	p. 208
4. Stop while moving in different directions.		4. Same mechanics as as 1-3 above.	p. 208

III. Culminating Activity

a. "Red Light-Green Light" with student as the "signal".	a. Children in single line at one end of the playing area with signal out in front.	a. Have you assumed a position to enable you to start quickly? Can you start and stop quickly on the signal?	p. 467

| SPECIFIC OBJECTIVES/EVALUATIVE CRITERIA | EQUIPMENT |

To perform the vertical throw, bending legs, keeping back
   straight, bringing ball up with two hands and extending
   arms in the direction of the throw.
To vary the height and speed of the vertical throw.
To use body parts in different ways to throw vertically.
To catch, lining up under ball, reaching up and pulling
   the ball in toward the body with two hands.

Rubber playground balls
Hoops

| ACTIVITY | PROCEDURES/ORGANIZATION | POINTS OF EMPHASIS | REFERENCES |

I. Opening Activity

a. "Free Time" with a ball. Roll, dribble, bounce, toss and catch the ball. (*FC) | a. General space. Each child with his/her own ball. | a. Free play - the joy of their own ball and choice of play. Keep the ball under control.

b. Fitness Activities | b. Self space. Exercises done in an enjoyable "can you" fashion.

1. Pushups - touch chest to ball. | | 1. Keep body straight, only chest may touch the ball.

2. Situps - hold ball on chest. | | 2. Knees bent, arms wrapped around ball on chest.

3. Side bends - hold ball over head, in hands. (*FS) | | 3. Torso should bend only to the side, arms extended with ball.

II. Motor Skills/Movement Concepts

a. Vertical tossing

1. Discuss and practice mechanics of the vertical throw.

2. Throw the ball to various heights.

3. Throw the ball using varieties in force.

4. Begin the throw at different levels.

5. Throw the ball while walking.

b. Catching skills

1. Catching a ball tossed vertically from various heights.

a. Self space

b. Best taught when integrated with each throwing activity.

1. Knees bent, back straight, ball raised with two hands, with fingers pointing in direction of desired flight on release.   p. 211

2. What did you do to maintain control as the ball went higher? Find the height where you have the most control?

3. How did you use body parts to increase force?

4. Same as 3 above as levels change.

5. Throwing the ball slightly in front of the body.

1. Line up under ball.   p. 215
Watch the ball into the hands.

2. Catching a ball tossed with different forces.

3. Catching a ball thrown vertically while walking.

2. Absorb force by "giving" with the hands.

3. Catch the ball in the fingers.

III. Culminating Activity
   a. "Hoop Tossing"

a. General space. Each child has a hoop.

1. Toss the ball vertically so it bounces in the hoop.

2. Toss at various heights so it bounces in the hoop.

3. Toss behind; beside; in back; and make it bounce in the hoop.

1. All tosses should be vertical. How did you adjust the toss so it landed in the hoop? p. 211

2. Maintain good mechanics when throwing in any variation. What adjustments did you make?

3. Follow through to ensure accuracy. What else did you do to adjust your throw?

42

| SPECIFIC OBJECTIVES/EVALUATIVE CRITERIA | EQUIPMENT |

To perform the vertical throw, knees flexed, back straight, hands reaching in direction of the throw.

To throw underhand with two hands on one side of the body, opposite foot forward and hands pointing in the direction of flight.

To adjust the underhand throw for various speeds, levels and distance.

To catch by lining up with the ball, reaching for the ball with two hands and bringing it in toward the body.

Rubber playground balls

| ACTIVITY | PROCEDURES/ORGANIZATION | POINTS OF EMPHASIS | REFERENCES |

I. Opening Activity
  a. Vertical throwing

a. Self space. Verbally review mechanics taught in previous class. Student demonstrations also useful.

  1. Throw and catch at different levels and heights.

  2. Throw and catch with different amounts of force.

  3. Throw and catch while walking.

1,2,3. Flex knees, keep body straight. Follow through by reaching in the direction of the throw. How did you adjust the throw to complete the task?

p. 211

II. Motor Skills/Movement Concepts

a. Underhand throwing (two hands)

    a. Self space, students spread around outside of gym facing the walls.

1. Throw at the wall. Step back one step if you catch it.

    1. Step more forcefully when farther from the wall. Follow through.   p. 213

2. Throw the ball with increasing force.

    2. How can you use your body to create more force?

3. Throw the ball at different levels.

    3. Anticipate the rebound for each level. Follow through in the direction of the level thrown.

4. Throw the ball quickly, slowly. (*FS)

    4. Maintain good mechanics as speed increases. How quickly can you throw and still maintain control?

b. Catching skills

    b. Best taught when integrated with each throwing activity.

1. Catching a ball thrown against the wall.

    1. Line up with the ball. to intercept its path.   p. 215

2. Catching a ball thrown with increasing force.

    2. Reach for the ball and absorb its force with hands and by stepping backward.

3. Catching a ball at different levels.

    3. Watch the ball into the hands.

III. Culminating Activity
    a. "Strideball"

a. In groups of 5 or 6
spaced in a circle.

a. Look for unguarded space.   p. 491
Flex knees, follow through.
Throw quickly.

SPECIFIC OBJECTIVES/EVALUATIVE CRITERIA	EQUIPMENT

To move, throw, and catch keeping the ball under control.   Rubber playground balls
To catch by lining up with the ball, reaching with two hands
  and pulling the ball in toward the body.
To catch a ball thrown at various levels and speeds, adjust-
  ing body position and distance and time of absorbing force.
To change direction to receive a ball.
To review the vertical and underhand throws, holding the ball in
  the fingers, stepping forward with the opposite foot, controlling
  force and following through in the direction of the throw.
To throw to a partner so the ball can be easily received.
To throw to an open space on a line.

ACTIVITY	PROCEDURES/ORGANIZATION	POINTS OF EMPHASIS	REFERENCES

I. Opening Activity
  a. Jog, throw and catch.   a. General space
     1. Using a vertical   1. Move so that body and ball
     throw.   avoid contact.

     2. Using an overhand   2. Keep ball close. How did you
     throw.   throw to keep the ball in control?

     3. Using an underhand   3. Use light force.
     throw.   (*FC)

  b. Fitness activities   b. Self space. Exercise done
                                in an enjoyable "can you"
                                fashion.

     1. Pushups - touching   1. Keep body straight; only
     chest to ball.   chest may touch ball.

2. Situps - holding
ball on chest.

3. Side bends - holding
ball over head.   (*FS)
(*FF)

2. Knees bent, arms wrapped
around ball on chest.

3. Torso should bend only to
the side, arms extended with ball.

II. Motor Skills/Movement
   Concepts
   a. Throw/catch with
   partner.

a. Self space with a partner.

   1. Directly back and
   forth.

1. Step and follow   p. 215
through toward partner when
throwing; give partner
good throw to catch. Reach
out to ball with both hands.

   2. Slightly to one side.

2. Move body in line with ball
by sliding to the right or left.

   3. At different levels.

3. Bend or reach to catch ball.

   4. Vertically or underhand,
   throws.

4. Position body in line with ball
to catch each type of throw. Absorb
the force of the throw. Which throw
was easier to catch? Why?

III. Culminating Activity
   a. "Goal Ball"
   1. Using the 2-hand
   underhand throw and
   rolling the ball.
   One person guards
   the line, and the
   other attempts to
   roll the ball over the
   line.

a. In partners, one guarding
a line 5-10 feet in length,
the other out in front 10
feet away. Change roles
every 2-3 minutes.

a. Lower body to keep the ball on
the floor. Can you direct the ball
to the empty space on the line?
Can you move quickly to prevent
the ball from going over the line?

SPECIFIC OBJECTIVES/EVALUATIVE CRITERIA	EQUIPMENT

To develop group interaction with each student working in unison with the others.

To develop fundamentaL movement skills of bending, lifting and swaying.

To develop locomotor skills of running, jogging, skipping and galloping.

To vary the range of movement in making ripples and waves.

Parachute
Foam balls
Plastic balls

ACTIVITY	PROCEDURES/ORGANIZATION	POINTS OF EMPHASIS	REFERENCES

I. Opening Activity			
a. Discussion of how to use parachute, how to grip, raise and lower, how to synchronize movements as a group.	a. Students seated around parachute.	a. Use overhand grip. Follow the signal of the teacher to initiate raising the parachute. Can we work together in raising and lowering the parachute?	
b. Making "waves" 1. Raise and lower the parachute with large arm movements.	b. Students standing, spread evenly around the parachute.	b. Stretch very high when raising the parachute. Let hands follow the parachute down slowly. Everyone lift together and come down together.	p. 288
2. Raise and hold for several seconds. (*FS)			
II. Motor Skills/Movement Concepts a. Raise the parachute taking one, then two, then three steps in	a. Students spread evenly around the parachute.	a. Move back out carefully as it comes down. See how high you can make it go.	p. 288

toward the center as it
goes up.

b. Raise the chute very
high, then pull the
edges down quickly to
form a bubble.

b. Same as above.

b. Hold it down tightly so that
no air leaks out.

c. Make ripples by shak-
ing the chute with small
arm movements at waist
level. (*FS)

c. Can you make ripples by shaking the parachute with small,
quick arm movements?

d. Vary waves and ripples.
Start making waves and
gradually reduce arm movements to make ripples.
Reverse the process.

d. Can you change from large to
small arm movements on the signal?

III. Culminating Activity
a. "Popcorn"
10 balls are placed on the
parachute. Children make
ripples causing the balls
to "pop" off the para-
chute. (*FC)

a. Can we get all the balls off?
Can we get all the balls off in
one minute?

b. "Igloo"
Students raise the para-
chute very high, then
get under it, pulling the
edges down tightly.
Stretch and relax. (*FF)

b. All students end up inside
the parachute. When the parachute finally falls, everyone comes out. If students
sit on the edge of the parachute, they can prevent air
leaks.

b. Can we pull the parachute
down quickly to trap the air
inside? A fun way to relax and
cool down.

p. 288

SPECIFIC OBJECTIVES/EVALUATIVE CRITERIA	EQUIPMENT

To form a variety of shapes with the rope (including letters and numbers)

To jump several times in succession, smoothly and rhythmically (2 beat jump), with side facing the rope and landing softly.

To jump over a rope while running, landing softly.

Jump ropes 6 to 8 feet in length

ACTIVITY	PROCEDURES/ORGANIZATION	POINTS OF EMPHASIS	REFERENCES

I. Opening Activity

a. Jog or skip throughout the gym jumping over ropes lying on the floor. (*FC)

a. Ropes scattered on the floor throughout general space, some curved, some in a circle.

a. Jog or skip under control so that you can jump over every rope without touching it. Land softly.

b. Stretch. Hold the rope in each hand, put the center around your feet. Pull your upper body forward with the rope. (*FF)

b. Students seated in general space, each with a rope.

b. Pull forward slowly on the rope, stretching the hamstring muscles.

II. Motor Skills/Movement Concepts

a. Jump a stationary rope. Teacher calls out the rhythm: Jump, jump; Jump, jump.

a. Self space. In groups of three, with a long rope on the floor. Children stand with one side to the rope.

a. Jump softly, with one jump over the rope and a second in place. Repeat several times. Your side should be facing the rope at all times. Can you keep

p. 291

b. "Cradle"
Two-beat jump on two feet.

b. Self space. In groups of three, two turners turn the rope back and forth, the third jumps. Change roles often.

b. Time the jump with the rope so that it is smooth and rhythmical.
Your side faces the rope each time. Land softly.

III. Culminating Activity
   a. Creating shapes
      1. Toss rope in the air letting it land on the floor. Copy the shape of the rope by making the same shape with your body.

1. Self space. This is also an opportunity to rest.

1. Use the legs and arms to copy loops and curls made by the rope.

      2. Make letters and numbers with the rope.

2. This works best when coordinated with letters and numbers being introduced by the classroom teacher.

2. Carefully create the straight and curved lines and corners. Can you make the same shape with your body?

SPECIFIC OBJECTIVES/EVALUATIVE CRITERIA	EQUIPMENT
To move in a variety of ways with equipment. To create an appropriate amount of force in controlling equipment and body movement. To work cooperatively and independently, with a variety of equipment at several sites.	Scooters Jump ropes Scoops A variety of balls

---

ACTIVITY	PROCEDURES/ORGANIZATION	POINTS OF EMPHASIS	REFERENCES
I. Opening Activity a. Introduce each station indicating what should be done and rules that apply.	a. Students seated in center of gym where they can see each station as teacher discusses it.	a. Emphasize that each station contains something previously taught. Have students recall what they learned with each piece of equipment. Emphasize controlling force to control one's movement and the equipment.	
II. Motor Skills/Movement Concepts a. Stations 1. Scooters: "Driving" on an obstacle course.	1. Scooters station will consist of an obstacle course of cones with tunnels, underpasses, bridges and pathways created with cones, wands, benches, mats and chairs.	1. Can you go through the course in a variety of ways without touching a marker and staying on the pathway? What different body parts can you use to create force to move the scooter.	p. 296

2. Scoops: tossing and catching.	2. Students have a play area designated by lines or cones.	2. Can you toss and catch the ball many different ways? How will you control and absorb the force?
		p. 286
3. Rope jumping variations. (*FC)	3. Each student with a rope, spread out in a large area.	3. Can you jump forward and backward? Can you jump several different ways? How long can you jump without missing? Can you land softly.
		p. 295
4. Balls	4. Any size or shape area is adequate. Change stations every 5 minutes. As the children change stations, have them jog a couple of laps around the outside of the stations before moving to the next station.	4. How many ways can you bounce and catch, toss and catch, dribble and roll the ball? Can you hit the target on the wall, then catch the ball? What different ways can you create and absorb force? Which balls required more force to move them?
		p. 276

Special Note:

Stations are an enjoyable way for children to use the equipment at nearly a 100% participation level. Organization in the first lesson often takes several minutes. It may be advantageous to do stations for two consecutive lessons, perhaps adding one or two new stations the second day.

Station activities provide the teacher with an ideal opportunity to work individually with students who require special attention.

SPECIFIC OBJECTIVES/EVALUATIVE CRITERIA	EQUIPMENT

To identify and understand safety precautions for tumbling activities.

To develop the concept and skill of "stretch" and "curl".

To slowly and smoothly perform and combine gymnastics movements.

To recognize the fitness components in animal walks.

Mats (one for every 2 to 3 students)

ACTIVITY	PROCEDURES/ORGANIZATION	POINTS OF EMPHASIS	REFERENCES

I. Opening Activity

a. Animal walks (*FS)

a. Self space on floor. Mats are not needed, so students may move in the spaces between the mats.

a. Which muscles are working?   p. 308

  1. Lame dog

  1. Can you walk on different combinations of body parts?

  2. Crab walk (*FS)

  2. Can you keep your back straight?

b. Stretch and animal walks (*FF)

b. Self space either on or off the mats.

b. Slow, static stretching.   p. 308

  1. Any combination of flexibility activities may be used, and discussion of the importance of flexible muscles in gymnastics should take place.

  1. Feel the muscles stretching. Which muscles are stretching on this exercise?

2. Ostrich

3. Inch worm

II. Motor Skills/Movement
Concept
a. Discussion of safety
in tumbling.

b. Stretch and curl
1. On your mat, start
in a stretched position,
then very slowly move
into a small curled
position.

2. Reverse that process.

c. Individual stunts

2. Can you keep your legs
straight?

3. Can you move your arms or
legs and keep the other limbs
still?

a. Students seated in group
with teacher.

1. Self space on a mat.

2. Same as above.

c. These stunts are done on
mats, 2-4 students per mat.
Mats should be situated so
that all students can
easily see the teacher and
demonstration area. Some
stunts may require a
demonstration.

a. A brief overview of safety.   pp. 303-306
The teaching of safety in gymnastics is ongoing and incorporated
into each activity.

1. Begin very stretched.
How slowly can you move?
How tightly can you curl?

2. Begin in a very tight curl.
How slowly can you move? How
long and high can you reach?

c. At first use a guided dis-   p. 312
covery "can you" approach.

1. Heel slap
2. Elevator
3. Log roll
4. Egg roll

1. Can you slap more than once?
2. Lean forward to get started.
3. Keep your body straight.
4. Keep your body curled.

III. Culminating Activity
    a. Movement combinations

        1. Can you combine an
        egg roll and a log
        roll? An elevator
        and an ostrich walk?

        2. What other combina-
        tions can you do with
        today's activities?

a. Self space on a mat.

a. Emphasize smooth transitions   p. 312
from one skill to another. Can
you change skills without stopping?

| SPECIFIC OBJECTIVES/EVALUATIVE CRITERIA | EQUIPMENT |

To use a variety of body parts for support and balance in
    performing stunts.   Mats
To recognize that a large base of support offers better balance
    than a small one.
To perform and combine stunts smoothly.

ACTIVITY	PROCEDURES/ORGANIZATION	POINTS OF EMPHASIS	REFERENCES

I. Opening Activity

a. Balance in a variety of ways.
   1. On one body part (smoothly).
   2. Change the body part.
   3. Balance on 2, then 3, then 4 body parts.
   4. Move the supporting parts closer together, farther apart.
   5. Balance on one body part while moving other body parts.   (*FS)

a. With 2-4 students on a mat, each can perform these balance stunts simultaneously.

a. Hold the balance position smoothly and steadily. Use unusual or creative ways to balance. Can you balance better with a wide or a narrow base of support? How does moving other body parts affect your balance?

p. 307

b. Stretch (*FF)

b. Self space on a mat.

b. Slow, static stretching. How can you stretch the muscles in your shoulders, in your back or in your stomach?

c. Review skills of previous lessons

c. Self space on a mat.

c. Emphasis in review sessions should be on quality of the movement.

pp. 309-312

1. Heel slap		1. Can you slap two times and land softly?
2. Log roll		2. Can you keep your body straight and roll in a straight line?
3. Elevator		3. Can you get up and down again smoothly?

II. Motor Skills/Movement Concepts

a. Animal walks	a. Self space on or around mats. Point out the students who most closely resemble the animal.	a. Move smoothly. Can you look just like the animal? p. 308
1. Snail		1. Can you curl and bring your hips and legs over your head?
2. Bear walk		2. Think left and then right as you move one side of the body and then the other.
3. Seal crawl (*FS)		3. Keep your body straight and relaxed.
4. Inch worm (*FF)		4. Keep your knees straight as you walk your feet up to your hands.

III. Culminating Activity

a. Combining skills after discussing skills covered in the last 3 lessons.

a. Self space on the mat.

a. Emphasize a smooth transition from one skill to another.

1. Can you combine a stretch and curl? A balance on two body parts with an animal walk?

2. What other combinations can you do?

SPECIFIC OBJECTIVES/EVALUATIVE CRITERIA	EQUIPMENT

To maintain balance in a variety of stunts.

To coordinate force and balance with a partner.

To perform and combine stunts smoothly.

To work with a partner in performing stunts.

Mats

ACTIVITY	PROCEDURES/ORGANIZATION	POINTS OF EMPHASIS	REFERENCES

I. Opening Activity

  a. Animal walks

    1. Gorilla walk

    2. Crab walk

    3. Bear walk (*FS)

a. On mats or area surrounding mats.

a. An enjoyable warmup activity, with emphasis on smooth and coordinated movements. Can you look just like (the animal)? What muscles are working in each activity?

p. 308

  b. Inch Worm (*FF)

b. How close can you move your feet to your hands? Keep your knees straight. Feel the stretch.

II. Motor Skills/Movement Concepts

  a. Individual stunts

    1. Jump and turn

a. Self space on the mats.

1. Can you land softly in a balanced position?

p. 311

    2. Thread the needle (*FF)

2. Can you step through your arms without letting go?

    3. Human rocker (*FS)

3. Can you make long, full rockers forward and back?

b. Partner stunts
   1. Wring the dishrag

   2. Partner get-up

III. Culminating Activity
   a. Combining stunts

      1. Can you wring
      the dishrag with a
      partner and then
      each do a jump and
      turn?

      2. A partner get-up
      and the bear walk?

      3. What other combi-
      nations can you do?

b. Partners together on a mat.

a. In partners together on a mat.

1. Can you make three   p. 310
smooth turns in a row?

2. Push smoothly and evenly
against each other.

a. Emphasize sharing space and
combining movements smoothly.

| SPECIFIC OBJECTIVES/EVALUATIVE CRITERIA | EQUIPMENT |

To use a variety and number of body parts to practice
static balance on the floor, lines on the floor, and
low balance beam.

To maintain dynamic balance while moving forward, backward
and sideways on lines on the floor and on a low balance
beam, focusing on the end of the line or balance beam.

To practice conscious relaxation by tightening and then
relaxing various body parts.

Lines taped or painted on the floor
(1 per student)
Low balance beams (3)
Mats under equipment

| ACTIVITY | PROCEDURES/ORGANIZATION | POINTS OF EMPHASIS | REFERENCES |

I. Opening Activity
  a. Stretching movement

ACTIVITY	PROCEDURES/ORGANIZATION	POINTS OF EMPHASIS	REFERENCES
1. Can you stretch isolated body parts, right and left sides, and whole body? Contrast stretching movements with curling. (*FF)	1. Self spaces on floor.	1. Where do you feel the stretching?	
2. Static balance. Can you balance on 4, 3, 2 or 1 body parts, at various levels, while stationary?	2. Self space	2. How did you adjust your balance as you balanced on different body parts? As you changed level?	p. 307

II. Motor Skills/Movement Concepts

a. Balance on lines on the floor. "Can you" approach with movement problems similar to those above. Once students have control of balance while stationary, encourage moving along lines - forward, backward, sideways, hopping, jumping, etc. with balance.

a. Each student finds own line on floor to use.

a. Emphasize use of arms held out at sides to help control balance, straight (like uncooked spaghetti) bodies and focusing on the end of the line, rather than at feet to help keep balance.

p. 331

b. Balance on low beams

b. At least 3 balance beams should be used to minimize time waiting for a turn . The beams may be different heights and widths. As children wait their turns, they may practice activities from lines on the floor.

1. Stationary balances (mirror games). The partner on line performs balances while staying balanced on the line. Partner on beam mirrors those balances. Change places.

1. In groups of three, one on a balance beam, one on a line on the floor, the third as spotter for the child on the beam. Spotter walks forward next to beam with arm extended in front of person on the beam. (Change roles.)

1. Movements should be done slowly, to optimize keeping balance. Which movements were easiest to mirror? Most difficult?

2. Locomotor movements. Students choose ways to move along beam - forward, backward, sideways, hopping, jumping, crawling, etc.

2. In partners, one on beam, one spotter. (Change roles.)

2. Encourage use of arms at sides, straight body, and focusing at end of balance beam to help keep balance. In which activities was balance easy to maintain? More difficult? Why?

p. 331

III. Culminating Activity
 a. Relaxation

a. Self space on floor, lying down, eyes closed. Turn lights off or down if possible.

1. Tension/relaxation. Can you tighten body parts so they are stiff as a board? Relax each one or slowly let it go soft like a rag doll. Repeat to whole body.

1. Can you feel the difference between tight and relaxed body parts?

2. Deep, rhythmic breathing.

2. Slowly breathe in and out, expanding chest in each breath.

SPECIFIC OBJECTIVES/EVALUATIVE CRITERIA	EQUIPMENT

To perform the dip walk on a low balance beam, focusing on end of beam and alternating dipping feet as they move forward.

To explore various movements and shapes on a low balance beam, adjusting body position to maintain balance.

To hang from various body parts under a horizontal bar.

To move under the horizontal bar in a variety of ways.

To assume a variety of positions under the horizontal bar.

To do a pull-up with the climbing rope, beginning close to the rope, keeping body straight and pulling up with a hand-over-hand motion.

Lines taped or painted on the floor, one per child.
Low balance beams
Horizontal bar
Mats under equipment
Climbing ropes

ACTIVITY	PROCEDURES/ORGANIZATION	POINTS OF EMPHASIS	REFERENCES

I. Opening Activity
  a. Locomotor warm-up
    1. Children move in relation to lines as directed by teacher, using locomotor skills. Can you jump up and down on the line? Can you jump back and forth, side to side over the line or leap over the line? Can you jog around the line clock-

a. Standing on individual lines.

a. Stress good body control and keeping a steady pace to best exercise the heart. Review points of balance from Lesson I.

wise/counterclockwise?
Can you walk/hop, etc.
like you were on a
tightrope?   (*FC)

   b. Stretches

      1. Can you stretch in
      the same direction as
      the line, trying to
      make body as long as
      the line?

      2. Can you stretch body
      across the line to make
      the letter X or T?

      3. Can you straddle sit
      with feet as far apart
      on line as possible?

      4. Curl body at the end
      of the line to make the
      letter I.   (*FF)

II. Motor Skills/Movement
Concepts
  a. Balance beam
     1. Review ways of
     balancing on balance
     beam (covered in
     Lesson 1). What are
     some ways that you
     balanced on the beam
     last time? What ways
     were easiest? Hardest?

b. Begin lying down, next
to line.

a. Seated on the floor.

b. Where do you feel the
stretching?

1. What helped you to keep   pp. 331-332
your balance when you were
walking on the beam? Where
did you look?

2. Demonstrate dip walk.

2. Head up, focus on end of beam, arms out at sides.

b. Horizontal bar
   1. Discuss safety procedures.

1. Seated on floor.

1. Always work with mats under the equipment. Grip the bars with thumbs opposite fingers. Take turns on equipment.   p. 334

2. Outline movement challenges.
   a) How many ways can you move under the bar?
   b) What body positions can you assume under the bar?

2. Seated on floor.

2. Children will take turns discovering new ways to solve problems. Encourage creative movement.   p. 334

c. Climbing ropes

c. Seated on floor.

c. Emphasize keeping body straight, pulling up with a hand-over-hand movement.   p. 340

III. Culminating Activity
   a. Movement at beam, horizontal bar and climbing ropes.

a. Seated around teacher. Class will be divided into 3 groups, one group at the bar, one group at the beam and the third at the climbing ropes. When all have had a turn at bars, group will switch places. Teacher will work at bar and signal switch.

1. Balance beam	1. Each child assumes the role of spotter for the child in front of him/her in line. Children waiting practice movements on lines on the floor.	1. Emphasize use of spotter, focusing on end of beam and controlling movements. Dip foot, pointing toes on each side of the beam as you move. What shapes can you make and still keep your balance? How did you do it?
2. Horizontal bar	2. As children wait for a turn at the bar, they practice assuming various body positions they will try on the bar - curled, stretched, bent, etc.	2. Encourage controlled movements and practice of body positions on the floor. What positions did you try? What ways did you move under the bar?
3. Climbing ropes	Seated on floor.	3. Begin close to the rope. Keep body straight. Pull up with overhand motion. What muscles were working?

SPECIFIC OBJECTIVES/EVALUATIVE CRITERIA	EQUIPMENT

To keep balance while stepping over and picking up objects
   on the balance beam by controlling movements and maintaining focus at the end of the beam.

To keep balance while carrying and moving with jugs of
   different weights on the balance beam by adjusting body
   position to keep center of gravity over base of support,
  and focusing on the end of the beam.

To swing on the rope and drop at the end of the backswing,
   keeping balance, landing softly.

To jump from the Swedish box, making different shapes with
   the body in the air and landing softly with good balance.

To perform a Skin the Cat on the horizontal bar by maintaining
   a tuck position and pushing off gently on the return.

Equipment:
Low balance beam
Swedish box with crash pad
Climbing rope
Horizontal bars
Mats under all equipment

ACTIVITY	PROCEDURES/ORGANIZATION	POINTS OF EMPHASIS	REFERENCES

I. Opening Activity
  a. Mirrors (*FF)
  Teacher moves slowly;
  include up/down and
  side/side movements,
  as well as swinging and
  stretching movements.
  Object is for students
  to duplicate teacher's
  actions as if they were
  the teacher's mirror.

a. Self space, students facing teacher.

a. Where do you feel the stretch?

II. Motor Skills/Movement
Concepts.
a. Stations

a. The tasks to be done provide practice and refinement of skills that have been introduced. Teacher works at horizontal bar spotting students there, but also keeps other students in full view.

1. Explain and demonstrate tasks to be done. Stations are:

1. Divided into 4 groups, move to equipment after explanation, rotating on teacher's signal. Teacher works at horizontal bar.

a) Balance beam. Pick up and step over bean bags; move and balance with weighted jugs held in different positions.

a) Emphasize use of spotter. How did you adjust your position for the added weight? Focus on the end of the beam?

p. 331

b) Swedish box. Climb up onto box and jump off onto crash pad. Encourage creativity in moving in the air to balanced landing.

b) What shapes can you make in the air? Land softly. Can you keep your balance on landing?

p. 344

c) Rope. Swing
and drop at the end
of backswing. Reach
high on rope, hold
feet up off mat while
swinging.

                                      c) Safe, balanced, soft   p. 341
landing.

d) Horizontal bar: d) Spot from side, moving   d) Keep a good tucked   p. 334
Skin the Cat   with child in the desired   position. Push off to
Using regular grip,   direction.   return to starting
tuck and pull legs up   position.
through arms to touch
floor. Gently push
with legs. Touch chin
for the return.

III. Culminating Activity
    a. Discuss activities.   a. Seated around teacher.   a. Reinforce all equally; insist
    Each child describes   on correct vocabulary and precise
    one movement that he/   descriptions.
    she did during class.

| SPECIFIC OBJECTIVES/EVALUATIVE CRITERIA | EQUIPMENT |

To move in a variety of ways in self and general space.   Music.
To assume a variety of body shapes.
To change the shape of body parts.
To move smoothly from one body shape to another.

| ACTIVITY | PROCEDURES/ORGANIZATION | POINTS OF EMPHASIS | REFERENCES |

I. Opening Activity
  a. Move creatively.

1. Find a space, but get there in an un- usual way.	1. Moving from a group to a self space.	1. Good phrases to use in- clude: "Show me a way I've never seen before..." Close your eyes and think of an un- usual way to move..."Move in an unusual way..."
2. Do that same move- ment, but only in self space.	2. Self space.	
3. Assume a body shape using your hands for balance and hold. (*FS)	3. Self space.	

II. Motor Skills/Movement Concepts
  a. Body shapes

	a. Self space.		
1. Make a body part rounded; another, etc.		1-3. Emphasize flow of the movements, one blending smoothly into another.	pp. 325, 375-378

2. Repeat 1, and keep
adding body parts until
you have 4 body parts
rounded.

3. Repeat 2, and add
body parts in sequence,
to the count of 8 in the
music. Unwind the body
parts to the same count.

3. Have a few children
show their sequences.

4. Slowly make the upper
half of the body round.
Slowly return to your
starting position.
Repeat with the lower
half of the body.

4. Encourage careful, smooth   p. 377
body movement of one half of
the body while the other half
remains still.

5. Make the entire body
round. Unwind slowly,
then make the body
round again.

5. Can you move smoothly?   p. 379
Listen to the music.

6. Walk through general
space while you make
your body round. Change
your round shape. Move
to your new shape.

6. Can you change to a new   p. 377
round shape? Can you move in
a new way in our new shape?

7. Slowly make your body
the opposite of round as
you find a self space.

III. Culminating Activity
    a. You are an acorn. Dig   a. Self space
    a hole in the soil and
    climb in. Cover yourself
    with dirt and wait for rain
    and sun. Then grow very
    slowly into a tall, sturdy
    oak tree!

7. Can you move and slowly
change your body shape?

a. The growing process is very
slow, so each seed must develop
in slow motion. Let each branch
and leaf develop slowly and smoothly.
What shapes will you be in as you
begin and grow?

SPECIFIC OBJECTIVES/EVALUATIVE CRITERIA	EQUIPMENT

To move in control to a variety of beats, tempos and rhythms.
To vary force of body movements.
To control the range of movement (large and small to the
   accompaniment).

Music
Drum

ACTIVITY	PROCEDURES/ORGANIZATION	POINTS OF EMPHASIS	REFERENCES

I. Opening Activity
   a. Move throughout
   space, changing your
   movement to match the
   changes in the music.

a. Scattered in general space.
Use a tape or record which has
a wide range of beats, rhythms
and loudness.

a. As the music becomes fast,
slow, loud, soft, "heavy", etc.,
the students should demonstrate
that in the movements of their
limbs and entire body.

II. Motor Skills/Movement
Concepts
a. Move with variations
in force.
   1. Pick a locomotor
   movement. Move through
   general space stiffly,
   loosely, forcefully,
   lightly.

1. Teacher signals the
change of movement.

1. What are some other ways   p. 377
you can move stiffly, etc.?
Maintain control of your
body throughout the movement.

   2. Move to the beat of
   the drum. When you
   hear a loud beat, accent
   that beat with a stronger
   movement.

2. Teacher can use various
techniques to lead them up
to the "explosion" or to
surprise them with the
"explosion".

2-3. How can you show an increase in force in your movements?

3. Repeat 2, but explode with the whole body on the loud beat.

4. As the drum beats loudly, move big. As the drum beats softly, move small.

b. Moving with variations in time.

1. As the drum beats fast, move fast. As the drum beats slowly, move slowly.

2. Combine slow and fast movement.

b. At first move in self space, then in general space.

2. Teacher beats a sequence of fast and slow beats. Children listen and then choose ways to move fast and slow.

b. While in self space, do the p. 379 movements with eyes closed. This gives more focus to the movement.
1. What ways did you move quickly? Slowly?

2. Can you smoothly change from fast to slow movements?

III. Culminating Activity
a. Combine time and force in locomotor movements.

1. Combine Activity II a. and b. Students vary locomotor movements from slow and light to forceful as they move first in self space and then in general space.

a. Moving in self and then general space as the teacher carefully changes the force and time of the drum beat. Use verbal cues at first to help children prepare for the change.

a. Encourage flowing transitions from one movement to another. Can Can you move slowly and forcefully?

1. Can you move slowly and forcefully? Quickly and lightly?

SPECIFIC OBJECTIVES/EVALUATIVE CRITERIA

EQUIPMENT

To use body movement to communicate ideas.

To vary body movements to create movement images.

To combine movements smoothly.

Music

Drum

ACTIVITY	PROCEDURES/ORGANIZATION	POINTS OF EMPHASIS	REFERENCES

I. Opening Activity
  a. Review of a variety
  of types of movements
  to music.
 	
  1. Fast, slow, heavy,
  light and soft.
 	
  2. Bending, stretching,
  twisting, curling and
  swaying.
 	
  3. Jerky, smooth,
  stiff and relaxed.
	a. Students moving at first
	in self space, then in general
	space as they combine non-
	locomotor and locomotor.
	Teacher can mix varieties of
	music and the rhythm drum.
		a. Smooth, controlled movements
		"Flowing" movements. Involve
		many body parts.
			Previous
			lessons

II. Motor Skills/Movement
Concepts
  a. Developing a movement
  story from an idea.
	a. Teacher presents a movement
	story from ideas on p. 382 or a
	favorite poem or story of the
	children.
			p. 382

1. With background music playing, children explore the types of movements and movement concepts important to the story.

2. Children select movements and movement concepts and move.

1. Scattered in general space. Teacher identifies movement concepts directly or through discussion.

2. Teacher reads the poem or story or explores elements of the idea selected.

1. Emphasize development of movements and application of movement concepts in smooth, controlled movements.

2. How can you move your body to convey the ideas without words?

UNIT: Singing Games/Folk Dances   LEVEL: I   LESSON: 1st of 8

| SPECIFIC OBJECTIVES/EVALUATIVE CRITERIA | EQUIPMENT |

To move body parts and the body in time to the music.
To move in relation to others, one behind the other.
To respond to musical phrasing in "Blue Bird" and "Did
    You Ever See A Lassie"

Records: "Bluebird"
    "Did You Ever See A Lassie"

| ACTIVITY | PROCEDURES/ORGANIZATION | POINTS OF EMPHASIS | REFERENCES |

I. Opening Activity
  a. Free movement to music
    1. Move any way you choose to the music.

    2. Specific locomotor movements (*FC)

    3. Nonlocomotor movements: Move various body parts to the beat.

1. Scattered in general space. Move in self space and then in general space.

2. In general space, children move on verbal cues from teacher.

3. In self space, teacher begins with a suggestion or 2 and then children explore on their own.

1. Listen carefully and move in time to the music. Can you move your whole body?

2. Can you skip to this rhythm? Can you jog, gallop, walk, etc. to this music?

3. What ways can we move body parts to the beat?

II. Motor Skills/Movement
Concepts

a. "Did You Ever See A Lassie"

    1. Walk through the action with music, singing the song.

a. Single circle, hands joined, the teacher in the center.

    1. Teacher does the action in the center first, then selects a child to go to the center.

p. 396

    1. Walk to the beat with small steps. Can you do the suggested movement to the beat? Be ready to change movements in time to the music. Can you move body parts in some of the ways we moved earlier?

b. Introduce skills for "Bluebird"

    1. Moving with a partner, one behind the other.

    1. With partners scattered in general space. Partners move on cues from the teacher.

    1. Can you walk to the music and move with your partner? Can you skip, etc.?

p. 396

    2. Perform "Bluebird". Walk through action first singing the song. Then dance and sing to the music.

    2. Single circle with one or more bluebirds. Teacher teaches words and demonstrates actions.

    2. Take small steps to move to the music. Can you stay with your partner? Listen carefully and be ready to change movements on each phrase.

SPECIFIC OBJECTIVES/EVALUATIVE CRITERIA	EQUIPMENT
To move in time to the beat and musical phrasing To maintain partner and group relationships in main- taining the circle. To reverse pathway with a partner and to the musical phrasing.	Records: "Did You Ever See A Lassie" "Bluebird", "Looby Lou" "Oats, Peas, Beans" "Peas Porridge Hot"

ACTIVITY	PROCEDURES/ORGANIZATION	POINTS OF EMPHASIS	REFERENCES
I. Opening Activity a.Moving in general space change the way you move on each phrase.	a. Scattered in general space	a. Listen carefully to the the music. What different ways can you move to the beat and each phrase.	p. 396

II. Motor Skills/Movement Concepts
a. Review the previously taught dances.
  1. "Looby Lou"
  2. "Oats, Pea, Beans"
	a. Single circle	a. Move with the beat of the music.	p. 344

b. "Peas Porridge Hot" 1. Moving to musical phrases. Move on the teacher's cues, re-versing pathway on the signal. Begin with a walk and gradually add other locomotor move-	b. Double circle of partners.	1. Can you adjust your steps to stay with your partner? Keep the circle spacing? Drop hands and reverse pathway?	

ments. Keep moving until
children are breathing
hard. (*FC)

2. Begin by teaching the
song and clapping action.

2. Clap on the beat so that   pp. 396-397
it sounds like one clap.

3. Add the chorus with the
reversing of the line of
direction.

3. Can you listen to the
music and be ready to reverse
pathway? Can you keep a good
circle as you move?

III. Culminating Activity
   a. Children's choice of
   any of the dances to do
   again, including: "Blue
   Bird", "Did You Ever See
   A Lassie", "Looby Lou",
   "Oats, Peas, Beans" or
   "Peas Porridge Hot"

a. In appropriate formation.

a. Move to the beat. Be ready   pp. 396-397
to change movements with the
music.

| SPECIFIC OBJECTIVES/EVALUATIVE CRITERIA | EQUIPMENT |

To move body parts or the whole body in time to the under-
   lying beat or musical phrasing.
To maintain the formation throughout the dance.
To adjust movements to stay with a partner.

Variety of music
"Seven Jumps" record

| ACTIVITY | PROCEDURES/ORGANIZATION | POINTS OF EMPHASIS | REFERENCES |

I. Opening Activity
a. Move to music, particularly galloping and skip-
ping. End in some body
shape and hold.   (*FC)

a. Scattered in general
space, moving to music of
"Seven Jumps" using verbal
cues or pauses in the music
to add skills.

a. Move to the underlying beat.   p. 410
Listen for cues to hold and
then move again. Change movement in some way each time.

b. Repeat a changing
pathway after each hold.

b. Can you move in a new path
each time?

c. Repeat b. but holding
a different stretched
position on each hold. (*FF)

c. Think about what you want to
do on the hold as you move smoothly
to the music.

**II. Motor Skills/Movement
Concepts**
a. "Head, shoulders,
knees and toes".

a. Scattered in general
space, but close to teacher.
Students follow teacher's
visual cues as they sing
along.

a. Move to the beat, smoothly
changing movements.

b. Danish Dance of
Greeting

    b. Single circle, partners
facing.

1. Go through actions
of Part I without
music, imitating
teacher's actions.

    1-4. Teacher cues
movements to music.

    1-3. Listen and move to
the music.

p. 399

2. Do Part I to the
music.

3. Add chorus, listen-
ing to the music and
responding to teacher's
cues without a change
of pathway.

4. Add change of path-
way with teacher's
cues.

    4. Listen to the music and be
ready to reverse path.

III. Culminating Activity
    a. Select one dance pre-
viously taught so that
review is brief.
        1. Sing the verses.

    a. Let students select a
dance of their choice.
Refer to text for descrip-
tion.

    a. Move to the rhythm and
phrasing of the song. Adjust
your steps to stay with your
partner.

2. Walk through the
steps, if needed.

3. Combine with the
music as a dance.

SPECIFIC OBJECTIVES/EVALUATIVE CRITERIA	EQUIPMENT

To learn the sticks at rest position. To listen and perform a variety of rhythmic patterns and tempos with rhythm sticks. To tap sticks in a rhythmic manner in a variety of ways. To perform sequences of two skills.	Rhythm sticks (2 per child) Music for even and uneven movements

---

ACTIVITY	PROCEDURES/ORGANIZATION	POINTS OF EMPHASIS	REFERENCES

ACTIVITY	PROCEDURES/ORGANIZATION	POINTS OF EMPHASIS	REFERENCES
I. Opening Activity a. Children move in general space to the beat of music using walking, running, skipping and galloping. (FC*)	a. Scattered in general space with music playing	a. Can you move to the beat? Listen carefully. Which movement fits the beat?	
II. Motor Skills/Movement Concepts. a. Introduce rhythm sticks and sticks at rest.	a. Seated near teacher. Teacher demonstrates sticks at rest.	a. We will be using rhythmic movements. Sticks will be at rest on the floor in front of you when the signal is given to stop activity.	pp. 442-443
b. Distribute sticks.	b. Students walk to place where sticks are kept and choose. Then sit in circle and place sticks at rest.	b. It is important to keep sticks quiet when the teacher or other students are talking.	
c. Demonstrate proper ways to hold sticks.	c. Seated in a circle.	c. Hold lower half of sticks with fingers between the thumb and index finger.	p. 443

d. Teacher taps short rhythms, hitting sticks together in front of the body. Students repeat same rhythm. Include steady beat, rests and faster/slower beats.

d. Seated in a circle.

d. Listen carefully to the rhythm. Can you copy it with your sticks?

p. 444

III. Culminating Activity

a. Tap sticks together.

a. Seated in a circle.

a. Tap sticks together in steady rhythm in front of body.

p. 443

b. Tap sticks on floor.

b. Tap sticks on floor in front of body, both at the same time.

p. 443

c. Tap right on left, left on right.

c. Tap right stick on left, then reverse. Do in counts of four each, then two, then one each (reversing with each tap).

p. 443

d. Tap sticks on floor at right side, then left side.

d. Use cue words "right" and "left" to indicate where to tap sticks. Tap them together on floor.

p. 444

e. Create sequence of two skills. Tap together (8), tap on floor (8), together (8), floor (8).

e. Teacher cues sequence.

e. Can you keep a steady beat?

f. Children suggest a new sequence of two skills of 8 hits each.

f. Teacher cues sequences.

f. Can we make our sticks sound like one pair of sticks?

| SPECIFIC OBJECTIVES/EVALUATIVE CRITERIA | EQUIPMENT |

To combine locomotor and non-locomotor movements in
   various rhythms.   A variety of records
To tap sticks in a variety of ways to the beat of the music.
To tap the sticks in various rhythms, varying time.
To smoothly combine two to four skills into a stick routine.

| ACTIVITY | PROCEDURES/ORGANIZATION | POINTS OF EMPHASIS | REFERENCES |

I. Opening Activity			
a. Even locomotor movements: moving and clapping to the beat. Try it as you walk, run, hop, jump. (*FC)	a. Scattered in general space.	a. Emphasize clapping and stepping on the beat.	
b. Uneven locomotor movements. Skip, slide and gallop, clapping the rhythm of movement.		b. Can you clap the uneven beat as you move?	
II. Motor Skills/Movement Concepts			
a. Review sticks at rest.	a. Seated in a circle with a pair of sticks.	a. Do you remember the sticks at rest position?	pp. 442-443
b. Review some of the ways the children tapped the sticks in previous lessons.		b. Can we tap together so that it sounds like one pair of sticks?	pp. 443-444

c. Children tap the rhythm of their names with the sticks. The groups asks the question, "What is your name?" The child responds verbally and then taps the response. Then all tap the rhythm.

c. Teacher begins with tapping the rhythm of his/her name.

c. Can you tap the rhythm of your name? Listen for the even and uneven taps.

d. Tap own sticks together, Tap partners sticks, Repeat for 8 counts. Repeat once more. What other ways can you tap the sticks?

d. With person next to you in the circle.

d. Can you stay with the beat as you tap your own and then your partner's sticks?

pp. 444-445

e. Children develop new ways to tap the sticks with a partner.

e. With person next to you in the circle. Share some of the ways.

e. In what ways can you tap the sticks with a partner?

pp. 385, 386

III. Culminating Activity
  a. Children develop a two-skill sequence with a partner (8 counts for each skill).

a. With a partner, each suggests one skill to use. Share them with the class. Several pairs performing at the same time.

a. Can you beat the sticks so that it sounds like one pair of sticks? (Some may be able to use uneven rhythms as well.)

| SPECIFIC OBJECTIVES/EVALUATIVE CRITERIA | EQUIPMENT |

To perform the following skills to a beat with a parachute:
  waves, mushrooms, igloos.

To perform a variety of locomotor movements with the parachute reversing pathways on each phrase.

To perform sequences of movements cooperatively and rhythmically with the parachute.

Parachute
Music of various tempos

| ACTIVITY | PROCEDURES/ORGANIZATION | POINTS OF EMPHASIS | REFERENCES |

I. Opening Activity

a. Locomotor warm-up. On signal "move", children move through general space, using their choice of locomotor skills to music. On signal "jump", all stop. Then "move", etc. (*FC)

    a. Scattered in general space, proceed to move through the room.

    a. Move with good body control around the room. Do you feel your heart and lungs working?

b. Move and Stretch. Move again but on the signal assume a stretched positions. Hold for eight beats of the music. (*FF)

    b. Where do you feel the stretch?

II. Motor Skills/Movement Concepts

a. Parachute Activities

1. Waves

a) Waist level. Start small, as ripples and get progressively larger. Start kneeling, then try standing, then jumping.

b) Bending and stretching. Bend at waist, lowering parachute to ankles (keep legs straight). Then stretch arms up and raise parachute over head.

2. Side to side. Move parachute rhythmically, side to side. Begin on signal and cue "left, right, left, right." Start slowly and get faster.

3. Locomotor skills, with a change of pathway. Practice each first, then give each a specific number of counts (for example, walk (8), reverse direction, walk (8).

1. Begin kneeling, then all stand. Teacher cues the count at first.

2. Standing around parachute, teacher giving cues.

3. Same as above, moving clockwise and counterclockwise around parachute. Teacher cues the changes.

a) Can you make 2 ripples to each beat? A large wave to 2 beats?   p. 288

b) Can we work together to raise the parachute on the count of 4? 8?

2. Can we move the parachute to the beat? Can we do it twice as fast? Half as fast?

3. Emphasize listening for signals to change direction and keeping the parachute taut. Listen to the music, move on each beat. Listen to the music, can you be ready to change?   p. 288

4. Mushroom. Start kneeling. All raise parachute overhead together, walk in two steps, out two steps and kneel again.	4. Around parachute, begin kneeling on one knee.	4. Emphasize going in and out together on the beat and taking the same number of steps. p. 288
5. Igloo. As with mushroom, all raise up together, step in together. Then pull parachute down behind body and sit down on the edge of parachute. Hold edge down firmly.	5. Same as above	5. Listen and move together to the beat. p. 288

III. Culminating Activity

a. Combine locomotor and parachute movements; i.e., walk 8 steps, mushroom 8 counts, walk 8 steps, reverse 8 steps. Children might suggest other combinations.	a. Around the parachute	a. Listen to the music and move ourselves and the parachute to the beat.

          SPECIFIC OBJECTIVES/EVALUATIVE CRITERIA   EQUIPMENT

To change pathways to avoid others while moving in general space.
To absorb force when stopping by assuming a forward/backward
   stride position, bending knees and bringing body weight
   over base.
To start from a forward/backward stride position, with knees
   bent and body leaning forward.

To move in a straight pathway.

  ACTIVITY   PROCEDURES/ORGANIZATION   POINTS OF EMPHASIS   REFERENCES

I. Opening Activity
   a." People Dodge". On a   a. Students running through   a. Be alert for crowded areas
   signal, students run, skip   general space within the   where collisions may occur.
   or gallop, dodging every   boundaries. Any fitness acti- Can you see the open pathways?
   one else. If a collision   vity may be substituted for   Control movement and change
   or contact occurs, those   inchworms or a variety may   pathways to avoid others.
   involved do two "inch-   be used. They should be used
   worms" then return to   in a positive way, not as a
   the game.(*FC) (*FS)   form of punishment.

   b. Rest and stretch. (*FF)   b. At one-minute intervals,   b. Discuss dodging techniques.
                                stop the game for rest,   Do the "inchworm" slowly. Do
                                stretching and discussion.   you feel which muscles are
                                Can be done in self space.   working?
                                                               do we stretch?

II. Motor Skills/Movement Concepts

a. Start and stop: moving in general space stopping and starting on signal.

a. Scattered in general space.

a. Stop by putting one foot in front of the other, bend knees, pull body back over feet. Start by putting one foot out in front of the other, knees bent, lean forward.

b. Start and stop: running in a straight line. On a signal students begin to run to opposite side. Each must run in a straight line so as not to move into his/her neighbor's pathway. On further signals they will stop and start up again until they reach the other side. Repeat coming back.

b. Students standing on the longest line (or side) of the gym or play area to start, then running straight across to opposite side.

b. Pick a point on the opposite side; run straight to that point. Can you stop quickly in a good balanced position?

III. Culminating Activity

a. Jet Pilot

a. In a single line

a. Be ready for a quick start.   p. 467
Run in a straight pathway. Stop on the end line with good control.

b. Red Light, Green Light

b. In a single line

b. Listen carefully for the   p. 467
signals to stop and start. Stop quickly in a balanced position.

c. Conscious relaxation

c. Self space

c. Cool down from dynamic game.   p.
Can you tense your _____ and then slowly relax, feeling the tension leaving your body?

SPECIFIC OBJECTIVES/EVALUATIVE CRITERIA	EQUIPMENT

To move within the boundaries of the play area.   Bowling pins
To use all areas of the available space.
To find and move into open spaces in the play area.
To control force by tagging softly.

ACTIVITY	PROCEDURES/ORGANIZATION	POINTS OF EMPHASIS	REFERENCES

I. Opening Activity
  a. Fitness Fun
    1. Inchworm
    2. Seal crawl
    3. Modified situps
    4. Sit and reach
    stretch (*FS) (*FF)

a. Each student in self space. These are fun strength build-ers that have been done before.

a. Enjoying a challenging strength builder. "Feeling" which muscles are working.

II. Motor Skills/Movement Concepts.
  a. Locating and defin-ing boundaries.
    1. Move in general space within the black lines.

    2. Cover all areas within the black lines.   (*FC)

a. Scattered in general space.

1. Can you move into all available space, but stay within the lines?

2. Can you cover all spaces, corners, sides, middle?

  b. Moving to an open space. Walk, run, skip and gallop in general

b. Scattered in general space.

b. Can you see the open spaces in which to move to avoid col-lisions with others?

space. On the signal,
stop and point to an
open space.

c. Tagging: Children
move in general space
tagging as many pins as
possible without knocking
them down. Those knocked
down stay down. Call time.
Repeat the activity.

b. Bowling pins and children
scattered in general space

c. Can you touch the pins
softly as you move quickly?
Control the force of running
as you control the force in
tagging. Can you beat your
record of pins standing?

III. Culminating Activity
a. Barnyard Upset

a. In a single line with a
farmer in front of the group.

a. Move within the boundaries.   p. 466
Can you see the open spaces to
to avoid the farmer? Remember
to tag softly. Stop with control.

b. Sharks and Barracudas

b. Half the class in a line
on one boundary line, the
other half on the opposite
line.

b. Stay within the boundaries.   p. 450
Tag softly. Be sure to stop
with control.

SPECIFIC OBJECTIVES/EVALUATIVE CRITERIA	EQUIPMENT

To throw overhand by gripping ball in fingers, using an overhand motion and pointing fingers where you want the ball to go. To put the ball in an empty space.	A small foam or "flying fleece" ball for each child

----

ACTIVITY	PROCEDURES/ORGANIZATION	POINTS OF EMPHASIS	REFERENCES

ACTIVITY	PROCEDURES/ORGANIZATION	POINTS OF EMPHASIS	REFERENCES
I. Opening Activity a. Skip, run, walk and gallop in general space. On the signal stop and point to the empty spaces. (*FC)	a. Scattered in general space.	a. Can you point to the empty spaces?	
II. Motor Skills/Movement Concepts a. Children practice the overhand throw, throwing and retrieving on signal.	a. Child stands straddling a line with side turned.	a. Grip ball in fingers, overhand motion, point to wall with fingers on release.	
b. Throwing to an empty space; one throws, the other moves in a limited space. Thrower attempts to get ball into empty space.	b. In partners, one guarding a wall space.	b. Can you find the empty space on the wall? Point to wall below head height of partner.	p. 463

III. Culminating Activity

a. Snowball. When signal to stop is given children, count the number of balls on their side. Repeat game, trying to have fewer balls on each side when signal to stop is given.

a. Children equally divided on each half of the gym.

a. Can you find the empty space? p. 491 Can you work together to cover space to close empty space? Throw balls quickly.

LEVEL II

SPECIFIC OBJECTIVES/EVALUATIVE CRITERIA   EQUIPMENT

To develop an awareness of body parts and their articulations.   Music
To identify the movements of body parts in performing motor   Hoops
 skills.
To move body parts in the same or opposite ways of a partner.
To control movements in working with a partner.

ACTIVITY	PROCEDURES/ORGANIZATION	POINTS OF EMPHASIS	REFERENCES
I. Opening Activity a. Musical hoops (*FC) Students jog to the music. When the music stops they place a body part in the hoop.	a. General space.	a. Put a different body part in the hoop each time.	
II. Movement Concepts a. Identify body parts: shin, thigh, ankle, wrist, shoulder, etc with children touching each part.	a. Self space	a. Identify less familiar body parts. Also ask for inside of thigh, behind the shoulder, left elbow, etc.	p. 164
b. Identify two adjoining body parts: Your hand and forearm are next to each other. Where are they attached? What other body parts are adjoining?	b. Self space.	b. What is the name of the body part which connects these body parts?	p. 164

c. Perform a walk. What body parts are used? What other motor skills can you do? What body parts are used? How did the body parts move?

c. Self space. Teacher directed at first, then student suggestions.

c. Where does the movement begin? What movements were necessary to perform the skill?

d. With a partner, one selects a skill and the other the moving parts.

d. In partners in general space.

d. How did the body part move? (flex, extend, rotate, etc)

e. Moving body parts in opposition to a partner. (*FF)

e. In partners in general space.

e. How did your partner move a body part? What is the opposite way you moved the part? Did you feel stretching in some body parts?

III. Culminating Activity
a. Move the ball to a partner in a variety of ways.

a. In general space, with a partner and a ball.

a. What body parts did you use to move the ball? How did they move? Did you control the ball so it was easily received by your partner?   p.137

SPECIFIC OBJECTIVES/EVALUATIVE CRITERIA	EQUIPMENT

To use different kinds of movements to communicate ideas to
    others.
To develop an awareness of body tension and the ability to
    perform conscious relaxation.

Music
Hoops

ACTIVITY	PROCEDURES/ORGANIZATION	POINTS OF EMPHASIS	REFERENCES

I. Opening activity
  a. Explore a variety of
  manipulative skills with a
  variety of locomotor skills.
    1. Carry a hoop on various
    body parts while jogging,
    skipping, hopping, etc. (*FS)

a. General space.

1. Be aware of others and
their hoops while moving.

1. Balance the hoop on a
number of different body
parts. Which muscles
were working?

    2. Can you roll the hoop with
    your left hand while you move
    in general space hopping on
    one foot? What other ways can
    you move a hoop?

2. Teacher directed at
first, then children's
suggestions.

2. Which body parts did you
use to control the hoop?

p. 167

II. Movement Concepts
  a. Use body language:
    1. Move to a variety
    of musical beats and
    rhythms, change move-
    movements to match the
    music.

a. General space.
1. music - fast, slow, soft,
lively, etc.

1. Can you make smooth
transitions from one type
of movement to another?
How did the movement change
as you moved to the different
kinds of music?

2. Tell something with your movement your partner can recognize.

2. In general space with a partner.

2. Use facial expressions as well as body movements Involve as many body parts and movements as possible.

p. 170

b. Muscle tension and relaxation. (*FR)
1. Match slow movements with a partner.

b. In general space with a partner.

1. Encourage leader to involve fine as well as large movements.

p. 171

2. Tell partner to tense and relax various muscles.

2. Watch the muscles as you tense and relax.

III. Culminating Activity
a. Explore using movement to communicate emotions: sad, tired, happy, angry, etc. with the use of tense and relaxed muscles.

a. In self space.

a. How did you use your body parts to convey emotions? Were they tense or relaxed?

p. 171

UNIT: Body Awareness   LEVEL: II   LESSON: 9th or 10

      SPECIFIC OBJECTIVES/EVALUATIVE CRITERIA   EQUIPMENT

To use the knowledge of body parts and their relationship
   while moving.
To use different kinds of movements to communicate with
   others.
To develop an awareness of body tension and relaxation.

   ACTIVITY   PROCEDURES/ORGANIZATION   POINTS OF EMPHASIS   REFERENCES

I. Opening Activity
   a. Explore the various ways   a. General space.   a. Challenge their creativity.
   to move across the room   Which body parts did you use
   using different body parts   for support?
   for support. (*FC) (*FS)

II. Movement Concepts
   a. Using body parts for
   body language.
   1. How would you carry   1. In self space.   1. Discuss mime and how it's   pp. 170-171
   something heavy, move a   done. Can you isolate body
   giant ball, lift a refriger-   parts in the movement?
   ator, etc?

   2. How would you crawl   2. In self space.   2. How can you change the
   into a tiny hole, step   dimensions of your body?
   over an electric fence, etc.

   3. Go over, through, under,   3. In general space with   3. Can you do it without
   around, etc. your partner's   a partner.   touching your partner?
   legs, arms, outstretched
   hands, etc.

103   Copyright © 1994 by Mosby–Year Book, Inc.

III. Culminating Activity
   a. Day at the Circus
   Select from a list of
   circus performers gener-
   ated from the class to
   imitate.

   a. In general space.

   a. What type of movements and
   body parts did you use to communicate your ideas?

   b. Tension and relaxa-
   tion of muscles. (*FR)

   b. In self space, teacher
   calling out body parts to
   first tense and then relax.

   b. Discuss the importance of   p. 171
   relaxation after dynamic
   activity. Emphasize slow, static
   stretching and relaxation.

SPECIFIC OBJECTIVES/EVALUATIVE CRITERIA	EQUIPMENT

To move within the boundaries of general space.	Parachute
To move in a variety of ways in general space.	Playground balls
To avoid others and objects while moving in general space.	

ACTIVITY	PROCEDURES/ORGANIZATION	POINTS OF EMPHASIS	REFERENCES

ACTIVITY	PROCEDURES/ORGANIZATION	POINTS OF EMPHASIS	REFERENCES
I. Opening Activity a. Students run throughout the space changing movements on the signal from the teacher. (*FC)	a. Scattered in general space.	a. Look for and be aware of open spaces to move into. What are some ways you moved in general space?	p. 176

II. Movement Concepts
  a. Move in a restricted space.
    1. Small groups move under the parachute. (*FS)
	1-2. Four students at a time move under the parachute while the others hold it up.	1. How much space did you cover before the parachute came down?	p. 176

2. Move in a variety of ways under the parachute.		2. What different ways did you move? Which enabled you to cover the most space?	p. 176
3. Jog, skip, gallop, etc. throughout the space; in half of the space; a quarter; in a circle. (*FC)	3. Scattered in a defined general space. Gradually diminish the size of space available.	3. Did you use all the space? How did your movements change to avoid others as the space changed in size?	p. 144

III. Culminating Activity
  a. Moving with balls
    1. In self space, how many things can you do with the ball?
	1. In self space.	1. Remember the ball increases your self space as long as it is controlled. How much space can you use as you	p. 176

2. Repeat some of the activities you just did, but moving with the ball in general space.

2. In general space.

2. How did you movements change to control the ball as you moved in general space? p. 176 Did the space seem smaller as you moved with the ball? Were you able to avoid others and other balls ?

SPECIFIC OBJECTIVES/EVALUATIVE CRITERIA   EQUIPMENT

To review the six directions.   Bean bags
To review the body parts which lead the direction of movement. Cones
To change body parts which lead.   Hoops
To move with objects and others in different directions.
To control movements when moving with a partner.

ACTIVITY	PROCEDURES/ORGANIZATION	POINTS OF EMPHASIS	REFERENCES

I. Opening Activity
   a. Walk, run, skip, gallop,   a. In general space.   a. Look for the empty spaces
   through general space. On   in which to move. Can you feel
   the signal, stop and assume   the muscles working as you hold?
   a balanced position on the
   number of body parts called
   by the teacher. (*FS)

II. Movement Concepts
   a. Move in various   a. In general space.
   directions?
      1. While moving in   1. What are some directions   p. 176
      general space change   in which you moved? Can you
      direction on the   change directions smoothly?
      signal.

      2. Pretend a string   2. What body parts lead?   p. 176
      is attached to a body
      part which is pulling
      you in the following
      directions: forward,

left, right, etc.
Then change the body
part which leads.

3. Begin moving in one
direction with one body
part leading. Continue
moving in that direction
but change the leading
body part.

b. Moving with others.

1. One calls a di-
rection and both
move in the direction.

2. Follow the leader.
Follower calls the di-
rection of movement.

III. Culminating Activity
a. With a hoop, move in
various directions. Can
you move in one direction
as you move the hoop in
another?

b. Relax and stretch.
Breathe comfortably as you

3. Can you lead with another
body part? Which body parts can
lead in each direction?

b. In general space with a
partner.

1. Can you move in the di-   p. 176
rection called? Can you move
together?

2. Can you change direction   p. 176
smoothly?

a. In general space with a
hoop.

a. Remember the hoop increases   p. 176
your self space. Which ways
did you control the hoop?

b. In self space.

b. Feel muscles stretching.

stretch and relax.

SPECIFIC OBJECTIVES/EVALUATIVE CRITERIA	EQUIPMENT

To review moving with objects in different directions.   Playground balls
To move with others in different ranges.

ACTIVITY	PROCEDURES/ORGANIZATION	POINTS OF EMPHASIS	REFERENCES

I. Opening Activity
  a. Move in various di-
  rections.
    1. Roll a ball while
    moving in different
    directions.

a. In general space with a
partner.

a. Plan movements and di-
rections before beginning.
Can you find many different
ways of moving the ball?
How did the skill change as
you changed direction?

p. 176

    2. Bounce a ball while
    moving in different
    directions.

    3. Blend a variety of
    directions and movements
    with the ball. (*FC)

3. How many different ways
can you move the ball as you
move backward, etc.?

II. Movement Concepts
  a. Explore range with a
  partner.
    1. How close can you
    get to your partner?
    How far apart?

a. In general space.

1. Awareness that all body
parts can be brought close
to partner. Did you use all
the space to get far apart?

p. 176

2. How far apart can you be and still touch fingers? Toes? (*FF)

2. Awareness of all body parts that can be moved far apart. Do you feel body parts stretching as you touch your fingers? Toes?

3. Can you move throughout the space, always staying as far from your partner as possible? As near?

3. In general space with a partner.

3. Can you watch your partner and others in the space as well? p. 176

III. Culminating Activity
  a. Contrasting ranges.
     1. Copy your partner's movements in the same range.

1. In self space, change leaders after one minute.

1. Can you copy your partner's movements exactly? p. 176

2. Do the opposite range of your partner's movements?

2. In self space with a partner.

2. Use many body parts to contrast range. p. 176

3. Moving in general space copying your partner's movements.

3. In general space with a partner.

3. Can you move in the same range as your partner?

4. Repeat #3 but vary the range of your partner's movements.

4. Can you vary the range and still move in the same way? What was the result of changing the range of movement?

SPECIFIC OBJECTIVES/EVALUATIVE CRITERIA	EQUIPMENT

To assume a variety of balanced positions.	Hoops
To balance objects and with objects.	Bean bags
To use the center of gravity and base of support to maintain balance.	Wands
To share ideas with a partner in creating an obstacle course.	

ACTIVITY	PROCEDURES/ORGANIZATION	POINTS OF EMPHASIS	REFERENCES

I. Opening Activity

a. Balance Tag: Two or more children are "it" and try to tag as many others as possible. To be safe students assume a balanced shape on 3 body parts. If tagged they assume a v-sit until a friend touches and frees them. (*FC)	a. Scattered in general space. Change "it" often.	a. Use a variety of 3-point balances. Can you feel the abdominals working in the v-sit?	

II. Movement Concepts

a. Balance with equipment. 1. Balance each piece of equipment (separately) on a variety of body parts.	a. Scattered in general space, with a hoop, bean bag, and wand.	1. Use different body parts and positions with each piece of equipment.	p. 185

2. Balance the pieces of equipment on each other in a variety of ways.

3. Balance on a piece of equipment. Now try another. Combine two pieces. Balance in different ways.

4. Balance on a piece of equipment while balancing another piece on a body part.

III. Culminating Activity
a. Balance obstacle course: Each pair of students creates an obstacle course, using their hoops, wands, and bean bags, which requires balance as the primary objective.

a. In general space with a partner.

2. How did you balance the objects? What did you learn about balancing different shapes, sizes, etc?

3. Which body parts offer the best balance points? Did this change as the size and shape of equipment pieces changed?

4. Can you shift your body weight, base of support, and center of gravity to help you find and maintain balance?

a. Each phase of the course must require balance to succeed. Did you have to change the base of support and move the center of gravity for success? Be sure to include ideas from each partner.

| SPECIFIC OBJECTIVES/EVALUATIVE CRITERIA | EQUIPMENT |

To vary time with the tempo of the music.

To vary movements with the rhythmic pattern of the drum.

To move to an imposed time.

To share ideas for moving with a partner.

A variety of records

Drum

ACTIVITY	PROCEDURES/ORGANIZATION	POINTS OF EMPHASIS	REFERENCES

I. Opening Activity

a. Moving to music. Using locomotor movements that go with the music. When the music changes, change the type of movement you do. (*FC)

a. In general space, music playing, varying from fast to slow.

a. How did your movements reflect the tempo of the music?

II. Movement Concepts

a. Discuss opening activity. Review the concept of time.

a. In a group; questions, answers, demonstrations.

a. Time varies during many activities and we can vary the speed of our movements.

b. Move to specific rhythms.

b. In general space.

1. Move to the drum beat, not only its speed but also its rhythm.

1. Can you respond to the speed and the rhythm of the drum?   p. 184

2. Move gradually into a curled position on 4 beats of the drum.

2. Break the movement into 4 equal parts.   p. 184

A stretched position.
A roll. A tall stand.
(*FF)

3. Do sit-ups to a 4-
beat count of the drum.
(4 beat up, 4 beats
down). (*FS)

III. Culminating Activity

a. Moving in slow motion.
One partner selects a movement (riding a bike, kicking a ball, etc.) the other
does the movement in slow
motion. (*FS)

b. Moving in fast motion.
Repeat above activity, but
moving at a faster speed
than normal.

3. Is it easier with a fast
or slow beat?

a. In general space with a
partner. Change leaders often.

a. Be as precise as possible
with the movement. What ideas did
your partner suggest? Were you
able to do them?

b. Move fast but maintain the
clarity of the movement. Were
some of the moves more difficult
than others? Why?

SPECIFIC OBJECTIVES/EVALUATIVE CRITERIA	EQUIPMENT

To vary force and speed while moving in general space.	Variety or records
To smoothly combine nonlocomotor and/or locomotor movements.	Drum
To smoothly combine movements with a change in speed or force.	

ACTIVITY	PROCEDURES/ORGANIZATION	POINTS OF EMPHASIS	REFERENCES

I. Opening Activity
  a. Blend speeds, force,
  and types of locomotor
  movement. As the music or
  drum beat changes, change
  the type of movement.

a. Scattered in general space.

a. Can you move smoothly from
one movement to the next without stopping? Can you increase
and decrease speed smoothly? Can
you vary force to match the speed
and beat?

II. Movement Concepts
  a. Combining movements
  into a sequence.

a. Scattered in general space.

p. 156

    1. Explore a variety
    of nonlocomotor move-
    ments - bend, stretch,
    push, pull, turn, twist,
    swing, sway ,etc. with
    body parts and the
    whole body.

1. How many ways can you move
body parts as you remain in
your self space?

    2. Combine two nonloco-
    motor movements into a
    sequence.

2. Can you smoothly move from
one movement to the next?

    3. Combine above with a
    locomotor movement.

3. Keep the movements in
sequence while moving forward.

4. Combine the 2 nonloco-
motor with 2 locomotor
movements into a smooth
sequence.

III. Culminating Activity
   a. Creating movements to a
   beat or to music.
      1. Using a drum, clap-
      ping, or music playing,
      create a series of 2 or
      more locomotor and 2
      or more nonlocomotor
      movements that flow to-
      gether to form a smooth
      sequence, with a change
      of force or time.

      2. Practice the sequence
      several times to be sure
      it is the same each time.

      3. Perform the sequence
      for the teacher and class-
      mates.

a. In general space, alone or
with a partner. Allow 4 to 6
minutes to prepare the sequence
then have the students show
what they have done.

3. Have one third of the
students perform at a
time.

4. Can you move smoothly from
nonlocomotor to locomotor
movements?

1. Select the locomotor
movements first and practice
them. Add the nonlocomotor
movements. Now a change of
force or time.

2. Blend the movements and
concepts together so they are
nonstop and flow smoothly. Use
the beat or music to tie it
together.

3. What did you like about the
ideas presented?

SPECIFIC OBJECTIVES/EVALUATIVE CRITERIA   EQUIPMENT

To jump vertically by assuming a deep crouch, forcefully   Hoops
  extending legs, reaching with arms for full body ex-   Bean bags
  tension and landing softly.   Benches
To jump horizontally by bending legs, taking off on two   Milk cartons
  feet, reaching forward with arms and legs extended,
  and landing softly.
To vary force in jump vertically and horizontally to cover
  various heights, distances and in different directions.

ACTIVITY	PROCEDURES/ORGANIZATION	POINTS OF EMPHASIS	REFERENCES

I. Opening Activity

a. Jog throughout the gym, jumping over all objects on the floor. (*FC)	a. General space with 30 to 40 objects on the floor (bean bags, milk cartons, cones, benches, hoops, etc.).	a. How did you jump differently over different objects?	
b. Stretch the jumping muscles (calves, quadriceps, hamstrings). (*FF)	b. Self space	b. Stretch slowly (10 to 15 seconds) each muscle group. A flexible muscle works better than a tight muscle.	

II. Motor Skills/Movement
Concepts

a. Jumping variations with a hoop. (*FS)	a. Self space, each student with a hoop.		
1. Jump in and out of the hoop forward, backward, sideways.		1. Take off on 2 feet, control jump and land softly.	p. 203

2. Jump over the hoop with a standing, two foot takeoff; a running, one foot takeoff.

3. Pretend the hoop is high and jump over it.

b. Jog in general space, jumping over everyone else's hoop.

III. Culminating Activity
a. Jumping stations
1. Long rope jumping

2. Vertical jump. Touching lines on the wall at various heights.

3. Four low hurdles. Plastic sticks placed across cones.

2. Flex ankles and knees to create more force. Swing arms forward and upward as you jump.

3. How can you create more force? Absorb force by bending the knees on landing.

b. General space

b. Control speed and timing so as not to touch any hoop. Land softly.

a. Six stations spaced comfortably in the gym. Students spend 2 to 3 minutes at each station, then rotate to the next.

1. Explore rope jumping variations. How many different ways can you jump the rope?

2. Crouch to begin, swing arms p. 201 upward forcefully, extend body, land softly.

3. Stay low as you run over the hurdles. Land softly and then move on.

4. Jump the brook.
A running jump across
a space by jumping
ropes lying on a mat.

4. How did your jump change as p. 201
the distance increased?

5. Standing broad jump.
Jump for distance; feet
and inches are marked
on a mat.

5. Flex ankles and knees to
begin; swing arms forcefully
forward and up. Land softly.

6. Jump the shot. Stu-
dents in a circle jumping
over a bean bag fastened to
a rope and twirled by a
 classmate. (*FS) (*FC)

6. Carefully watch the shot as p.291
it approaches. Jump only high
enough to clear the shot (3 to
5 inches).

SPECIFIC OBJECTIVES/EVALUATIVE CRITERIA	EQUIPMENT

To leap by taking off on one foot, arms driving in opposition
   to legs, extending legs in flight and landing softly.

To leap in a variety of directions, levels and ranges.

To hop, taking off on one foot, using arms for added height
   and balance, and landing softly on same foot.

To hop in a variety of levels and ranges.

To smoothly combine the skills of hop, leap and jump into a
   single movement.

To coach and encourage a partner's efforts.

EQUIPMENT

Bean bags
Hoops
Jump ropes
Cones
Plastic tubes

ACTIVITY	PROCEDURES/ORGANIZATION	POINTS OF EMPHASIS	REFERENCES

I. Opening Activity

a. Jog throughout the gym, leaping over every line.

   a. General space

   a. Look for lines in open areas. Head up. Time steps so that your feet never touch the lines. Take off on one foot, land softly on the other.

b. Rest and stretch

   b. Static stretching of the quad- p. 183 ricep and hamstring groups.

c. Jog throughout the gym leaping over every space formed by two lines.

   c. Same as a. above.

d. Rest and stretch.
(*FC) (*FS)

   d. Same as b. above.

II. Motor Skills/Movement Concepts

a. Leaping

1. Leaping over objects of increasing width (bean bag, hoop, jump rope).	1. Each student has various sized objects. Students may join together, increasing the objects they must leap over.	1. What do you need to do to leap farther? p. 204
2. Leaping over objects of different heights.	2. Set up hurdles with various size cones and plastic tubes as cross bars.	2. What do you need to do to leap higher?
3. Leap over a partner in various positions (lying flat, on hands and knees).	3. Students working with a partner.	3. Safety of partner comes first! Arm swing and leg force will create longer, higher flight.

b. Hopping

1. Hop in general space around objects.	1. In general space, objects (hoops, bean bags, cones, etc.) scattered in the space.	1. Take off on one foot, p. 204 land softly on the same foot. Use arms for height and balance.
2. Hop in general space over objects.		2. How did you change your hop to increase distance? Height?

III. Culminating Activity

a. Create the "hop, step, jump".

1. Discuss blending separate movements into a movement pattern or sequence.	1. Students in self space but facing the teacher at the front of the gym.	1. Flow from one movement to another. Do each part correctly - think it through.

2. Hop, then walk with two huge steps.

2. Students in self space, teacher working with individual.

2. When landing on the hop, continue forward movement with a large walking step.

3. Hop, then leap with a huge leap.

3. Self space

3. Same as above, but use hop momentum to create a leap instead of a walk.

4. Hop, then leap. This time finish the leap with one more step to two feet (a jump). Practice this sequence several times, each time striving for more distance.

4. Self space

4. Same as above, adding a   p. 204 jump at the end of the leap. The jump is started from one foot, landing on two feet. Develop a sense of rhythm in the three parts.

5. Compete with self for the longest hop-skip-jump. (*FS)

5. In self space. Choose a partner who is close by.

5. Compete with self as you and your partner work together, coaching each other to cover more more distance. Establish flow and rhythm of the three parts together.

SPECIFIC OBJECTIVES/EVALUATIVE CRITERIA	EQUIPMENT

To review the gallop to the beat, and in various directions
  and pathways.
To skip in a variety of directions, pathways and speeds.
To imitate the skipping rhythm of a partner.

Rhythm drum
Variety of music
Rubber playground balls
Bean bags, cones or hoops

ACTIVITY	PROCEDURES/ORGANIZATION	POINTS OF EMPHASIS	REFERENCES

I. Opening Activity

a. Gallop to the beat
of a drum. (*FC)

a. General space

a. Vary the speed of the beat; students should adjust their speed to that of the drum beat.

p. 206

b. Gallop to the rhythm
of music with a strong
galloping beat. (*FC)

b. General space. Music
stops each minute for 1
minute of stretching.

b. Vary the direction and path-ways. How did you begin to change direction and pathway while maintaining the gallop?

c. Flexibility exercises
for quadriceps, ham-
strings, lower back.(*FF)

c. Self space each time the
music stops. Teacher demonstrates and leads. Students
may lead if the class has
learned the exercise pre-
viously.

c. One muscle group during each
break in the music. Slow,
static stretching.

II. Motor Skills/Movement
Concepts
a. Skipping variations
1. Skip in three dif-
ferent pathways.

a. General space

1. Can you keep the rhythm
as you change the pathway?
How did you initiate a change
in pathway?

p. 206

123

2. Skip in three different directions.

2. Can you skip rhythmically while going sideways and backward? How did the skip change as you moved in different directions?

3. Skip at three different levels. Begin skipping as low as you can, gradually raising the level of your skip until you skip as high as you can. Now gradually change to skip once again at the low level.

3. How high can you skip? How low can you skip? Can you keep the skip rhythmical as you change level?

4. Skip with a partner.
   a) Holding hands.
   b) Following your partner.

4. Choose a partner close by. Scattered in general space.

4. Can you skip in the same rhythm as well as in the same pathways and directions? How did you adjust your skip to stay with your partner?

III. Culminating Activity
   a. Skipping challenges
      1. How few skips can you do while crossing the gym?

      2. In how small a circle can you skip?

a. General space. Teacher provides verbal challenges at first. Also, give students a chance to offer challenges. It is particularly fun when two students create a challenge together.

p. 206

1-5. During each challenge students should maintain mechanics, rhythm and flow in their skipping. How did your skip change in each challenge?

3. Can you skip while moving in a circular pathway?

4. Can you and a partner skip in a straight pathway while facing each other?

5. Can you skip and dribble a ball; toss and catch a ball; move the ball around your body?

| SPECIFIC OBJECTIVES/EVALUATIVE CRITERIA | EQUIPMENT |

To dodge by bending knees and shifting body weight in the   Traffic cones
   new direction of movement.
To dodge around both stationary and moving objects.
To dodge in different directions and pathways and at
   different speeds.

| ACTIVITY | PROCEDURES/ORGANIZATION | POINTS OF EMPHASIS | REFERENCES |

I. Opening Activity
   a. Fitness stations
      1. Pullups/flexed
         arm hang.

   a. Stations set up around the
   gym, each with a capacity for
   several children. Students
   move from station to station
   on signal. Signal change when
   all students have finished their
   turns.

   1. Do as many pullups as possible. If unable to do pullups,
   hold flexed arm position as
   long as possible. A clock or
   watch is necessary for timing.

      2. Modified situps

   2. Done with a partner. Do as   p. 258, Ch. 17
   many as possible in 30 seconds,
   then switch.

      3. Seal crawl

   3. Do the seal crawl up to and
   around a marker, then back.

      4. Standing broad
         jump (*FS)

   4. Have several mats with feet
   and inch marks indicated with
   masking tape.

II. Motor Skills/Movement
    Concepts
   a. Discussion of dodging   a. Single group with teacher.   a. Stress importance of anti-   pp. 208-209
                                                                        cipating collisions and obsta-
                                                                        cles. Bend knees and shift body
                                                                        weight in the new direction.

b. Run through general space, dodging other people.

b. General space

b-d. Can you anticipate the movements of others, cones, and balls to perform a good dodge? What is different about dodging stationary and moving obstacles?

c. Run through general space, dodging other people and the traffic cones.

c. General space with cones scattered throughout the space.

d. Dodge rolling balls while running. (*FC)

d. Half the class running in general space, half the class rolling balls across gym.

e. One attempts to move to a spot in the gym moving and dodging his/her partner.

e. Choose a partner close by. Scattered in general space.

e. Can you fake a dodge in one direction and then move in another?

III. Culminating Activity
a. Gophers in the Garden

a. Lines of bean bags in the shape of garden rows. Two or three games should be played simultaneously to keep participation level high.

a. Gopher should make the path difficult to follow. Gardener must watch the path carefully. Can you fake your dodge and move in a new pathway?

p. 478

127

SPECIFIC OBJECTIVES/EVALUATIVE CRITERIA	EQUIPMENT

To take-off by bending and extending legs, pushing off with feet
  and swinging arms to increase force.

To land softly, bending knees, hips and ankles to absorb force.   Platforms, benches or bleachers

To land using a variety of body parts.   Hoops

To land in various positions.   Mats

To review dodging by keeping body low, bending knees and   Sticks and cones
  moving body weight in new direction.

ACTIVITY	PROCEDURES/ORGANIZATION	POINTS OF EMPHASIS	REFERENCES

I. Opening Activity

a. People Dodge. Students run through general space, dodging other people. If two people collide or make contact, they stop and stretch for 15 seconds, then resume play. Demonstrate two or three flexibility exercises they may choose from. (*FC, FF)

a. Move into open spaces. Keep center of gravity low, knees bent to change directions quickly. Stretching is a way to help the muscles perform better during the game. Stretch slowly.

II. Motor Skills/Movement Concepts

a. Landing from different forms of flight (leap, hop, jump).

a. General space

a. How did you land so that your feet did not make any noise?   p. 209

b. Landing when jumping from (a bench, bleachers, etc.) of various heights.

b. General space

b. How did the height change the way you landed?

III. Culminating Activity
a. Jumping/landing stations

a. Stations placed around the gym. Rotate to next station every 2 to 3 minutes.

p. 209

1. Jump from a stage (platform, bench, bleacher, etc.) into a hoop on a mat.

1. Several platforms of increasing height is best. Students progress to the height they are comfortable jumping from.

1. Bend knees, absorb force to maintain balance in hoop.

2. Hurdles

2. Plastic sticks placed on 12" to 20" cones.

2. Leap over the hurdles low, land softly, continue running as foot lands. p. 353

3. Running jump for distance.

3. Jump onto a mat that has feet and inches marked off.

3. Land on two feet, bending knees into a crouch on landing. How did you change your jump to jump farther? How did your landing change? p. 209

4. Jump for height.

4. A bar or long jump rope supported by two posts (or chairs), with a landing mat on the opposite side.

4. Land on hands and feet. Control take-off and flight so that a safe landing on hands and feet is possible.

5. Vertical jump. (*FS)

5. Vertical jump to touch lines on the wall of increasing height.

5. Swing arms and flex knees for more height. Land with knees flexed, facing in the same direction as the take-off. p. 254

SPECIFIC OBJECTIVES/EVALUATIVE CRITERIA

EQUIPMENT

To develop an awareness of the movement potential of each body
  part to bend, stretch, twist and turn.
To use many body parts in bending, twisting, stretching and turning activities.
To feel the tension and relaxation of muscles involved in bending
  and stretching.

ACTIVITY	PROCEDURES/ORGANIZATION	POINTS OF EMPHASIS	REFERENCES

I. Opening Activity

  a. Locomotor movements, pathways, directions, levels.

1. On verbal cues from teacher, students move through general space using the locomotor movement, pathway, direction and level indicated.	1. General space	1-2. Maintain good rhythm and form during each movement.	
2. Repeat above, but partner directed or led.	2. Partner may use verbal cues, give a demonstration that must be followed, or lead the part- ner through the challenge.		

II. Motor Skills/Movement
  Concepts
  a. Nonlocomotor move-
  ments:

1. Bend different body parts, then stretch those parts.

1. Self space, teacher giving verbal cues and demonstration when needed.

1. Feel the tension and muscle flexion. How many different body parts can you bend and stretch?

p. 209

2. Jump and stretch - land and bend.

2. Same as above.

2. Try it several times, stretching higher and bending more each time.

3. Twist several different body parts.

3. Same as above.

3-4. Some parts twist, others will not. Which ones twist?

4 Twist several different body parts at the same time.

4. Same as above.

5. Move through the gym, twist and turn your body and its parts.

5. General space.

5. Can you twist some body parts while the whole body moves and turns?

6. Move through the gym, bend and stretch your body and its parts. (*FF)

6. General space.

6. Can you feel your muscles bend and stretch as the whole body moves?

p. 170

III. Culminating Activity
    a. "Sculptor". One partner is the artist, the other is the clay. The artist bends, stretches, twists, turns and moves each body part to make his/her "masterpiece".

a. Students working with a partner.

a. Try to include each of the non-locomotor movement qualities discussed. Clay partner will really have to feel his muscles and bones being placed into position and hold them there.

p. 170

SPECIFIC OBJECTIVES/EVALUATIVE CRITERIA	EQUIPMENT

To develop the overhand throw by turning the side in the direction of the throw, using an overhand motion and following through in the direction of the throw. To adjust the overhand throw for different levels and distances. To throw overhand varying the force. To catch a ball thrown at various levels speeds and distances by lining up with the ball, reaching out and pulling the the ball in with two hands.	Nerf balls or fleece balls Hoops

---

ACTIVITY	PROCEDURES/ORGANIZATION	POINTS OF EMPHASIS	REFERENCES

ACTIVITY	PROCEDURES/ORGANIZATION	POINTS OF EMPHASIS	REFERENCES
I. Opening Activity a. "Jog and Toss". Students jog throughout gym tossing and catching their ball. The teacher gives cues to change locomotor movements, pathways or directions. (*FC)	a. General space, each student with his/her own nerf or fleece ball.	a. Move into open areas to avoid collisions. Can you control the ball as you move in general space?	
b. Stretch and rest. Students stretch various muscle groups used in running and/or throwing. (*FF) II. Motor Skills/Movement Concepts a. Overhand throwing	b. General space, teacher giving direction/demonstration.	b. Slow, static stretching. Can you reach the ball to your toes with your legs straight? How far down your back can you reach the ball?	p. 183 p. 214

1. Throw the ball at the wall at different levels.

2. Aim for specific spots on the wall.

b. Overhand throwing to a partner.
1. Throw smoothly so a partner can catch it.

2. Throw to partner at different levels.

3. Throw to partner at different distances.

1. Students spread out evenly around the gym facing the wall.

2. Same as above, using blocks, tiles or other targets on the wall.

b. General space. Spread out so that pairs do not intersect pathways.

1. Side facing direction of throw, overhand motion and follow through in direction of throw. How did you adjust throw to throw to different levels?

2. End pointing fingers to target.

p. 214

1. Throw directly to your partner's hands. Throw with a force your partner can handle. Line up with ball, reach out to pull it in with two hands to catch.

2. As the levels change, the receiver must move body in front of ball, focus on ball and absorb the force.

3. As distance increases, the step becomes more important to impact force. Use the entire arm/shoulder muscle group in the throw. Catching at longer distances requires more movement to get in line with the ball.

III. Culminating Activity

a. "Target Shoot". One partner throws the nerf ball overhand through the hoop. For each successful throw, the hoop holder moves one step back. The object is to see how far away each can be and still throw through the hoop. (*FS)

a. One partner holds the hoop over his/her head. Second partner throws the ball through the hoop. When thrower misses three times, they change places.

a. Step toward the hoop with opposite foot when throwing. Follow through with throwing hand in the direction of the throw. Aim care-

---

SPECIFIC OBJECTIVES/EVALUATIVE CRITERIA	EQUIPMENT

To throw sidearm by leading with elbow, stepping toward
   target with opposite foot and following through in the
   direction of the throw.

To throw sidearm at different levels and distances.

To throw sidearm varying the force.

To catch a ball thrown at different levels, speeds and distances by moving in line with the ball, reaching out
   and absorbing force in pulling it in toward the body.

To review the underhand and overhand throws by stepping
   forward on opposite foot and following through in the
   direction of the throw.

Nerf balls or fleece balls
Hoops

ACTIVITY	PROCEDURES/ORGANIZATION	POINTS OF EMPHASIS	REFERENCES

I. Opening Activity

a. "Partner Catch. Play catch with a partner from various levels and distances using overhand and underhand techniques.

   a. General space with a partner.

   a. Plan the technique, level, speed, etc. before you make the throw. How many ways can you change the throw and still get it to a partner?

   pp. 214-215

b. "Target Shoot". Review from previous lesson.

   b. In partners with a hoop.

   b. Step toward the hoop with the opposite foot when throwing. Follow through in the direction of the throw.

II. Motor Skills/Movement
   Concepts
   a. Sidearm throwing

   p. 215

1. Throw at the wall at different levels and forces.

1. Students spread out evenly around the gym, facing the walls.

1. Lead with elbow, step and and follow through. How high can you throw it using the sidearm?   p. 214

2. Hit target spots on the wall.

2. Same as above.

2. Follow through in the direction of the throw. Step toward the target with the opposite foot.

b. Discuss different throwing techniques; compare underhand, overhand, sidearm; review demonstration of catching.

b. Students seated in a group.

b. How does technique vary in each of the throws? What are the similarities? What are the important aspects of catching?   p. 214

c. Throw and catch with a partner.
   1. Throw from different distances using each throwing technique.

1. Students lined up evenly along a line facing their partners.

1. As the distance increases, which throw is more accurate? Provides more force? Control throw so that your partner can easily catch it.   p. 215

III. Culminating Activity
   a. "Boundary Ball"

a. Divided into two teams, each scattered on one-half of the court.

a. Throw at the appropriate level (below head height). Throw (aim) into the open spaces. Use the throwing technique which will best get the ball across the boundary line (it may vary depending on where opponents stand).   p. 491

   b. Relax and stretch. (*FF)

b. Self space

b. Slow, static stretching of the arm and shoulder muscle groups. "Cooling down" from the game.   p. 258, Ch. 17

136

SPECIFIC OBJECTIVES/EVALUATIVE CRITERIA	EQUIPMENT

To practice catching, moving in the direction of the throw
  to line up with it.
To catch a ball thrown at different levels, speeds and
  pathways.
To throw a ball overhand, underhand and sidearm at different
  levels and speeds, adjusting arm swing and follow-through.
To strike a ball by hitting the ball with the hand in an
  underhand motion and following through in the direction
  of the hit.
To throw to a moving target by placing ball ahead of receiver.

Rubber playground balls
Nerf balls
Fleece balls

ACTIVITY	PROCEDURES/ORGANIZATION	POINTS OF EMPHASIS	REFERENCES

I. Opening Activity
  a. Partners jog together
  and toss a ball back and
  forth. Vary the throws
  using underhand, sidearm
  and overhand. Vary the
  type of locomotor move-
  ment. (*FC)

a. Partners moving together
(5 to 8 feet apart) through
general space.

a. Where did you throw the ball
so that your moving partner
could catch it?

II. Motor Skills/Movement
  Concepts
  a. Catch a ball.
    1. Throw each ball
    against the wall and
    catch it.

1. Scattered in general
space, each student has a
nerf ball and a playground
ball.

1. Which ball was easier to
catch? How did you change
the force with each ball?
Extend hands to meet ball.
Absorb force by pulling back
as ball enters hands.

p. 215

2. Throw each verti-
cally and catch.

2. Same as above.

2. Move into position under   p. 211
the ball. How did you adjust
for the nerf ball? The playground ball?

b. Striking a ball -
discuss and demonstrate.
(*FS)

b. Drop ball and hit with under-   p. 216
hand motion. End pointing hand
in direction of throw.

c. Strike a ball.
1. Bounce the ball,
then hit it against
the wall with one hand.

c. Scattered facing the wall
with a playground or nerf
ball.

1. How did you adjust hit to
project ball to different
levels? Experiment with hitting ball with a fist and an
open hand.

2. Toss it vertically,
then hit it with one
hand against the wall.

2. Can you hit the ball without a bounce first?

III. Culminating Activity
a. "Four Square". Part-
ners attempt to hit the
ball back and forth over
the lines.

a. In partners, separated by
a line on the floor, or each
in a box.

a. Can you and your partner   p. 576
have 5 successive hits before
missing? Can you control the
force to keep the ball moving?

b. Relax and stretch.
(*FF)

b. Self space

b. Slow static stretching of
quadricep, abdominal and hamstring muscle groups. "Cool
down" from the game.

138

| SPECIFIC OBJECTIVES/EVALUATIVE CRITERIA | EQUIPMENT |

To strike a ball with the hand with an underhand movement,   A variety of nerf and playground balls.
    controlling force and following through in the direction
    of the hit.
To throw overhand, controlling level and force.
To catch, adjusting position to line up with an oncoming ball,
    absorbing force by reaching out and pulling it in.
To roll a ball underhand with accuracy by bending legs and
    following through in the direction of the throw.

| ACTIVITY | PROCEDURES/ORGANIZATION | POINTS OF EMPHASIS | REFERENCES |

I. Opening Activity
   a. Individual ball hand-   a. Scattered in general space,   a. How many different ways can
      ling: moving in general   children select the type of   you control the ball as you move
      space with a variety of   ball they wish to work with.   through general space?
      ball skills.

II. Motor Skills/Movement
    Concepts
    a. Ball handling stations.   a. In 4 small groups. Rotate
                                   stations every 5-7 minutes.
       1. Wall targets.   1. Targets varying in height   1. How did you adjust throw   p. 215
       Throw to targets vary-   on the wall.   for level and distance?
       ing in level and dis-
       tance. After 3 suc-
       cessful throws to
       target, step back to
       increase distance.

2. Four-square. Keep track of number of consecutive hits.

2. Small courts or lines to separate partners.

2. Can you control force to keep ball going?

p. 576

3. Bowling

3. Sets of 3-5 pins set up for each 2 children. One sets pins, one bowls; change after 2 tries to hit all pins.

3. How did you direct throw to pins? Could you get a spare?

4. Partner throwing (overhand, underhand, sidearm) and catching. Throwing to partner's left or right.

4. In partners.

4. Can you throw the ball to make your partner move to receive it? Can you move to line up with the ball?

p. 216

SPECIFIC OBJECTIVES/EVALUATIVE CRITERIA	EQUIPMENT
To move in a variety of pathways and directions. To vary pathway of an object while moving in space To move with objects in various pathways.	Hoops Balls Ribbons

----

ACTIVITY	PROCEDURES/ORGANIZATION	POINTS OF EMPHASIS	REFERENCES

I. Opening Activity

a. Moving in various pathways and directions in general space.

a. Scattered in general space with a hoop. Change movement on signal.

a. In what pathways did you move? What directions?

II. Motor Skills/Movement Concepts

a. Hoop activities

1. Move in general space with a hoop.

a. Scattered in general space with a hoop. Change movement on signal.

1. What ways can you move with your hoop?

2. Move with your hoop in a forward direction. Now backward. To the right. Left. Up. Down.

2. What ways can you move in in each direction with your hoop?

3. Moving in different pathways.

a) Move in a straight path; a curved path.

a) How did you get your hoop to follow the desired path?

141

b) Choose two points
in the room. Move with
your hoop from one to
the other.

b. Ball activities. Repeat
hoop activities a. 1-3 but with
a ball.

III. Culminating Activity
a. Ribbons
1. Move ribbon in a
variety of pathways in
the air in front of you.
To the side. Above you.

2. Move through general
space moving in a path
similar to that of your
ribbon.

3. Move through general
space in a path differ-
ent from the path of the
ribbon.

b) Can you move your body
in one pathway and the hoop
in another?

b. There may be more variety   pp. 276-277
in responses with ball.

1. In self space.

2. In general space.

3. In general space. After
exploring, children show
some of their responses to
the class.

1. How would you describe   p. 290
the path of your ribbon?

2. What design do you make
on the floor as you move?
In the air?

3. What combinations were
most interesting?

SPECIFIC OBJECTIVES/EVALUATIVE CRITERIA	EQUIPMENT

To develop dynamic balance on stilts, keeping center of gravity over stilts and looking at a spot ahead.

To balance by centering base of support over balance board.

To balance while moving through various obstacles.

To maintain balance while balancing objects.

Tin can stilts
Balance boards
Bean bags
Jugs filled with varying amounts of sand.
Foam balls

ACTIVITY	PROCEDURES/ORGANIZATION	POINTS OF EMPHASIS	REFERENCES

I. Opening Activity
  a. Fitness fun.

1. Wheelbarrow walk. (*FS)	1. In general space. Change positions several times.	1. Follow slowly behind partner.	p. 311
2. Mule kick. (*FS)	2. Self space.	2. How long can you kick your feet while balancing on your hands?	p. 309

II. Motor Skills/Movement Concepts

a. Stilt walk	a. Self and general space. If not enough stilts are available, partners may take turns.	a. Keep the center of gravity over the cans. Smaller steps are easiest. Look ahead as you move.	p. 296
b. Balance boards 1. Balance on board.	b. In partners or groups. Two take turns on board other two perform tasks on one foot, switch roles.	1. Partner helps by holding balancer's hand until he/she seems to be balanced.	p. 296

2. Try putting feet in
different positions
on the board.

2. Which position worked best?

3. Balance on board
balancing bean bags on
various body parts.

3-4. What did you do to keep
balanced as you balanced
objects?

4. Balance on board
while holding one or
two jugs containing un-
equal amounts of sand.

5. Catch a ball thrown
by a partner while
balancing.

5. How did you adjust balance
in catching and throwing ball?

III. Culminating Activity
a. Balance obstacle course.
Set up an obstacle course
with objects to go around,
over lines to straddle or
cross, etc.

a. Organize class into groups
to begin at different places
in the obstacle course.

a. Which obstacles were the
most challenging? How did
you adjust your balance?

p. 247

SPECIFIC OBJECTIVES/EVALUATIVE CRITERIA	EQUIPMENT

To control force in using a variety of body parts to hit a
  balloon to a partner.
To balance on stilts keeping feet centered on cans and looking
  forward in direction of movement.
To adjust balance position performing tasks from a balance board.
To control a ball while moving through an obstacle course.
To jump long ropes in a variety of ways keeping jumping rhythm
  going, changing skills smoothly and landing softly.

Balloons
Tin can stilts
Balance boards
Discs/cones/balls/bean bags
Playground balls

ACTIVITY	PROCEDURES/ORGANIZATION	POINTS OF EMPHASIS	REFERENCES

I. Opening Activity
   a. Introduce each station,
   indicating what should be
   done and any rules that
   apply.

a. Students seated as teacher
explains stations. These stations are selected for, and
best used for, an outdoor
set-up.

a. What are some of the activities we have done in previous
lessons?

II. Motor Skills/Movement
   Concepts
   a. Stations
      1. Balloons: explore
      ways of hitting bal-
      loon to partner.

a. Students divided into small
groups. Rotate to next station after 5-7 minutes.

1. How many ways can you
hit balloon to partner?
How many consecutive hits
can you perform without
missing? How softly can
hit the balloon? How hard,
keeping it under control?

p. 275

2. Stilts obstacle course. An obstacle course of cones, 3-foot to 4-foot high cross bar, ropes, hoops, etc. Students move under, over and through.

2. Can you move through the course without touching any of the markers, hoops or bars? Can you move through the course keeping your balance? p. 296

3. Long ropes. Jump in a variety of ways: feet in various positions, turning, touching the ground, etc.

3. In groups of 3, 2 turners and 1 jumper.

3. Can you combine 2 or 3 different jumps without stopping? p. 291

4. Balls obstacle course. Each student with a ball and an obstacle course of cones, high bars, low bars and natural obstacles (trees, bushes, swing sets, etc.) through, over and under which each must move. (*FC)

4. Scattered in course to begin at different places.

4. Can you steer your ball through the course with your feet? Can you dribble your ball through the course? Can you roll your ball through the course? pp. 276-277

5. Balance boards. How many ways can you balance? Can you and a partner play catch with a bean bag while balancing?

5. Each student with a balance board.

5. Keep feet spread equally on each side of the board. p. 296

SPECIFIC OBJECTIVES/EVALUATIVE CRITERIA	EQUIPMENT

To move safely in gymnastic activities by allowing
   sufficient space for the activity.

To review the forward roll, tucking chin, maintaining
   tuck position and pushing equally with hands.

To move smoothly from one movement or support to another.

Mats
Short jump ropes

ACTIVITY	PROCEDURES/ORGANIZATION	POINTS OF EMPHASIS	REFERENCES

ACTIVITY	PROCEDURES/ORGANIZATION	POINTS OF EMPHASIS	REFERENCES
I. Opening Activity a. Rope jumping (*FC)	a. Self space, each student with a rope.	a. Encourage the use of variety of jumping skills taught in previous lessons.	
b. Stretches (*FF)	b. Stretching exercises can take place during rest between jumping bouts.	b. Discuss how flexible muscles allow for greater range of motion. Explore "how far" different muscles will stretch.	
II. Motor Skills/Movement Concepts a. Individual stunts	a. Self space on a mat.	a. Review safety. Be sure you have enough space to move without collisions.	
1. Single leg circles.		1. Bend the inside leg and keep the back straight. Can you change supporting hand smoothly?	p. 310
2. Coffee grinder.		2. Keep body straight, slowly turning supporting hand.	p. 310

3. Forward roll. (*FS)

3. Children find a space at one side of the mat and then work across the mat.

3. Review skills taught pre- p. 312
viously. Tuck head, maintain tuck position, push
equally with hands. What
body parts support the body
throughout the skill?

III. Culminating Activity
   a. Partner stunts.
      1. Monkey walk

a. Partners on a mat.

1. Hold legs tightly around p. 311
partner's waist. Walk slowly.
What body parts were used for
support?

      2. Eskimo roll.

2. Review skills of the for- p. 260
ward roll, applying them to
Eskimo roll. Maintain tight
grasp with hands. What body
parts were used for support?

SPECIFIC OBJECTIVES/EVALUATIVE CRITERIA	EQUIPMENT

To move the body with changing body supports.

To roll forward keeping head and body tucked, pushing with hands and coming up to feet.

To do a backward roll maintaining a tuck position, pushing with hands at shoulders, fingers pointing in direction of movement and coming back up to feet.

To perform a back straddle roll keeping legs straight, pulling them over the head, head tucked, and pushing with hands.

To combine movements smoothly.

Mats

ACTIVITY	PROCEDURES/ORGANIZATION	POINTS OF EMPHASIS	REFERENCES

I. Opening Activity

a. Review animal walks.
1. Gorilla walk
2. Bear walk
3. Bear dance
4. Lame dog
5. Snail (*FS)

a. Self space on or around mats. Students can recall and select their favorites.

a. Smooth, coordinated movements. What is the base of support? Smooth flow throughout the movement range.

p. 308

b. Stretches (*FF)

b. Self space. Students may have the opportunity to lead or suggest different exercises.

b. Slow, static stretching. Stretching challenges are fun. Can you stretch further than you did last time? How far can you reach and stretch?

p. 183

c. Review forward roll.

c. Roll across mats; two or three students can work on a mat simultaneously.

c. Keep head and body in a tuck. Push with hands. Come up to feet. What body parts were used for support?

p. 312

II. Motor Skills/Movement
Concepts.

a. Backward roll

a. Roll across mats. Those having difficulty are spotted by the teacher, lifting to support neck.

a. Push with the hands. Keep in tucked position. Where did supporting parts change?

p. 316

b. Backward straddle roll

b. Same as above, but only one person at a time as the straddle requires more room.

b. Keep legs straight and pull them over the head. Push off with hands.

p. 316

III. Culminating Activity

a. Develop a routine. Blend a forward roll, half turn and backward roll together in a continuous sequence of movements.

a. Students will need to take turns working down the length of the mat.

a-b. Discuss and emphasize the flow of movements. Make the movement non-stop. Begin and finish the sequence with good posture and form.

p. 327

b. What other combinations of two skills from previous lessons can you combine?

SPECIFIC OBJECTIVES/EVALUATIVE CRITERIA   EQUIPMENT

To review rolls keeping body tucked and moving smoothly   Mats
   throughout the roll.   Music
To perform a cartwheel by keeping body straight and placing
   hands and feet in sequence - hand, hand, foot, foot.

ACTIVITY	PROCEDURES/ORGANIZATION	POINTS OF EMPHASIS	REFERENCES

I. Opening Activity

a. Locomotor Warmup. Students skip, gallop, jog, hop, leap and jump in the spaces between the mats. (*FC)

    a. Students move in the spaces between the mats. Occasionally, on signal from the teacher, students may leap or jump over the mats.

    a. Discuss the importance of warmup and warm muscles for gymnastics. Make movements controlled, smooth and free-flowing.

b. Stretches (*FF)

    b. Self space on a mat. Students may lead or suggest the exercises.

    b. Slow, static stretching. Can you stretch further than you could before? Offer specific stretching incentives or goals, particularly for those who have difficulty.

II. Motor Skills/Movement Concepts

a. Review roll variations.
   1. Forward roll
   2. Log roll
   3. Egg roll
   4. Backward roll

    a. Self space, spending only one or two minutes on each.

    a. Review the key points of each roll briefly. Look for tight tucks, smooth movements, control. Emphasize a good start and finish position (Olympic form!!).

    pp. 312, 313, 316

b. Cartwheel

b. May be done on a mat or on a line on the floor.

b. Make the cartwheel high and straight. Strength in arms needs to be emphasized. Maintain the hand, hand, foot, foot sequence.

p. 316

III. Culminating Activity

a. Free time to work on stunts students need work on or enjoy most.

a. Students working at mats in groups, partners or alone.

a. Work safely and care- fully. Help a friend who is having difficulty.

b. Combining stunts. Combine 2 to 3 stunts covered in the unit into a routine. Can you include a change in direction, level or pathway?

b. Children may work indi- vidually or with a partner.

b. Can you blend several stunts into a flowing routine? Can you coordinate your move- ments with a partner? What other concepts did you use?

p. 328

SPECIFIC OBJECTIVES/EVALUATIVE CRITERIA	EQUIPMENT

To keep balance while walking over an obstacle on a low balance beam, focusing on end of beam.

To move from a low to high level while moving across a low balance beam, using arms for balance.

To swing across mat over an obstacle and drop off, reaching high on rope and landing softly.

To jump off a Swedish box and land with legs bent to absorb force and hold landing.

To perform the sloth walk gripping bar with hands and legs and moving with a hand-over-hand motion.

To perform a front support mount on the horizontal bar, springing with legs, pushing with hands and ending with body and arms straight and hips resting against the bar.

To relax tense muscles.

Equipment:
Rope
Swedish box and crash pad
Low balance beam
Horizontal bar
Mats under all equipment

ACTIVITY	PROCEDURES/ORGANIZATION	POINTS OF EMPHASIS	REFERENCES

I. Opening Activity

a. Bent knee situps (*FS)	a. Self space. Class counts together as they perform sit-ups.	a. Knees bent, arms crossed over chest and holding shoulders.	
b. Pushups (*FS)	b. Self space	b. Body straight with hands underneath shoulders, lower body to touch nose to floor.	
c. Stretches (*FF)	c. Self space	c. Slow, gentle stretches; name muscles as they are being stretched.	

II. Motor Skills/Movement Concepts.

a. Obstacle course

1. Explain and demonstrate each part of course. Then begin activity.

    a) Balance beam: walk over obstacle on low

    b) Ropes: swing across mat and drop off. beam.

    c) Swedish box: jump off and land with good balance.

    d) Horizontal bar: sloth walk.

1. Seated where all parts of the obstacle course are visible. Small groups move to various places on the course and begin moving. Locomotor skills between apparatus may also be included.

a) Focus on end of beam; use arms for balance.

b) Reach high on rope; land softly.

c) Bend knees and hold landing.

d) Grip bar with hands and legs; use a hand-over-hand movement to pull you along.

pp. 382, 335, 336

2. Slightly change selected tasks along the course.

    a) Horizontal bar: perform front support mount.

    b) Beam: move changing level from low to high.

    c) Ropes: swing over an obstacle and drop off.

2. Signal for students to stop, give new directions and signal for them to begin again.

a) Jump to pull up with arms straight, hips on bar - body extended.

b) Focus on end of beam; use arms for balance.

c) Lift body over obstacle; land softly.

pp. 231, 334, 344

III. Culminating Activity
    a. Relaxation

1. Lie down on floor, eyes closed.	1. Self space	1. Feel the muscles that you have worked today. Where are they? Now think about them and make them feel as relaxed as you can.
2. Deep, rhythmic breathing.	2. Self space	2. Expand the abdomen with each breath; with each breath feel muscles relax.

SPECIFIC OBJECTIVES/EVALUATIVE CRITERIA	EQUIPMENT

To perform as many pullups as possible with the rope,
   pulling up with hand-over-hand motion and keeping
   body straight.

To perform a two-foot takeoff, landing with both feet
   on the board simultaneously and pushing off with
   both feet to spring into the air.

To review the front support mount, pushing off with
   both feet and pushing with arms until they are straight
   and hips are resting against the bar.

To perform toe touches on the beam, with toes pointed and
   focusing on the end of the beam.

To perform a back hip pullover on the horizontal bar by
   keeping upper body in close to bar as leg kicks up and over.

To combine skills smoothly so movement is continuous from one
   skill to the next.

Horizontal bar
Hanging rope
High balance beam
Springboard

ACTIVITY	PROCEDURES/ORGANIZATION	POINTS OF EMPHASIS	REFERENCES

I. Opening Activity
   a. "Simon Says"
      (*FC) (*FF)

a. Self spaces, facing "Simon". Teacher or student leader.

a. Include locomotor movements and stretches. Encourage good listening skills and holding stretches.

II. Motor Skills/Movement
   Concepts
   a. Station work
      1. Ropes: pullups
         on rope.

a. Seated in group where all equipment is visible for demonstration. Divide into 4 groups. Rotate every 5-7 minutes.

1. Reach up, gripping rope. Keep body straight. Pull hand over hand until standing.

p. 340

2. Springboard: two-foot takeoff from springboard.

   a) Front support on high beam

   b) Toe touches on high beam

4. Horizontal bar: back hip pullover on horizontal bar.

2. Did you land with both feet simultaneously on the springboard. Emphasize a balanced landing, with legs bent.   p. 344

   a) Spring with legs and push with arms until arms are straight and hips are resting against beam. Hands may stay on beam or momentarily extend to the sides.   p. 332

   b) Walking forward, touch toes briefly on beam before taking weight onto that foot. Repeat, walking backwards.   p. 332

4. Kick up and over the bar with one leg, bending the arms to keep body close to the bar and lifting body under and over bar to end in a front support position.   p. 334

III. Culminating Activity
  a. Skill combinations

a. As students work at stations, encourage combining skills from this and previous lessons. Provide opportunity for some to show combinations either before changing stations or at the end of class.

a. Can you smoothly combine 2 skills? Did any combinations use a change of level? Direction?

SPECIFIC OBJECTIVES/EVALUATIVE CRITERIA	EQUIPMENT

To perform the rollover dismount on the horizontal bar, gripping bar with regular grip, leaning forward to begin circling and ending in a standing position.

To combine movements smoothly on the horizontal bar and balance beam, with a change in level or direction.

To hold an arabesque for 3 seconds on the balance beam, balancing on one foot, with other leg lifted back as high as possible and back arched.

To dismount the beam with a straddle jump, assuming a straddle position, toes pointed in the air and landing softly.

To perform a bent arm hang on a hanging rope, reaching high up on rope and holding the bent arm position.

To perform a squat mount, taking off with two feet, pushing with hands to bring feet up onto the box.

Jump ropes, one per student
Horizontal bar
Hanging rope
High balance beam
Mats under apparatus
Music
Vaulting box

ACTIVITY	PROCEDURES/ORGANIZATION	POINTS OF EMPHASIS	REFERENCES

I. Opening Activity

a. Rope jumping to music. Try jumping backward or on one foot while keeping rhythm. (*FC)

a. Self space

a. Jump rhythmically, keeping the beat of the music while jumping.

b. Stretches, using jump ropes. Fold jump ropes in half, and use for side bends and long sitting and straddle stretches. (*FF)

b. Self space

b. How far down your leg can you reach with your rope? What muscles do you feel stretching?

II. Motor Skills/Movement
   Concepts
   a. Stations

a. Seated in group where all equipment is visible for demonstration and explanation. Divide into 3 groups. Rotate every 7-8 minutes. Teacher stays at vaulting station.

1. Beam:
   a) Straddle jump from high beam.

a) Assume a straddle in the air, toes pointed before landing. Land softly, bending legs to hold a balanced position.   p. 334

   b) Arabesque on high beam

b) Point back toe, work for good extension of body, arms and legs.   p. 321

2. Horizontal bar: rollover dismount

2. With a regular grip, lean forward over bar to begin to circle the bar. As legs come around, they leave the bar and the performer lands in a standing position.   p. 336

3. Ropes: bent arm hand

3. Reach up with hands, grabbing the rope overhead. Spring with feet, lift with arms and hold the body off the mat as long as possible.   p. 340

4. Vaulting squat
mount

4. Teacher stands in front
of and to the side of the
box (opposite side from
performer). Spot at closest
arm to check momentum.

4. Use 2-foot takeoff. Push
with hands to bring feet up
on box.

III. Culminating Activity
a. Skill combinations.
Combine 2 or more
skills from this and
previous lessons.
previous lessons.

a. Encourage combining skills
as they work. Have some children share combinations throughout the class or at the end.

a. Can you combine skills
smoothly? Did you use a change
of level or direction?

SPECIFIC OBJECTIVES/EVALUATIVE CRITERIA	EQUIPMENT

To combine a variety of body shapes and movements in
   general space.

To create shapes at various levels and to change levels
   smoothly.

To move with a partner changing shape and level.

Music

ACTIVITY	PROCEDURES/ORGANIZATION	POINTS OF EMPHASIS	REFERENCES

| I. Opening Activity
  a. Body shapes
    1. Move to space using an unusual shape.
    2. Move to another space using a different shape.
    3. Move back to your own self space using both shapes on the way. | a. Self and general space, with music playing. | a. Use many body parts in creating your shape. Can you keep that shape even as you move? How would you describe your shape? | p. 375
376
377 |
| II. Motor Skills/Movement Concepts
  a. Change body shapes and levels.
    1. Explore a variety of body shapes at the low level. Medium level. High level.

    2. Combine 3 shapes at one level. | a. Self space, with music playing. | 1. What shapes can you make at the low level? Medium? High?

2. Can you smoothly change shape as you stay at the level you've chosen? | p. 377 |

3. Combine one shape
at each level.

III. Culminating Activity
    a. Blend shapes and levels
with a partner.
      1. Move in self or
general space; decide
on 3 shapes to do in
sequence.

      2. Repeat sequence
changing level on
each shape.

      3. Perform sequence.
Add another concept,
such as a change in
direction, as you re-
peat the sequence again.

      4. Children perform
sequences.

a. With a partner in general
space, music playing.

4. One-third of the class
at a line.

3. Can you make each shape and
level flow smoothly to the next?

p. 377

1. Can you move smoothly from
one shape to the next? Time
movements with a partner?

2. Which shapes worked best
at what level? Did some work
best at one level or another?

3. What concept did you use?
How did it make your sequence
more interesting?

4. What did you like about the
sequences? Are there some
ideas you'd like to try?

| SPECIFIC OBJECTIVES/EVALUATIVE CRITERIA | EQUIPMENT |

To respond to a variety of rhythmic patterns.
To move in a variety of ways to a rhythmic pattern.
To teach a partner a rhythmic pattern.

Music
Rhythm instruments

ACTIVITY	PROCEDURES/ORGANIZATION	POINTS OF EMPHASIS	REFERENCES

ACTIVITY	PROCEDURES/ORGANIZATION	POINTS OF EMPHASIS	REFERENCES
I. Opening Activity a. Clap to various rhythms.	a. Children in a group. Use several musical selections.	a. Listen to how the rhythm repeats itself. Pick up the accenting beat with a louder clap.	p. 381
b. Repeat a rhythm.	b. Leader claps out a rhythmic pattern, children repeat it.	b. Listen to the entire sequence, then repeat it. Does it sound like one person is clapping?	

II. Motor Skills/Movement Concepts
  a. Moving to a rhythmic pattern.
    1. Teacher beats a rhythmic pattern with a drum or in response to some music. Children explore a variety of ways to move to the rhythm.
	a. Children moving in general space.	1. How many ways did you move to the rhythm? Which ways did you like best?	p. 381

2. Child claps a rhythmic pattern (his/her name, a nursery rhyme, etc.) and then moves to it.

2. If needed, children may draw a suggestion from a box. Then move in general space.

2. How did you fit the move-   p. 381
ments to the rhythmic pattern?

III. Culminating Activity
    a. Moving to a partner's rhythmic pattern.

a. In partners in general space.

      1. Show your partner your favorite movement performed in a.2. Clap rhythm first, then move to it.

1. What movements did your partner use? How did they fit the rhythm?

      2. Teach each other your pattern and movements.

2. Can you perform the move-ments smoothly and in time to the rhythmic pattern?

| SPECIFIC OBJECTIVES/EVALUATIVE CRITERIA | EQUIPMENT |

To respond to musical phrasing with a variety of locomotor
   movements.

To smoothly combine movements into a movement sequence.

To combine locomotor or non-locomotor movements and space
   concepts into a movement sequence.

Music

| ACTIVITY | PROCEDURES/ORGANIZATION | POINTS OF EMPHASIS | REFERENCES |

I. Opening Activity
   a. Variety of locomotor
   movements to music. (*FC)

a. General space. Students
change type of movement on
each phrase. Teacher cues
phrases at first.

a. Anticipate the end of the
phrase. Make the change from
one locomotor movement to
another as smoothly as possible.

p. 381

   b. Repeat, but when
   music stops, hold a
   funny shape while balancing on one foot.   (*FS)

b. Hold pose for one phrase.

b. Involve as many body parts
as possible. Make a different shape each time. What
muscles do you feel working?

II. Motor Skills/Movement
   Concepts
   a. Creating a dance
     1. Working alone, each
     student creates a
     series of movements,
     one for each phrase.
     Begin with a 2-phrase
     sequence, then a 4-
     phrase sequence.

1. Students working in
self space with music
playing in background.

1. Make the movements flow
with the music and fit the
phrase.

2. Repeat sequence (2 or 4 phrase). As sequence is repeated, add a change in level, direction or pathway.

3. Each student selects a friend to watch the end product and offer helpful hints.

b. Showing the dance to the class.

2. Informal match-ups with a friend. Each watches the other.

b. Students in a group with teacher. At first take volunteers, then select those who may want to but need encouragement.

2. Could you add a smooth change of level, etc. to your smooth change of movement?

3. Offer your friend hints on how to make it smoother, more rhythmical.

b. Have a definite start and finish to the dance. What combinations did you especially like? What made them interesting?

SPECIFIC OBJECTIVES/EVALUATIVE CRITERIA
EQUIPMENT

To move to the beat of the music.   Folkcraft 1191, 1198
To respond to musical phrasing.
To move with a partner and a group in time to the music.
To make an arch by facing a partner and raising joined hands.

ACTIVITY	PROCEDURES/ORGANIZATION	POINTS OF EMPHASIS	REFERENCES

I. Opening Activity
   a. Students skip, gallop,   a. In general space.   a. Carefully listen to and
   jog, etc. to the beat of   move to the beat of the music.
   the music. When music   Select an unusual balance posi-
   stops, they hold a bal-   tion. What muscles are working
   ance position in the   as you balance?
   nearest hoop. (*FC) (*FS)

II. Motor Skills/Movement
   Concepts
   a. A Hunting We Will Go   a. In lines of 4-6 couples. a. Can you move to the beat?   p. 397
      1. Teach song   Stay with your partner?

      2. Teach movements and   2. Can you and your partner
      perform to song.   face and raise hands for an
                                                            arch through which the other
                                                            children will go?

b. Grand Old Duke of York
1. Teach song

2. Teach movements and perform to music.

c. The Snail: teach movements and perform to music.

b. In lines of 4-6 couples.

c. One line with hands joined. Teacher leads the first time. Then break into 2 groups with student leaders. Change leaders.

b. Can you move to the beat? Stay with your partner? Can you change movement on each new phrase?

c. Can you move with the group to the music's beat?

p. 398

p. 399

SPECIFIC OBJECTIVES/EVALUATIVE CRITERIA   EQUIPMENT

To control the size of steps taken to stay with a partner.   Records: Merit Audio Visual 1041
To move to the beat and musical phrasing
To respond to a change in tempo.

| ACTIVITY | PROCEDURES/ORGANIZATION | POINTS OF EMPHASIS | REFERENCES |

I. Opening Activity			
a. Review dances taught in last lesson.		a. Can you move to the beat and the musical phrasing?	
b. Children's choice of previously learned dance.		b. Can you move to the beat and musical phrasing? How did you adjust steps to stay with partner?	
II. Motor Skills/Movement Concepts			
a. Carousel			
1. Teach to changing tempo.	1. Single circle	1. How did steps and slides change as tempo changed?	p. 405
2. Teach movements with partner.	2. Double circle, children in outside circle with hands on partner's shoulders.	2. How did you adjust steps to stay with partner? To set the pace?	
3. Put together and perform to music.		3. Can you stay with the beat? Anticipate the change in tempo?	

| SPECIFIC OBJECTIVES/EVALUATIVE CRITERIA | EQUIPMENT |

To move to the beat and musical phrasing.
To change movements smoothly.
To perform step-draw with a partner, controlling size of
   steps to stay with partner and maintain formation.

Record: Merit Audio Visual 1041

| ACTIVITY | PROCEDURES/ORGANIZATION | POINTS OF EMPHASIS | REFERENCES |

I. Opening Activity
  a. Move to music.
    1. Jog, walk and skip.

  a. General space

    1. Can you change locomotor -
    movement as the type or beat
    of the music changes?

    2. Select locomotor
    movement and change
    movement on each
    phrase. (*FC)

    2. Can you anticipate the end
    of one phrase and the begin-
    of a new one ? Change move
    ments smoothly?

II. Motor Skills/Movement
    Concepts
  a. Kinderpolka
    1. Practice step-
    draw to music.

  a. Single circle of partners.

    1. Cue step-close, step-   p. 406
    close. Can you take small
    steps to maintain circle
    formation and stay with
    partner?

    2. Teach dance move-
    ments and perform to
    music.

    2. Can you move with partner
    and the phrasing?

III. Culminating Activity
   a. Children's choices of
   previously taught dances.

a. Emphasize moving on the beat
and anticipating the phrasing.
Can you smoothly change movements?

SPECIFIC OBJECTIVES/EVALUATIVE CRITERIA	EQUIPMENT

To move in a variety of pathways in and out of the hoops.

To assume a variety of body shapes with hoops.

To perform nonlocomotor movements with hoops to the
beat of the music.

To perform locomotor skills with hoops to the beat of
the music.

To smoothly combine nonlocomotor with locomotor movements
with hoops to the beat of the music.

Hoops, one per child

ACTIVITY	PROCEDURES/ORGANIZATION	POINTS OF EMPHASIS	REFERENCES

I. Opening Activity
a. Walk, hop and jump in
hoops scattered on floor.
Select a path to follow.
Repeat in a new path.
(*FC)

a. Students move in and out
of hoops in general space.
Music playing.

a. Can you control your movements so that hoops are not
touched? What path did you
follow as you moved in and
out of the hoops?

b. Movement problems.
Can you:
  1. Curl up in hoop?
  2. Stretch over and
  around hoop?
  3. Stretch hoop over
  head and to sides?
  (*FF)

b. Students select a hoop.
Self spaces in hoops.
Music playing.

b. What other activities could
you do? What body shapes did
you use? What muscles did you
feel stretching?

II. Motor Skills/Movement
Concepts
a. Introduce hoops as
rhythmic tools.

a. Seated inside hoops,
scattered around room.

a. Compare rhythmic use of hoops
to use of body parts, balls, etc.
that have been taught previously.

b. Non-locomotor hoop
skills. Can you:
   1. Move hoop over
   head, side to side;
   up and down to
   beat of music?
   2. Circle hoop in
   front of body?
   3. Lunge to sides, moving hoop rhythmically?
   4. Roll hoop on wrist?
   5. What other ways can
   you move to the beat in
   your self space?

b. Self space

b. Use hoop as extension of   p. 438
body; keep the steady beat of
the music with the hoop.

c. Locomotor hoop skills.
Can you:
   1. Walk around hoop while
   holding it vertically on
   floor?
   2. Jump back and forth
   through hoops as jump-
   ing rope?
   3. Roll hoop away, catch
   up to it on beat?
   4. Roll hoop to one side
   then the other, stepping
   to sides as it rolls?

c. Moving through general
space.

c. Release and catch hoop on   p. 438
the beat; move feet in rhythm
with music.

III. Culminating Activity
   a. Combining movements:
   combine one nonlocomotor
   and one locomotor hoop
   activity with a partner
   into a movement sequence.

a. With a partner.

a. Could you smoothly change   p. 438
movements with your hoop?
Move to the beat? Can you
move with a partner?

| SPECIFIC OBJECTIVES/EVALUATIVE CRITERIA | EQUIPMENT |

To smoothly combine ball and locomotor movements.
To perform ball skills rhythmically in self and general space.
To roll and bounce a ball on the beat, with a partner.
To combine ball and locomotor skills in various pathways.

Balls in a variety of sizes; all
should be soft and with some bounce
Music - tape or record with various
tempos, 2/4 or 4/4 time.

| ACTIVITY | PROCEDURES/ORGANIZATION | POINTS OF EMPHASIS | REFERENCES |

I. Opening Activity
   a. Locomotor warm-up.
   Use locomotor skills,
   move rhythmically
   throughout general
   space; change direction
   on the beginning of a
   phrase. (*FC)

a. Scattered in general
space. Music playing.

a. Keep the steady beat of the
music while moving and changing
direction.

   b. Stretches. Imitate
   animals, athletes and
   shapes. (*FF)

b. In general space. Move
to teacher and student suggestions.

b. Stretches should be full and
relaxed. In what muscles do you
feel stretching?

II. Motor Skills/Movement
    Concepts
   a. Body and ball move-
   ments. Students demonstrate ways they moved
   hands/arms rhythmically
   and how they could in-
   clude use of ball in same
   or similar movements.

a. In self space.

a. Balls can be used as extension of body or moved separately.
Can you move arms and hands on
the beat?

174

b. Problem solving with balls in self space. Can you:

   1. Make designs with ball, use left and right and variety of levels?

   2. Bounce ball in front of body and catch it; at sides and catch it?

   3. Toss ball in air with two-hand underhand motion and catch it?

   4. Bounce, bounce, bounce, catch, bounce, catch?

   5. Roll the ball from one hand to the other, side to side?

c. Problem solving in general space.
   1. Make a design with the ball as you move through space.

   2. Throw the ball vertically in the air and slightly forward; move under it and catch it.

b. In self space.

c. In general space.

b. Use body to show ball's path and to release and absorb force of ball.
p. 437

c. Actions should begin before the beat so that the throw or contact on the bounce will be on the beat.
p. 437

3. Execute a ball skill
in place, stop, do a
locomotor movement,
stop, repeat.

4. Execute a ball skill
as you skip, slide and
gallop.

5. Execute ball skills
while moving in various
pathways.

III. Culminating Activity
a. Ball skills with a
partner.

a. Partners scattered throughout room, sitting and facing
each other.

1. Roll the ball to
a partner, catch
and hold.

1. Time movements so that   p. 438
delivery is on the beat.

2. Roll the ball to
partner, stretching
arm and ball high
over head on catch.

2. If you catch the ball
before it is time to return
it, what could you do with it?

3. Bounce ball to
partner, catch and
hold. Repeat.

3. Hold appropriate amount of
time so that bounce is on the
beat; action should start
before the beat so that the
bounce will be on the beat.

4. Bounce ball three
times to self, then
to partner.

4. Does it sound like one ball
bouncing?

SPECIFIC OBJECTIVES/EVALUATIVE CRITERIA	EQUIPMENT

To move with balls to the beat of the accompaniment.
To change level and direction while moving with a ball.
To smoothly combine ball skills into a movement sequence.

Balls in a variety of sizes
Music in 2/4, 3/4 and 4/4 meters.

ACTIVITY	PROCEDURES/ORGANIZATION	POINTS OF EMPHASIS	REFERENCES

I. Opening Activity
 a. Free ball exploration. Children explore ball skills from previous lesson and others of their choice.

a. In self space, music playing. Each child with a ball.

a. Can you move the ball to the beat of the music?

 b. Stretching with a ball. Children suggest a variety of stretches with a ball.

b. In self space

b. In what muscles do you feel stretching?

II. Motor Skills/Movement Concepts
 a. Moving with a ball.
  1. Explore ball skills as in a. above, but moving in general space.

a. In general space

1. Can you move the ball and your body through space in time to the music?

p. 437

  2. Repeat, changing direction as you move.

2. Can you change direction on the beat?

3. Explore ball skills
changing level.

b. Movement sequence
1. Combine 3 ball
skills.

2. Add a change of
direction or level.

3. Share combinations
with a partner. Teach
your partner your com-
bination.

b. In general space

3. With a partner in
general space.

3. Can you move the ball to
the beat at the low level?
Medium? High? Can you
change level smoothly?

p. 438

1. Can you put 3 ball skills
together? Can you change
from one to the next without
hesitating?

2. Can you move the ball to
the beat? Change direction
or level to the beat?

3. Can you teach your sequence
to your partner? What suggestions do you have for each other?

SPECIFIC OBJECTIVES/EVALUATIVE CRITERIA   EQUIPMENT

To recognize available pathways in which to move.   Hoops
To intercept or close pathways of others.   Medicine ball

| ACTIVITY | PROCEDURES/ORGANIZATION | POINTS OF EMPHASIS | REFERENCES |

I . Opening Activity
  a. Fitness stations
    1. Flexed arm hang
    2. Standing broad jump
    3. Sit and reach
       stretch
    4. Medicine ball toss
    5. Modified situps
    (*FS) (*FF)

a. Five stations spread out in the gym, each able to handle 4-6 children. It may be helpful to have students working with partners.

a. Work carefully at each station doing each activity slowly and thoroughly. Feel that muscle group that is working at each station.

II. Motor Skills/Movement
  Concepts
  a. Using hoops (15-20) as safety areas, half the students try to re-main free by avoiding the tags of the others. When tag occurs, those players switch roles.

a. Hoops scattered randomly throughout general space. Game begins with half the class in their own hoops with the other half ready to give chase.

a. Taggers must anticipate the pathway of runners and cut them off before they reach a hoop. Taggers and runners must avoid collisions with other players. Runners must stop effectively in a hoop to avoid overrunning it.

III. Culminating Activity
  a. Sharks and Minnows

a. Single line with one person as the shark out in front.

a. Minnows, can you see the available pathways? Seaweed, can you close paths to the minnows?

SPECIFIC OBJECTIVES/EVALUATIVE CRITERIA	EQUIPMENT

To throw a ball at the appropriate level below an
   opponent's waist.

To recognize the path to throw the ball to intercept
   another person.

To anticipate the pathway of the ball to avoid being hit.

Foam balls

ACTIVITY	PROCEDURES/ORGANIZATION	POINTS OF EMPHASIS	REFERENCES

I. Opening Activity

ACTIVITY	PROCEDURES/ORGANIZATION	POINTS OF EMPHASIS	REFERENCES
a. Free time with a ball.	a. Each student in general space with own ball.	a. Enjoy the free choice of activity with the ball, but play safely and under control. Can you control the ball in your self space?	
b. Fitness activities with a ball 1. "Inchworm" on the ball. Hands balanced on the ball, walk feet backward until arms and legs are extended.	b. Self space, each student with own ball.	a. Using a ball to perform fitness activities and adds an enjoyable dimension to fitness. Can you feel the muscles working? Muscles being stretched?	
2. Situps with a ball. From a lying position on the back, bring the ball forward over the head to the feet, and return.			

3. Side bends. Hold the ball over head, arms extended, bend slowly to each side for 3 seconds. (*FS) (*FF)

II. Motor Skills/Movement Concepts

a. One throws toward the wall trying to roll the ball between the legs of the other, who slides slowly at first and then with more speed.

a. In partners with a wall space.

a. Were you able to control the ball to the low level? How did you throw the ball to intercept the path of your partner?

p. 464

b. Discuss techniques used to throw.

b. Group discussion

b. Point out successful methods. Why did certain techniques fail?

III. Culminating Activity

a. Bull in a ring

a. In a circle, one-fourth of the group scattered inside the circle.

a. Throw a level below the waist. If the person is moving, anticipate his/her pathway with the throw. Dodgers should fake directions.

p. 493

b. Stretch and relax

b. Self space

b. Cool down, relax muscles from the game.

181

| SPECIFIC OBJECTIVES/EVALUATIVE CRITERIA | EQUIPMENT |

To throw the ball, pointing fingers where you want the ball to go. To position oneself to close space to a ball.	Indian pins Hoops Playground balls Medicine ball

---

| ACTIVITY | PROCEDURES/ORGANIZATION | POINTS OF EMPHASIS | REFERENCES |

I. Opening Activity

a. Fitness stations
   1. Flexed arm hang
   2. Standing broad jump
   3. Sit and reach
     stretch
   4. Medicine ball toss
   5. Modified situps
   (*FS) (*FF)
	a. Five stations spread out around the gym. This is a repeat of previous lessons and little time should be needed to organize. Students should be able to work well independently.	a. Work toward improving performance of previous lessons where these stations were used. Discuss use of improvement as a goal in fitness.	

II. Motor Skills/Movement Concepts

a. Two throwers attempt to roll or throw the ball in the low level to each other. The third attempts to intercept.	a. In groups of three.	a. What position enabled you to guard the space? How did you direct your throw to your partner?	p. 463

III. Culminating Activity
   a. Boundary ball

a. Class divided into two
groups, each group scattered
in one-half of the playing
area. Discuss limitations
in dealing with game role
as thrower and guard. Help
them problem solve solutions.

a. Aim the ball at a low
level. How did you position
yourselves to guard the space?
What difficulties did you have
in guarding your space and in
throwing the ball?

p. 491

   b. Repeat game with
      adjustments for child-
      ren's suggestions.

LEVEL III

SPECIFIC OBJECTIVES/EVALUATIVE CRITERIA   EQUIPMENT

To throw a disc with a cross body backhand by grasping disc   Discs
   as a fan, thumb on top, index finger on the rim, turning   Hoops
   side, bringing disc across in front of the body, stepping
   forward on forward motion and following through in direction of flight.
To throw a disc with a side arm throw, grasping disc with
   thumb on top, middle and index fingers extended on the
   bottom, side turned in direction of throw, hips leading
   forward motion and snapping wrist on release.
To throw a disc at various levels and pathways, directing
   flight with arm action and follow through.
To participate in the activity of Frisbee Golf, following
   golf etiquette.

ACTIVITY   PROCEDURES/ORGANIZATION   POINTS OF EMPHASIS   REFERENCES

I. Opening Activity
   a. Moving in general   a. 9-12 numbered hoops scat-   a. What ways did you move from
   space on frisbee golf   tered throughout the playing   one hoop to the next? Did you
   course, changing move-   area. Students scattered   go to the hoops in sequence?
   ment as you move from   near hoops.
   one hole to the next.
   (*FC)

   b. Stretches.   (*FF)   b. In self space with a   b. Could you extend your stretch
                             disc. Teacher and student   with your disc?
                             suggested stretches.

II. Motor Skills/Movement
    Concepts

a. Throwing the disc:
   1. Cross body back-
   hand.

a. Scattered at one end of
the playing area. Throw and
retrieve on signal (unless a
very large space is available).

1. Grasp disc with thumb on   p. 278
top, index finger on rim,
turn side, bring disc across
body, step forward, bring arm
forward, release, follow
through in direction of flight.

   2. Side arm throw.

2. Thumb on top, index and   p. 278
middle fingers extended on
bottom of disc; side turned,
hips lead forward motion,
snap wrist on release.

b. Explore flights and
pathways.
   1. Explore throwing the
   disc at various levels.

1. How did you direct the   p. 279
disc for a high flight?
Medium? Low? Which covered
the greatest distance?

   2. Explore throwing disc
   in various pathways.

2. How did you direct the   p. 279
disc in various pathways?

III. Culminating Activity
   a. Frisbee golf: counting throws to get discs
   to each hold.

a. Children divided into
groups of 3 or 4, beginning at
various holes. Each player
has a disc, and a score card,
with a pencil.

a. How can you get the disc   p. 281
to each hole in the least
number of throws? Golf etiquette: take turns, player
farthest from hole throws
first. Wait until players
ahead finish a hole before
beginning play at that hole.
Add your total score, Add your
groups total score and sign
both score cards.

    SPECIFIC OBJECTIVES/EVALUATIVE CRITERIA   EQUIPMENT

To toss one scarf across the front of the chest and catch   Juggling scarves
    it with the other hand with a downward motion of the hand.
To juggle two scarves, tossing second scarf when first reaches
    the height of its flight and catching each with the hand
    not throwing it, while receiving, throwing, and catching tips
    from partner.
To juggle three scarves, adding a third scarf when the second
    scarf reaches the top of its flight.

    ACTIVITY   PROCEDURES/ORGANIZATION   POINTS OF EMPHASIS   REFERENCES

ACTIVITY	PROCEDURES/ORGANIZATION	POINTS OF EMPHASIS	REFERENCES
I. Opening Activity a. Moving in general space tossing scarf with one hand, catching with the other. (*FC)	a. In general space, each child with a scarf.	a. Can you toss with one hand and reach up to catch with the other? Watch out for others and their scarves to avoid collisions.	
b. Stretching. (*FF)	b. In self space with a scarf. Students and teachers suggest stretches.	b. What ways can you stretch with your scarf?	
II. Motor Skills/Movement Concepts a. Throwing and catching one scarf.	a. In self space with a scarf.	a. Toss scarf in front of chest. Catch with a downward motion with the other hand.	p. 285

b. Throwing and catching
two scarves.

b-c. In partners, one throws
the other coaches. Change
throwers after one minute.
Repeat several times.

b. Begin second scarf when
first reaches top of its toss.
Think toss-toss-catch-catch.
Can you repeat this sequence
three times without missing?

p. 285

c. Juggling 3 scarves.

c. Begin third scarf when
second reaches top of its
flight. Think toss-toss-toss-
catch-catch-toss-catch.

p. 285

III. Culminating Activity
a. Juggling challenge:
each tries to keep
scarves going in sequence
for 1, 2, 3 times, etc.
Each child sets own
challenge.

a. In partners. Partner
helps count. (Some may
wish to try two scarves at
first.)

a. Did you reach your challenge? Try a new one? Did
you control the force to
keep throws equal?

p. 285

SPECIFIC OBJECTIVES/EVALUATIVE CRITERIA	EQUIPMENT

To identify safety precautions for stunts and tumbling, in assuming responsibility for the safety of self and others.

To safely share space with others, always moving away from others.

To work cooperatively with others in the centipede, skin the snake and walking chair.

To roll backward and forward, keeping tucked, pushing with hands and coming up to a stand.

To roll sideways, keeping body straight for a log roll and curled for an egg roll.

To smoothly combine two types of roll with a partner, moving either in unison, opposition or in sequence.

Mats, one for every 3-4 students
Music

ACTIVITY	PROCEDURES/ORGANIZATION	POINTS OF EMPHASIS	REFERENCES

I. Opening Activity

a. Aerobics: rhythmic warm-up to music. Students follow leader, jogging, jumping, dance steps and rhythmically circling and stretching body parts. (*FC)

a. Self space on mats, music playing.

a. Keep steady pace to best work heart; make movements through full range of motion to properly warm up.

p. 250

b. Stretches. Teacher tells which muscles will be worked in class; students show stretches for those muscles. (*FF)

b. Self space on mats.

b. Slow, gentle stretches. Review muscle names.

c. Safety discussion.

c. Discuss safety. Assume responsibility for safety of others. Share mat space where appropriate.

II. Motor Skills/Movement Concepts

a. Review roll variations:

a. Seated on mats for review, then working with 2-3 students on a mat, moving across mat.

a. Always work so that movement is away from others. Always move under control. — p. 304

    1. Forward roll.

1. Rounded body, push with hands. Come up to a stand. — p. 312

    2. Backward roll.

2. Fingers point in direction of movement. Push with hands; come up to a stand. — p. 316

    3. Log/egg roll.

3. Smooth rolling; keep body straight/curled. — p. 312

b. Partner rolls. Work with a partner to combine 2 types of rolls.

b. Working with a partner on a mat.

b. What combinations can you do together? Can you work in unison? Opposition? In sequence? Can you move smoothly in one continuous movement? Have a definite beginning and ending.

III. Culminating Activity

a. Large group stunts:

    1. Centipede.

1. Groups of 4-5 on a mat.

1. Mount centipede properly; all move forward together. — p. 312

    2. Skin the snake forward with a roll.

2. Start at the end of a mat and move forward.

2. As each person comes to front, he/she rolls and lies down. — p. 311

3. Walking chair.

3. Each group of 4 to 8 students forms a small circle on mat. (Can also be accomplish in a straight line.)

3. Groups must form tight circle; all move legs together. Did you work together as a group.

p. 312

4. Whole class walking chair.

4. Whole class forms circle in area where floor surface is flat (either on floor or where mats are pushed together).

4. Group forms tight circle and moves with unity. It may be helpful to use a leader to give the step command. Was it helpful to have a leader give commands?

| SPECIFIC OBJECTIVES/EVALUATIVE CRITERIA | EQUIPMENT |

To review the straight arm support, straddle seat and
   straddle travel, keeping arms and body straight, toes
   pointed and eyes looking straight ahead.

To perform a back and front leaning rest with arms straight,
   body extended and toes pointed.

To review the jump and turn from the springboard using a
   two-foot takeoff, extending body in the air, turning
   head, wrapping arms and landing softly.

To review a tuck, pike and straddle jump from the springboard
   taking off with two feet and maintaining body position in
   the air before landing softly.

To review a front support mount on the beam, pushing with hands,
   pushing with hands to straighten arms and body in front
   support position.

To review and learn moves on the beam, focusing on good body
   posture and focusing on the end of the beam.

To perform a body wave with a smooth flow of body movement
   throughout the wave.

To review knee scale dismount, pushing with hands and swinging
   leg to raise body off the beam and landing softly with side
   to beam.

To climb the rope alternately, supporting the body with hands
   and then feet and coming down in a hand-under-hand fashion.

Equipment:
Individual jump ropes
Springboard and crash pad
High beam, parallel bars
and hanging rope
Mats underneath equipment
Vaulting bench

| ACTIVITY | PROCEDURES/ORGANIZATION | POINTS OF EMPHASIS | REFERENCES |

I. Opening Activity
  a. Rope jumping. (*FC)

a. Self space, each student
   with an individual rope.

a. Jump at steady pace for
duration of activity; practice skills previously learned.
Land softly.

b. Stretches. (*FF)   b. Same as above.   b. Fold rope in half and use to aid stretching to sides and long sitting and straddle stretches.

II. Motor Skills/Movement Concepts

a. Parallel bars: a. Group seated where all equipment is visible, various students demonstrating skills. Then divide into groups for station work.

1. Review jump to straight arm support on parallel bars.

1. Spring with feet and push with arms, finish with the body straight and extended.   p. 337

2. Review swing to straddle seat.

2. Swing body from hips, end straddling bars, legs extended, toes pointed.   p. 338

3. Review straddle travel.

3. Support with arms, swing through to straddle seat; regrasp, swinging legs back and free of bars.   p. 339

4. Introduce back foot leaning rest.

4. Swing both legs forward and up onto bar, finishing with legs extended and straight arms, head up and back straight.   p. 338

5. Introduce front foot leaning rest.

5. Lift legs to the bars behind, finishing with legs extended straight behind, straight arms and feet, head up and back slightly arched.   p. 288

b. Springboard:
1. Review jump half turn from springboard.

b. Same as above.

1. Two foot takeoff, turn head, wrap arms to turn in air, land softly.

2. Review tuck, pike and straddle jumps.

2. Two foot takeoff, hold position, land softly.

p. 334

c. Beam:
1. Review front support mount.

c. Same as above

1. Jump, pushing with hands to pull body to beam. End with arms straight, legs extended, toes pointed.

p. 332

2. Review locomotor movements.

2. Body erect, eyes focused on end of beam.

3. Introduce body wave (to be performed on beam, previously learned as a floor exercise skill).

3. Begin with lift of arms. Move smoothly throughout the wave.

p. 329

4. Review knee scale dismount.

4. Push with hands as leg swings down and up to lift body from beam. End with side next to beam.

p. 334

5. Introduce step-hop (to be performed on beam, previously learned as a floor exercise.

5. Step forward on one foot-then hop on that foot, lifting opposite knee upward. Repeat.

p. 332

d. Hanging ropes:
1. Review bent arm
hang.

1. Reach up with hands and   p. 340
and grasp the rope over head.
Spring with feet, lift with
arms, and hold body off mat
with bent arms for as long
as possible.

2. Review climbing.

2. Extend legs to raise   p. 340
body, supporting body weight
alternately with hands and
then feet. Come down hand-
under-hand fashion.

III. Culminating Activity
a. Student demonstra-
tions of individual
skills or combinations.

a. Seated at stations.
Students volunteer to
show skills.

a. What did you like about the
skills shown? Do we need to review skills again?

SPECIFIC OBJECTIVES/EVALUATIVE CRITERIA	EQUIPMENT

To perform a movement sequence on the high beam, moving smoothly from one skill to the next and changing level and direction.	High beam Parallel bars Springboard and Swedish
To perform a routine on the parallel bars, smoothly connecting a mount, movement over the bars, a balance, and a dismount.	box or low horse Two hanging ropes Mats underneath equipment
To perform the straddle vault, with a two-foot takeoff, legs and toes extended in a straddle position and a controlled landing.	
To perform the "skin the cat" using two hanging ropes, pulling up and over in a tuck and tucking chin on return.	

ACTIVITY	PROCEDURES/ORGANIZATION	POINTS OF EMPHASIS	REFERENCES

I. Opening Activity a. Pushups, situps and wall sits. (*FS)	a. Self space	a. In a given amount of time, students do as many pushups and situps as they can; hold the wall sit for as long as possible.	
b. Stretches. (*FF)	b. Self space	b. Stretch given muscles on own, hold comfortable position for slow count of eight. What muscles do you feel stretching?	

II. Motor Skills/Movement
Concepts

a. Beam sequence: students compose a routine that includes a mount, dismount, a change in level and direction, at least one turn and one balance.

a. Seated where all equipment is visible, then divided into groups for station work.

a. Make the movements flow from one to the next.

pp. 331-334

b. Skill combinations on parallel bars, including a mount, movement on the bar and dismount.

b. Sequence the movements smoothly.

pp. 337-340

c. Ropes: skin the cat using two ropes.

c. Swing both legs up and between the arms. Stay tucked, tuck the chin to return to starting position.

p. 335

d. Vaulting: wolf vault.

d. Two-foot takeoff, place both hands on the horse. The body assumes a squat position with one leg and a straddle with the other.

p. 345

III. Culminating Activity
a. Students demonstrate skills and routines.

a. Seated at stations. Students volunteer to show skills and routines.

a. What did you like about the presentations?

SPECIFIC OBJECTIVES/EVALUATIVE CRITERIA	EQUIPMENT

To perform an activity (sequence or vaults) with good form, moving smoothly from one skill to the next, with a definite beginning and ending.	Parallel bars Ropes Vault and springboard Balance beam Mats underneath equipment

---

ACTIVITY	PROCEDURES/ORGANIZATION	POINTS OF EMPHASIS	REFERENCES

ACTIVITY	PROCEDURES/ORGANIZATION	POINTS OF EMPHASIS
I. Opening Activity a. Warmups.	a. Self spaces.	a. Choose warmups to help you prepare for the equipment that you will use during the class.
II. Motor Skills/Movement Concepts a. Practice skills and sequences that will be tested later in class.	a. Students work individually on equipment. Students' choice of equipment and skills.	a. Emphasize a good beginning and ending and smooth transitions.
III. Culminating Activity a. Evaluation of skills.	a. Students work individually on equipment. Teacher rotates to students as they are ready.	a. Did the combinations have continuity of movement? Was student focusing on good technique?

| SPECIFIC OBJECTIVES/EVALUATIVE CRITERIA | EQUIPMENT |

To run 200 yards at an even pace, with rhythmical breathing,
  arms swinging forward and backward and a comfortable
  stride.
To perform a long jump taking off on one foot, extending
  arms and legs forward on the takeoff and landing with
  body flexed and weight slightly forward.
To measure a long jump from the takeoff board to the
  first point of contact on landing.

Soft landing area (sand or mats)
Cones or markers
Measuring tape
Low (18-20 inch) hurdles
Cones with plastic sticks to
use as hurdles

| ACTIVITY | PROCEDURES/ORGANIZATION | POINTS OF EMPHASIS | REFERENCES |

I. Opening Activity
  a. 200-yard jog. (*FC)

  a. Jog around a marked oval or cross-country course. A cross-country loop through trees or around obstacles adds an element of fun.

  a. Steady, even pace with forward/backward arm swing and comfortable stride. Begin easy; find a comfortable speed to maintain the distance.

  p. 351

  b. Stretches.   (*FF)

  b. Self space

  b. Slow, static stretches of the running muscles: hamstrings calves, quadriceps. Can you feel the muscles stretching?

II. Motor Skills/Movement
  Concepts
  a. Endurance running.

  a. Group discussion of warm-up run. Discuss what happened; how they felt and how they will run next time.

  a. Select a pace that can be maintained for the distance; comfortable stride, arms swing forward/backward, breathing is rhythmical.

b. Long jump: 1. Introduce and practice skill.	b. Group demonstration/discussion. Then divide into 4 jumping groups. Work with a partner who watches for fouls and marks landing distance	b. Select jumping leg to take off on. Jump up at a 45-degree angle. Measure run in so that same takeoff foot is used every time. Legs and arms reach forward on takeoff. Absorb force in landing, with body flexed and weight moving forward. p. 356
2. Teach measuring of jumps.	2. Group demonstration/ discussion.	2. All jumps are measured from takeoff line to the spot of nearest body contact in landing.

III. Culminating Activity
a. Student choice

1. Long jump for distance.	1. Several jumping areas to maximize participation. Students take turns marking, measuring, coaching and jumping. Measuring tape provided for each jumping area.	1. One-foot takeoff. Reach with arms and legs. Land with weight forward.
2. Distance running.	2. Oval for students to run.	2. Alternate running with stretching. Run comfortably to prevent soreness. Set a pace. Swing arms forward and backward. Comfortable stride.

         SPECIFIC OBJECTIVES/EVALUATIVE CRITERIA   EQUIPMENT

To run 300 yards at an even pace, swinging arms forward   Soft landing area (sand or mats)
  and backward, breathing rhythmically and with a com-   Cones or markers
  fortable stride.   Low (18-20 inch) hurdles
To review sprinting 50 yards, running in a straight line,   Cones with plastic tubes
  arms driving, head up and continuing at top speed   to use as hurdles
  beyond the finish line.   Measuring tapes
To long jump for distance, taking off on one foot, reach-
  ing forward with arms and legs and landing in a balanced
  position.
To run over three hurdles, leading with the same foot, reaching with opposite hand and staying low to the hurdle.

| ACTIVITY | PROCEDURES/ORGANIZATION | POINTS OF EMPHASIS | REFERENCES |

I. Opening Activity
   a. Distance running. (*FC)   a. Students have choice of   a. Arms swing at sides.   p. 351
                                    running 1-3 laps. Running   Run on balls of feet. Did
                                    with a partner is helpful.   you maintain a steady pace?

   b. Stretches.   (*FF)   b. Self space as soon as   b. Slow, static stretching of
                                    each student finishes the   running muscle groups: quad-
                                    run. A regular pattern or   riceps, hamstrings and calves.
                                    group of stretches should
                                    be done each lesson.

II. Motor Skills/Movement
    Concepts
    a. Hurdling: intro-   a. Group demonstration/dis-   a. Always lead with the same   p. 353
       duction/demonstration/   cussion.   leg. Run, not jump, over
       practice.   the hurdles. Reach with hand

opposite lead leg. Can you
continue running after you
clear the hurdle and lead with
the same leg on the next?

b. Long jump review.	b. Group seated for demonstration/discussion.	b. Always use the same take-off leg. Reach with arms and legs after takeoff. Land with weight balanced. — p. 356
c. Sprinting review.	c. Group seated for demonstration/discussion.	c. Use standing start. Drive with arms. Run in a straight line. Run past finish line at full speed. — pp. 349-350

III. Culminating Activity
    a. Stations:

a. Students divided into groups which rotate randomly to each station.

a. Emphasize good form from points above. Students can coach each other by watching for key elements. Time and measuring offer wonderful self-improvement motivation. Can you improve your scores from last time? Did you recieve encouragement or coaching tips from your group?

      1. Sprinting.

1. Sprint once over 50 yards.

      2. Hurdling.

2. Sprint once over 50 yards with three hurdles.

      3. Long jump.

3. Each partner takes one jump, then marks and measures for partner.

      4. Distance running.
      (*FS) (*FC)

4. Each student determines how many laps to run, but the total for the class period should be approximately 300 yards.

SPECIFIC OBJECTIVES/EVALUATIVE CRITERIA | EQUIPMENT

SPECIFIC OBJECTIVES/EVALUATIVE CRITERIA	EQUIPMENT
To run a distance of 400 yards at an even pace, comfortable stride and arms swinging forward and backward.	Long jump landing area
To sprint 50 yards in a straight line, arms driving, knees lifted and running at full speed past the finish line.	18-20 inch hurdles Cones/markers High jump standards Batons
To long jump for distance, taking off from one foot, driving forward with arms and legs, head up and landing in a balanced position.	Measuring tapes Stop watch
To run 50 yards over three hurdles for time using the same lead leg and reaching with opposite hand.	
To high jump using the scissors technique, forcefully thrusting takeoff leg and swinging arms upward to clear bar.	
To throw a soccer ball for distance using a two-hand overhand throw and a forceful step forward to impart force.	
To perform a shuttle relay from a standing start, extending baton to next runner with right hand and moving quickly past receiver.	
To measure and time individuals, groups at appropriate stations.	

ACTIVITY	PROCEDURES/ORGANIZATION	POINTS OF EMPHASIS	REFERENCES
I. Opening Activity a. Distance run. (*FC)	a. A 200-yard oval or cross country course.	a. To complete the 200-yard course nonstop or in a personal best time. Run in a steady, even pace.	p. 351
b. Stretches. (*FF)	b. Each student individually upon completing run.	b. Stretching helps performance in jumping and hurdling events. Slow, static stretching.	

II. Motor Skills/Movement
Concepts

a. Stations:

a. Seated for review, then students in groups. Each group measures and times itself. Groups rotate to event.

1. High jump.

1. Forcefully thrust take-off leg, swinging arms upward to clear the bar.

p. 354

2. Long jump.

2. One foot takeoff, reach with arms and legs, head up, landing in a balanced position.

p. 356

3. 50-yard dash.

3. Standing start, arms drive, lift knees, run at full speed past finish line.

pp. 349-350

4. 400-yard run.

4. Set pace, easy arm swing and comfortable stride. Breathe rhythmically.

p. 351

5. 50-yard hurdles.

5. Lead with same leg. Run over hurdles and reaching with opposite hand.

p. 353

6. Soccer ball throw.

6. Two-hand overhand throw with a forceful step forward on release.

p. 357

b. Shuttle run.

b. Groups divided into shuttle relay teams.

b. Standing start, extend baton, passing from right hand to right hand of next runner. Quickly move to the right and past the next runner.

SPECIFIC OBJECTIVES/EVALUATIVE CRITERIA	EQUIPMENT

To explore a variety of potential body shapes.
To explore a variety of ways to move through general
　space, assuming different shapes.
To create a dance with changing body shapes and movements
　to tell a story, to perform to the class.
To create a sequence of movements in a flowing manner.

Music of many varieties

ACTIVITY	PROCEDURES/ORGANIZATION	POINTS OF EMPHASIS	REFERENCES

I. Opening Activity
　a. Creative fitness
　activities.
　　1. Do the following
　　in an unusual body
　　shape.
　　　a) Pushups.
　　　b) Hamstrings.
　　　c) Situps.
　　　d) Jumping jacks. (*FS)

a. Self space

a. Encourage student to develop a way "we have never seen before." Be sure the correct muscle group is being used. Stretching should be slow and steady. What muscles do you feel are working?

II. Motor Skills/Movement
　Concepts
　a. Body shapes in move-
　ment.
　　1. Move from one
　　place to another,
　　making three shapes
　　on the way.

a. Self and general space. Once the problem is posed, allow several minutes for the creation of the movement. Much individual assistance will be needed.

a. Change the positions in a smooth flow. Make each posi-tion and movement last one-third of the distance travel-ed. Begin with simple shapes, then become more complex.

pp. 375-376

205

2. Repeat and use 3
types of movement as
well.

III. Culminating Activity

a. Make up a story which
you can present with
changing body shapes.

b. Make up a dance to
tell your story, with
one or more children
moving and one tell-
ing the story.

a. With a partner or in a
group of 3. Have a few
story ideas available for
those having difficulty.
(Stress Creativity)

b. With partner. Ask for
a few volunteers to share
their stories and move-
ments.

a. What types of shapes could
you use to convey the story?

b. What ideas did the shapes
portray? Use movements between the shapes. Was the
story funny? Scary?

UNIT: Creative Dance   LEVEL: III   LESSON: 3rd of 6

| SPECIFIC OBJECTIVES/EVALUATIVE CRITERIA | EQUIPMENT |

To move to the beat and musical phrasing.   Music
To accent a beat with body movements.
To create an 8-beat movement sequence accenting different beats.
To volunteerly, present your dance.

| ACTIVITY | PROCEDURES/ORGANIZATION | POINTS OF EMPHASIS | REFERENCES |

I. Opening Activity
   a. Locomotor warm-up.   a. In general space, music   a. Can you move to the music
   Students move in   playing.   and phrasing? What ways did
   general space with a   you like best?
   partner to music. One
   chooses a movement for
   one phrase, the other
   for the next, etc. (*FC)

   b. Everyone "melts" to   b. In self space, music   b. What muscles do you feel
   the floor, then "grows"   playing.   stretching? Can you stretch
   to a fully stretched   slowly and smoothly to the
   position. When all are   music?
   fully stretched, the
   signal is given to re-
   start. (*FF)

II. Motor Skills/Movement Concepts

a. Accenting the first beat: moving in general space to music in a way of their choice. Accent the first beat of each measure in some way. Change movements on the teacher's signal.

a. In general space.

a. What did you do to accent the beat? Use more force? Bigger emphasized movement? Add non-locomotor movements? Change direction, etc.?

b. Repeat a. but accent the second beat, then third and finally fourth beat.

b. In general space.

b. What difficulties did you have accenting different beats?

III. Culminating Activity

a. Create a dance sequence of 4 measures. Accent one beat in each measure in some way(s) of your choice. Repeat the sequence with accent on a different beat.

a. Seated so that all can see. Discuss possible movement sequences, then work in groups of 3.

a. Choose the movements you will use first. What are some movements you could use? What beats can you accent easily?

b. Dance presentations.

b. Ask volunteers to show their ideas, with group seated so all can see.

b. What movements did you like best? How did they accent the beat? Did the movements flow?

p. 382

SPECIFIC OBJECTIVES/EVALUATIVE CRITERIA   EQUIPMENT

To move, responding to changes in tempo, beat,   Music
   loudness and rhythm.   Drum
To contrast jerky and smooth locomotor and non-
   locomotor movements.
To create a dance using a variety of body movements
   with a change in force and tempo and an interesting floor pattern.

ACTIVITY   PROCEDURES/ORGANIZATION   POINTS OF EMPHASIS   REFERENCES

I. Opening Activity
  a. Moving to a drum beat
  with frequent changes in
  tempo, beat, loudness and
  rhythm.   (*FC)

    a. Students moving first in self space, then through general space. Beat on rim of drum as well as drum head to contrast the sound.

    a. Let your body respond to the changes in the drum beat. Pretend you are greatly affected by even the slightest changes. Encourage the use of many body parts in the movement; for example, small extremities for soft sounds, large body parts for loud sounds.

II. Motor Skills/Movement
  Concepts
  a. Using force and time
  in different ways.
    1. Move a body part
    very smoothly. Now
    sharply.

    a. Self space.

    a. Explore how the same movement can be done but with differences in force and time. Can you blend the different movements together?   p. 380

2. Repeat, but move
to another place
both ways.

3. Begin moving body
part in a very jerky
manner and gradually
smooth it out.

   b. Balancing and moving.   b. Self space.
      1. Repeat the above,
      but do the movements
      while balancing on one
      or two body parts.

      2. Change the balanc-
      ing body parts during
      the movement. (*FS)

III. Culminating Activity
   a. Create a dance: a. After a discussion about
      1. Choose and practice the dance project, students
      the movements to be   may work alone, in pairs
      used.   or in small groups. Ask for
                     volunteers the last 5 minutes
      2. Add a change in   to show their dances.
      force.

      3. Add a change in
      tempo.

      4. Use an interesting
      floor pattern.

3. Can you feel the contrast from jerky
to smooth movements.

b. Which types of movement enabled you to keep your balance?
Work on control and flow of
movement to enhance kbalance.

1. Choose locomotor and/or non-
locomotor movements.

2. How can you show a contrast in force?

3. How can you show a change
in tempo?

4. Can you choose a floor pat-
that adds to the excitement of
your dance?

SPECIFIC OBJECTIVES/EVALUATIVE CRITERIA   EQUIPMENT

To skip, gallop, walk and jog to a specific beat and rhythm.
To maintain a position to a hold in the music.
To move in a variety of ways to the chorus.
To do the bleking step alternately springing on one foot
 and extending the opposite heel forward.
To step-hop in even rhythm.

Records: miscellaneous music
"La Raspa"
Seven Jumps"

ACTIVITY	PROCEDURES/ORGANIZATION	POINTS OF EMPHASIS	REFERENCES
I. Opening Activity			

a. Fitness and music. A combination of traditional calisthenic exercises done to popular music, randomly choreographed by the teacher or done impromptu:
  1. Run in place.
  2. Sliding sideways.
  3. Jumping jacks.
  4. Pushups.
  5. Situps.
  6. Arm circles.
  7. Flexibility.
(*FS) (*FC) (*FF)
	a. Students in self space, spread out, facing and following the lead of the teacher.	a. Make exercise enjoyable. Stay with the beat whenever possible. Work many muscle groups. Stretch to soft music at the end.	

II. Motor Skills/Movement Concepts			
a. Seven jumps: 1. Practice the step-hop.	1. Students in general space.	1. Step-hop in even rhythm.	pp. 410-411

2. Perform 7 jumps, with step-hop on the chorus.	2. Students in single circle; imitate actions of teacher.	2. Can you maintain your position for the hold in the music. Step-hop to the beat? Reverse path on the second phrase of the chorus.
		pp. 410-411

III. Culminating Activity
  a. La Raspa:

1. Teach the bleking step.	1. Students in general space, no music.	
		p. 389
2. Perform dance. On chorus, students do a right and then left elbow swing.	2. In general space. Pick someone close by as a partner.	2. Can you move to the beat and phrasing?
		p. 409
3. Repeat dance, skipping on the chorus. Repeat dance again with an elbow swing on chorus. On every chorus students move individually to teacher or student suggestions, changing partners each time.	3. On chorus, skip or perform other movements in general space individually, meeting a new partner.	3. Can you time movements to the beat and phrasing? Can you anticipate the end of the phrase to get a partner and be ready to begin the dance again?

SPECIFIC OBJECTIVES/EVALUATIVE CRITERIA	EQUIPMENT

To move to the beat and musical phrasing, adjusting steps to stay with a partner.	Records: Ace of Diamonds
	La Raspa
To review La Raspa, responding to slow, slow, quick, quick, quick rhythm of the bleking.	Dances from previous lessons
To perform the front-to-front, back-to-back polka, turning after every two slides.	

ACTIVITY	PROCEDURES/ORGANIZATION	POINTS OF EMPHASIS	REFERENCES

ACTIVITY	PROCEDURES/ORGANIZATION	POINTS OF EMPHASIS	REFERENCES
I. Opening Activity a. Review new dances from Lesson 2. (*FC)	a. With partner in dance formation.	a. Can you move with your partner? To the beat and phrasing?	
II. Motor Skills/Movement Concepts a. Ace of Diamonds 1. Develop polka step, review 4 slides, (back-to-back, front-to-front) from last lesson. Then reduce to 2 slides.	1. In general space with a partner, holding inside hands, facing each other.	1. Adjust steps to slide with partner, swing joined arms forward to change from front to back.	p. 407
2. Teach dance steps. Listen to music. Put dance together.	2. Double circle, partners facing. Teaching cues steps and changes.	2. Take small steps to stay with partner. Listen to music to move with phrasing.	

III. Culminating Activity

a. Review La Raspa. One option on the chorus is the front-to-front, back-to-back polka.

a. In general space with a partner. Students and teacher suggest movements for chorus (on preceding bleking step).

a. Can you move to the music - slow-slow, quick, quick, quick - with the bleking? Anticipate end of phrase to begin again?

p. 409

b. Students' choice of any dance.

b. Formation called for in the dance chosen.

b. Can you move to the phrasing without cuing?

SPECIFIC OBJECTIVES/EVALUATIVE CRITERIA   EQUIPMENT

To respond to musical phrasing.   Records: Oh, Susanna
To move in general space to the musical beat on the   Dances from previous lessons
  "scatter" signal.   Square dance music (no calls)
To dance the circle, swing and promenade steps.
To learn some of the history and heritage of American
  square dance.
To find partners quickly on the signal "partners all".

| ACTIVITY | PROCEDURES/ORGANIZATION | POINTS OF EMPHASIS | REFERENCES |

I. Opening Activity			
a. Students' choice of dance to review. (*FC)	a. In formation of dance chosen.	a. Listen and move to musical phrasing. Can you do it without cuing?	
II. Motor Skills/Movement Concepts			
a. Introduction to square dancing.	a. Group discussion.	a. Review the history and heritage of square dancing.	
b. Introduction to square dance figures.	b. With a partner in general space. (Teacher establishes first partners if necessary.)		
1. Honor your partner. Honor your corner.		1. Acknowledge partner with nod, etc., turn to someone close by as you stay with partner and acknowledge that person.	p. 390
2. Swing your partner. Swing your corner.		2. Right elbow swing. Adjust steps to move comfortably with partner. Left elbow to corner, then return to partner.	p. 390

Copyright © 1994 by Mosby–Year Book, Inc.

3. Promenade.

4. Do-si-do.

3. Side by side, right hands p. 390
joined, left hands joined.

4. Walk forward, passing right p. 390
shoulders with your partner.
Continue to face same path, but
move back to place, passing left
shoulders.

b. Practice figures.
Students do figures
called for by teacher.
On signal to "scatter,"
move in general space
to the beat. On signal
"partners all," get a
new partner, responding
to figures called for
by teacher. Repeat
several times.

b. In general space with a
partner.

b. Listen to calls and cuing.
Quickly find a partner on the
signal to begin again. Always
move to the beat, adjusting
steps to also move with partner.

III. Culminating Activity
a. Oh Susanna (substi-
tuting partner swing
or other figures learned
today for the grand
right and left). Teach
song and steps; listen
to music; put dance
together.

a. Single circle of part-
ners, facing the center.

a. (If boy-girl partners are not
used, refer to parts as person
on right or left). Listen and
move to the beat and phrasing.

SPECIFIC OBJECTIVES/EVALUATIVE CRITERIA	EQUIPMENT
To create and perform with control rhythmic bouncing and catching combinations and rhythmic tossing and bouncing combinations to the beat of the accompaniment.	Balls that bounce(in a variety of sizes and textures)
To create and perform a movement sequence of sixteen counts that combines ball skills in self space, locomotor movements, a definite beginning and end, and contrast in levels, moving to the beat of the music.	Drum Music

---

ACTIVITY	PROCEDURES/ORGANIZATION	POINTS OF EMPHASIS	REFERENCES
I. Opening Activity a. Locomotor warm-up. Use locomotor skills, move rhythmically through general space, change direction and level on signal. (*FC)	a. Moving throughout room.	a. Keep steady beat of drum; avoid collisions with others; make changes in direction and level very noticeable.	
b. Stretches/curls. Stay in self space, stretch and then curl, change from one to the other on signal. (*FF)	b. Self space.	b. Encourage whole body movements, right/left sides of body and isolated body parts. Explore stretches and curls on own before changing on signal.	
II. Motor Skills/Movement Concepts a. Review individual ball skills. Discussion/	a. Seated in group with teacher.	a. What ball skills can you do to music?	

217

demonstration of ball
skills that the students
remember from previous
lessons.

b. Bouncing/catching
combinations.

b. Self space, each student
with a ball. Music playing.

b. Can you make your own
combinations of bouncing and
catching rhythms; for example,
bounce, bounce, bounce, catch,
bounce, catch? Can you bounce
and catch right on the beat?

p. 438

c. Throwing/bouncing
combinations.

c. In self space, each
student with a ball.

c. Control ball so that
bounces are all performed
in self space. For example,
bounce, throw, bounce, bounce,
throw, throw.

p. 437

d. Execute a bounce or
throw; stop. Do a loco-
motor movement using
the same number of beats,
stop and repeat.

d. Moving in general space
with a ball.

d. Locomotor movement and ball
skill should take equal number
of beats to perform, such as
four bounces, four steps.

pp. 437-
438

e. Using same format as
above, execute ball skill
on one level and loco-
motor skill on a contrasting level, such as four
high tosses, four low
sliding steps repeated
over and over, giving the
idea of high/low/high/low.

e. Moving in general space
with a ball.

e. Can you repeat the
sequence several times?
Can you change level smoothly?

pp. 437-
438

III. Culminating Activity

a. Create sequence of 16 counts, following format in Activity II, e.

b. Groups of four students at a time perform sequence.

a. Seated in self space for directions. Moving throughout room to create sequence.

b. Audience seated around perimeter of space, performers using empty spaces in room. Performers do not have to begin and end together. Drum beat starts and students begin when ready. Teacher cues beginning.

a. Give the sequence a definite beginning and ending.

b. Reinforce creativity of sequences, contrast in levels, good beginning and endings. What did you especially like about the sequence?

SPECIFIC OBJECTIVES/EVALUATIVE CRITERIA	EQUIPMENT

To smoothly combine ball and locomotor skills and move
   to the beat of the accompaniment.

To perform ball skills with a change in level, speed,
   rhythm, direction and pathway.

To create a ball sequence incorporating concepts of space
   and/or time.

Balls that bounce (in a variety
of sizes and textures)
Music

ACTIVITY	PROCEDURES/ORGANIZATION	POINTS OF EMPHASIS	REFERENCES

I. Opening Activity

a. Station activities. Students perform abdominal and upper body exercises, tasks that require cardiovascular endurance and a variety of stretches in a station format. (*FF) (*FC) (*FS)

a. Stations are set up before students arrive. At each station there are cards with tasks to be performed. Students rotate through all stations on their own. Music playing.

a. Recognize individual fitness levels of students. Provide help and encouragement whenever necessary. Each task should include at least three levels of performance so that students can perform activity at appropriate level or pace.

II. Motor Skills/Movement Concepts

a. Free exploration with balls.

a-f. Self and general space, Each student with a ball. Music playing.

a. What ball skills can you do in self space? General space? What movements do you combine to move in general space with the ball? Did you move on the beat?

p. 437

b. Repeat activities
with a change in level.

c. Repeat, changing speed.

d. Repeat, changing the
rhythm of movements.

e. Repeat, changing
direction.

f. Repeat, changing
pathway.

III. Culminating Activity
a. Create a sequence of
2-4 ball skills, includ-
ing 2 of the following:
change in level, direc-
tion, pathway, speed,
rhythm. Repeat sequence
at least once.

b. Perform sequence for
class, 4 students at
at a time.

a. Seated for directions,
working in self space to
create sequence.

b. Audience seated on perimeter of room; performers
scattered throughout room.

b. What did you do to control   p. 437
the ball at each level?

c. Can you control your move-   p. 437
ments and the ball as you
changed speed?

d. Can you combine even and   p. 438
uneven rhythms?

e. How did you change direction
as you moved with the ball?

f. What ball skills worked   p. 437
best in the various paths?

a. Good ball control; smooth
flow from one skill to the
next and in variations of
each concept.

b. Reinforce creativity, good
ball control. What concepts
were used? What did you like
best?

SPECIFIC OBJECTIVES/EVALUATIVE CRITERIA	EQUIPMENT

To perform ball skills with a partner, each person using a ball rhythmically and with control, and moving to the beat of the music. To create a ball skills sequence with a partner, including 2-4 ball skills and changes in level and force.	Balls that bounce (in a variety of sizes and textures) Music of moderate tempo

---

ACTIVITY	PROCEDURES/ORGANIZATION	POINTS OF EMPHASIS	REFERENCES

ACTIVITY	PROCEDURES/ORGANIZATION	POINTS OF EMPHASIS
I. Opening Activity a. Moving in general space dribbling a ball, responding to changes in speed, etc. as signaled by the teacher. (*FC)		a. Can you make it sound like one ball bouncing? Control the ball, avoiding others?
b. Stretches on own. (*FF)	b. Self space.	b. Discuss importance of flexibility as a component of fitness. Stretch slowly and comfortably.
II. Motor Skills/Movement Concepts a. Partner warm-up review with balls. Begin close together, partners facing; toss, roll and bounce back and forth. Gradually get farther apart.	a. Partners sharing ball, scattered throughout space. Groups should not cross each others' paths. Music playing.	a. Can you control the force of the ball to get it to partner so that it can be easily received? Move the ball to the beat?

222

b. Partner skills:
partner with a ball.
   1. Roll to each
   other, both releasing
   at the same time.

   2. Bounce to each
   other, both releasing
   at the same time.

   3. Same as #1 and #2,
   tossing the balls.

c. Partner skills. Explore the following:
   1. Changing level
   with the balls, moving each in the same
   and different levels.

   2. Changing force
   (hard or soft). Example: hard bounce,
   soft throw.

III. Culminating Activity
   a. Create sequence with
   both partners using 2
   balls. Include individual
   and partner ball skills, a
   change in level and force.
   Sequence should be at
   least 16 counts or 4
   different skills.

b. Partner without ball
should get one that is similar in size to first ball.
Music playing.

b. Timing is important; verbal
cues to release at the same
time are helpful. Control is
also important. Try to keep
beat of music while coordinating
releases and catches.

   1. What levels can you use with
   control? Did the ball change
   levels?

   2. Can you contrast the force
   in working with the ball?

a. Select skills; practice   p. 438
first, then add other concepts.
Did you move to the beat?
Control balls to partner so
they could be easily controlled?

b. Demonstration of sequences.

b. Several sets of partners at a time.

b. What ball skills used did you especially like? In what creative ways did they use the concepts?

SPECIFIC OBJECTIVES/EVALUATIVE CRITERIA	EQUIPMENT

To perform the following individual rhythmic rope skills: double beat, single beat, horizontal swing, overhead and side swing, maintaining rhythm, landing softly and moving rope with control to the beat of the music.

To perform a variety of skills with a long jump rope, coordinating jump and movements with rope's rhythm, and landing softly

EQUIPMENT

Individual jump ropes
Long jump ropes
Music record or tape with 2/4 or 4/4 time

ACTIVITY	PROCEDURES/ORGANIZATION	POINTS OF EMPHASIS	REFERENCES

I. Opening Activity
a. Individual rope jumping. (*FC)

a. Each child with a short rope, self space.

a. Practice skills previously learned. Can you maintain the the rhythm of the rope and jump?

b. Stretches. As a group, teacher leading. (*FF)

b. Self space. Jump ropes on floor nearby.

b. Slow, static stretches for the muscles most used in rope jumping.

II. Motor Skills/Movement Concepts
a. Rhythmic jumping with long ropes.

   1. Turn rope to rhythm of music.

   2. Jump in and establish rhythm.

a. Groups of 3 or 4, one long rope per group. Music playing.

p. 290

1. Can you make the rope touch the floor on the beat?

2. Move into rope as rope passes your eyes.

3. Practice two and one-beat jumping rhythms.

3. Can you maintain a 2-beat jump rhythm? Jump only when rope passes under your feet?

p. 291

b. Rhythmic jumping with individual ropes.
   1. Double beat
   2. Single beat

b. Seated in self space for explanation; working in self space with ropes. Music playing.

1-2. Are you comfortable jumping in rhythm with either double or single beat consistently? Can you jump a specific number of jumps?

3. Horizontal swing over head.
4. Side swing.

3-4. Can you trace the same path in the air in performing swings?

5. Combine 2 of the above.

5. Can you combine skills without stopping?

III. Culminating Activity
   a. Choice time. Students choose short or long ropes to practice rhythms, skills and combinations.

a. Scattered individually and in small groups throughout space. Music playing.

a. What skills can you do comfortably? Can you combine 2 or 3 skills and maintain the rhythm of jumping?

p. 441

| SPECIFIC OBJECTIVES/EVALUATIVE CRITERIA | EQUIPMENT |

To turn the rope to the beat of the music.

To jump rhythmically in a long jump rope, alone and
with others.

To combine skills smoothly while jumping the long rope.

Individual jump ropes
Long jump ropes (one for
every 3-4 students)
Music records or tapes
in 2/4 or 4/4 time

| ACTIVITY | PROCEDURES/ORGANIZATION | POINTS OF EMPHASIS | REFERENCES |

I. Opening Activity
a. Individual rope
jumping (*FC)

a. Self space. Music
playing.

a. Encourage continuous rhythmic
jumps.

b. Stretches. As a
group, students lead-
ing. (*FF)

b. Self space. Ropes on
floor nearby.

b. Appropriate stretches for
muscles used in rope jumping.

II. Motor Skills/Movement
Concepts
a. Review long rope
skills practiced in
Lesson #1.

a. Seated for explanation,
then divided into groups of
3 or 4, with one long rope.
Music playing.

p. 291

    1. Turn rope to
the beat.

1. Can you make the rope
touch the floor on the beat?

    2. Jump into moving
rope and establish
rhythm.

2. Can you follow rope's
rhythm to get in and to jump?

    3. Two and one-beat
jumping.

3. Can you adjust to 2- or 1-
beat jumping?

b. Introduce and prac-
tice long rope skills,
combining 2 skills on
each turn.

b. Seated for explanation
of long ropes. Teacher and
students offer suggestions.
Then practice in groups.
Music playing.

b. What are some long rope
skills that you could use for
rhythmic jumping? What skills
can you combine? Can you change
skills smoothly? Remember to
time rope with the music.

pp. 291,
441

III. Culminating Activity
a. Partner and group
jumps.

1. Select 2 skills
and jump with a part-
ner. Try a new com-
bination each turn.

1. Students seated at long
ropes for discussion. Then
practice with music playing.

1. Can two of you jump
together? What 2 skills can
you combine? Can you change
skills smoothly to the beat?

p. 442

2. Try combinations
you did with partners
in groups of 3 or 4.

2. Combine groups for group
jumps.

2. Move into the rope one at
a time. Then start your combination together.

SPECIFIC OBJECTIVES/EVALUATIVE CRITERIA	EQUIPMENT

To practice rhythmic single and double bounces using individual jump ropes and jumping rhythmically to the beat of the music.

To change jumping on each phrase of the music.

To combine rope jumping skills with a partner, synchronizing jumps to the beat and musical phrasing.

To write and perform a 2-phrase combination with a partner.

Individual jump ropes
Music records or tapes 2/4 or 4/4 time
Poster of rope jumping skills
Pencils and paper

ACTIVITY	PROCEDURES/ORGANIZATION	POINTS OF EMPHASIS	REFERENCES

I. Opening Activity

a. Individual rope jumping. Practice/review jump rope skills previously learned. (*FC)

a. Self space, each student with an individual rope. Music playing.

a. Can you perform rhythmic jumps to music?

b. Stretches. (*FF)

b. Self space, jump ropes on floor nearby.

b. Slow, static stretches to maintain most efficient movement in muscles.

II. Motor Skills/Movement Concepts

a. Review skills from previous lesson; discover new rhythmic jumping skills. Select a skill and practice for one musical phrase. Then try another.

a. Seated in self space for explanation, working in self space and moving through general space for discovery time. Use poster of rope jumping skills. Music playing. Teacher cues phrases at first.

a. What are some of the rope jumping skills you know to do with short ropes? Can they be done to the one- and two-beat jumps we did yesterday? Listen and jump to the beat. Change the way you jump on each phrase.

p. 291

III. Culminating Activity

a. Develop a 2-phrase combination with a partner.

  1. Select possible skills to combine and write them down. Think of several combinations.

  2. Practice/decide on final combination.

  3. Demonstration of sequences.

a. Seated for explanation. Then working with a partner in general space.

  3. Several sets of partners perform at a time. Others seated.

p. 441

  1. What skills can you combine smoothly, keeping the rhythm and also performing for one whole phrase?

  2. Could you jump in the same rhythm? Change skills smoothly on the end of each phrase? Can you repeat the sequence without stopping?

  3. What skills were combined? Which combinations would you like to try?

| SPECIFIC OBJECTIVES/EVALUATIVE CRITERIA | EQUIPMENT |

To hold sticks between thumbs and finger pads.

To hit sticks in a variety of ways to the beat of 3/4 time.

To flip sticks, controlling force, turning them in the air and regrasping them easily.

To perform a 24 count combination of 4 skills (with others) and to the 3/4 beat.

Rhythm sticks, two for each student
Music in 3/4 time

| ACTIVITY | PROCEDURES/ORGANIZATION | POINTS OF EMPHASIS | REFERENCES |

I. Opening Activity

a. Locomotor movements. Move to the beat in different ways, accenting one or more beats, changing direction, level, pathway, rhythm, etc., combining locomotor and non-locomotor movements. (*FC)

a. In general space. Music playing. Teacher signals when to change movement (phrasing).

a. Move to the beat. Can you change without stopping or hesitating? Can you smoothly combine locomotor and non-locomotor movements?

b. Stretches. (*FF)

b. Self space. Students take turns choosing stretches. Class stretches together.

b. Hold stretches in comfortable position for slow count of six.

II. Motor Skills/Movement Concepts

a. Skill activities.
1. Review grip and sticks at rest. Ex-

a. Seated in general space, each student with two sticks.

1. Hold sticks with thumb and finger pads, sticks at

p. 443

plore different ways
of hitting sticks to
3/4 time rhythm of
music.

b. Share skills used.
Volunteers demonstrate
skills.

b. Seated in general space.

c. New skills
1. Flip sticks in
front of body. Touch
the tips to the floor,
turn (flip) sticks
toward you and regrasp,
touching ends to the
floor. Practice first
without music, then to
the beat.

c. In general space.

2. Flip sticks out to
sides. Those who are
successful with flip-
ping can try the same
skill, but flipping
sticks with one stick
at each side of the body.

III. Culminating Activity
a. 24 count stick routine.
Group performs 24 count
routine together. Prac-
tice each part separately,
then combine parts. Then
half performs as other
half watches.

rest in front of you on the
floor or quietly in your hands.
Can you hit on the beat?

b. What skills did you enjoy
most? Which skills did you
do easily to the beat?

1. Can you flip and re-
grasp in time to the beat?

p. 444

2. Can you see sticks as
well? Control flip to regrasp easily.

p. 444

a. Seated in a circle. Students suggest movements for
6 counts. Teacher cuing.

a. Can we make it sound like
one pair of sticks? Were we
all together on the beat?

p. 444

SPECIFIC OBJECTIVES/EVALUATIVE CRITERIA	EQUIPMENT
To learn lummi sticks song and skills. To perform skills to a 3/4 rhythm. To perform a stick exchange on the beat of the 3/4 music, gently passing sticks perpendicularly to partner.	Rhythm sticks, 2 for each student Music in 3/4 time

---

ACTIVITY	PROCEDURES/ORGANIZATION	POINTS OF EMPHASIS	REFERENCES
I. Opening Activity a. Move in general space to 3/4 time in a variety of ways. (*FC)	a. In general space. Music playing. Teacher signals when to change movements.	a. Move to beat. Change movement smoothly on the signal.	
II. Motor Skills/Movement Concepts a. Lummi sticks song and rhythm. 1. Teach history and song to lummi sticks.	1. Seated in general space.	1. From Northwest Washington Indians, similar to game of Maori Indians of New Zealand. Can you repeat words in rhythm?	p. 444
2. Singing song and tapping sticks to 3/4 beat.	2. Seated in general space.	2. Can you tap sticks on the beat as you sing?	
b. Lummi sticks skills 1. Hit tails to floor. Hit own sticks together, hit partner's right stick.	b. Facing a partner, singing song.	b. Can you make it sound like one pair of sticks? Hit exactly on the beat?	p. 444

233

Repeat, but hit partner's left stick on beat 3. Repeat sequence through the song, alternating hitting partner's right and left sticks.

2. Hit tails to floor. Hit own sticks together Hit partner's right stick, then partner's left stick on beat 4. Repeat to the end of the song.

3. Repeat #1 but with a toss to partner instead of hitting his/her stick.

3. Pass stick perpendicularly and gently into the air.

4. Repeat #2 but with 2 tosses - right, then left instead of hits.

4. Pass sticks perpendicularly and gently. Decide where each stick will go so that they do not hit each other.

5. Repeat #1 but toss 2 sticks at the same time.

5. Decide who will go on the inside and outside to avoid hitting sticks.

III. Culminating Activity
   a. Demonstrations

a. Seated with partner so all can see. Several may go at the same time. Everyone singing.

a. Can you move your sticks on the beat? With your partner?

SPECIFIC OBJECTIVES/EVALUATIVE CRITERIA	EQUIPMENT
To review lummi stick skills in groups of four, making up combinations of skills and moving sticks to the beat. To write combinations in 3/4 and 4/4 rhythm phrases. To volunteer to present to the class.	Rhythm sticks, 2 per student Music in 4/4 and 3/4 time Pencils and paper

---

ACTIVITY	PROCEDURES/ORGANIZATION	POINTS OF EMPHASIS	REFERENCES
I. Opening Activity a. Jogging in general space to music. Change movement on each phrase.	a. In general space. 3/4 and 4/4 music playing. Teacher cues at first.	a. Can you move and change on each phrase? Listen and plan what change you'll do so you can begin on the first beat of the phrase. How did the phrases change in 4/4 and 3/4?	
b. Stretches. (*FF)	b. Self space. Students and teacher suggest stretches.		
II. Motor Skills/Movement Concepts a. Review lummi sticks. Make up own combinations of skills.	a. In general space, in groups of 4.	a. Stay on the beat. What skills can you do? How can you pass sticks with 4 people?	pp. 444-445
III. Culminating Activity a. Begin work on group routines. Combine skills to make up a routine in 24 counts to either 3/4 or 4/4. Can use some lummi stick or other skills.	a. In groups of 4, 3/4 and 4/4 music playing. Pencil and paper to write down combinations. Volunteers can show some combinations at the end of the lesson.	a. Include the following 1. Determine skills to use and number of repetitions. 2. Group formation.	pp. 444-445

SPECIFIC OBJECTIVES/EVALUATIVE CRITERIA
EQUIPMENT

To review dribble, pushing ball slightly ahead with finger
   pads, looking up to see where one is going.
To dribble in a variety of levels, directions and pathways.
To shoot with a soft arc, extending the legs to create force,
   keeping the elbow into create a base and following through
   toward the basket.
To review bounce and chest passes, pushing equally with 2
   hands, stepping forward to increase force, following
   through in direction of pass and controlling force so
   that ball is easily received.
To guard a space using hands to cover as much space as
   possible and moving to intercept the pathway of the ball.
To move within the boundaries of the court.

Junior basketballs and
utility balls
Basketball hoops 7'-8' high

ACTIVITY	PROCEDURES/ORGANIZATION	POINTS OF EMPHASIS	REFERENCES

I. Opening Activity
 a. Dribbling

| 1. Review dribble in self space using each hand. Explore level. | 1. In self space, each child with a ball. | 1. Can you control the ball by pushing with finger pads? How low can you dribble? Can you dribble with either hand? | p. 501 |
| 2. Dribble in general space, changing hands, directions and pathways. (*FC) | 2. In general space. | 2. Push balls lightly ahead. What did you do to change direction while dribbling? Pathway? What part of your hand is pushing the ball? | p. 501 |

b. Free shooting.	b. In groups, each child with a ball, at each basket.	b. How did you control the ball to make a basket? How did you control force? Did you use any other body parts to assist with the force on the ball? Where is your elbow? p. 507
II. Motor Skills/Movement Concepts a. Defensive play: to stay between an opponent and the goal. Guard attempts to intercept passes to a wall.	a. In pairs, 1 thrower and 1 guard, with a wall space.	a. Hands up to protect as much space as possible. Passing: push equally with both hands, step to increase force, follow through in direction of throw and control force. pp. 510-511
b. Dribbling within court boundaries.	b. Divided into teams, placed on courts for endball. Each player has a ball.	b. Can you move and keep the the ball within your court? Try to use all the space, but stay in bounds. p. 512
III. Culminating Activity a. Endball.	a. Small courts of 8 players (4 per team.)	a. Move ball quickly with soft passes. Dribble to get into a good position to pass. On defense: hands up and be ready to move to intercept the path of the ball. p. 518

SPECIFIC OBJECTIVES/EVALUATIVE CRITERIA	EQUIPMENT

To shoot, controlling force and following through to basket.
To develop control of force in passing while stepping for-
  ward and snapping the wrists.
To move to an open space to receive a pass.
To pass to a space in front of a moving receiver.
To develop the defensive skills of staying between ball and
  goal, moving to cut off pathways.

Junior basketballs and
utility balls
12 cones
Basketball hoops 7'-8' high

ACTIVITY	PROCEDURES/ORGANIZATION	POINTS OF EMPHASIS	REFERENCES

I. Opening Activity
a. Basketball fitness
activities:

1. Partner push.

1. Students with partners randomly spread near center. A partner sitting holding a ball; B partner standing behind; B partner presses down on ball while A extends arms up.

1. Ball in fingers, not palms. Partner B allows ball to come up slowly with constant, even pressure.

2. Partner push. (*FS)

2. Same as above, but Partner A is squatting and comes to a stand with pressure down from B.

2. Partner A keeps back straight, arms flexed.

b. Free shooting.

b. Randomly divided into groups at each basket. Each student with a ball.

b. Emphasize a high arc and a light touch to get ball to basket. Hands follow through toward basket. Finger pads on the ball, not whole hand.

II. Motor Skills/Movement Concepts
a. Review passing (chest/bounce).

1. Partner passing.

1. Randomly spread in general space with a partner. Short distance apart, passing back and forth, varying the types of passes.

1. One foot in front, stepping with that foot when releasing ball. Snap wrist when passing. Control force so it can be easily received.

pp. 503-507

2. Moving to an open space to receive ball. Passing and dribbling. Partners pass and dribble, receiver moving to an open space, calling "yes" to receive pass.

2. Randomly spread in general space, with a partner.

2. Did you pass ahead of moving receiver? Control force for an easy catch? Did you see the open spaces to move to receive the pass?

p. 512

b. Review defensive play: staying between an opponent and the goal. Passer attempts to throw to wall, guard tries to intercept.

b. In pairs, 1 passer and 1 guard, with a wall space.

b. What position best enabled you to close pathways? What did you do with your hands? Your legs?

p. 511

III. Culminating Activity
a. Basket Endball.

a. Games of 8 players per team.

1. Move to an open space to receive the ball.

p. 518

2. Pass ahead of moving receiver.

3. Position yourself between ball and goal on defense.

| SPECIFIC OBJECTIVES/EVALUATIVE CRITERIA | EQUIPMENT |

To protect the ball while dribbling by keeping body
  between ball and opponent.

To perform a bounce pass with a forward step, arms extended
  to chest level of receiver.

To perform a bounce pass to avoid interruption by an opponent.

To shoot with a good arc, elbows in, soft release; knees bent
  and force created from legs.

Junior basketballs and
utility balls

Basketball hoops 7'-8' high

ACTIVITY	PROCEDURES/ORGANIZATION	POINTS OF EMPHASIS	REFERENCES

I. Opening Activity
  a. Review shooting skills.

1. Free shooting time.	1. Partners sharing a ball, taking turns shooting.	1. Shoot a variety of shots from just outside the key area, soft touch and follow through to basket.	pp. 507-509
2. Stretching.	2. Individual stretching.	2. Slow, easy stretches for muscles involved in basketball.	

II. Motor Skills/Movement
   Concepts
  a. Review dribble:

1. Discussion/demonstration/practice. Change hands on signal.	1. Group with teacher. Select a student to demonstrate, then scattered in general space. Each student has a ball.	1. Dribble at hip height. Press ball down with fingers. Look forward. Did you use all the space available?	p. 501

2. Protect ball while dribbling. Players without a ball try to knock ball away from those dribbling. Defense may only touch the ball when it is not in player's hand.

2. All but 3 or 4 have a ball in general space.

2. How did you keep ball away from those trying to knock it away? Use all the space.

p. 511

III. Culminating Activity
   a. Zone basketball

a. Small games of 8-10 players (4-5 per team).

a. Use all the space available. Pass quickly. Move to an open space to receive ball. Protect ball from defense. Where does defense want to be?

p. 518

SPECIFIC OBJECTIVES/EVALUATIVE CRITERIA	EQUIPMENT

To hold the hockey stick with top hand, shaking hands with
  stick and bottom hand placed several inches below.
To push the puck in a forehand manner, keeping stick
  low and beginning stroke with stick on the puck.
To dribble with the side-to-side dribble, with gentle
  taps to keep puck close.
To push a puck to a teammate, controlling force so that
  it can be easily received.
To receive a pass, giving with stick on contact to control
  the puck.

Floor hockey sticks
Plastic pucks/balls
Eye protectors
Shin guards

ACTIVITY	PROCEDURES/ORGANIZATION	POINTS OF EMPHASIS	REFERENCES

I. Opening Activity
a. Moving in general
space holding sticks
down, touching the
floor.

a. In general space with
sticks.

a. Stick increases self space.
Can you avoid others and their
sticks?

b. Stretches. (*FF)

b. Self space, with student
leaders. Sticks on floor
next to student.

b. Slow, static stretches.
Emphasis on quadriceps and hamstring groups.

II. Motor Skills/Movement
Concepts
a. Stick handling: hold-
ing the stick.

a. Group seated for demon-
stration/discussion.

a. Always keep the stick low
to the ground. Left hand at
the top of the stick as if
shaking hands. Right hand
4"-8" below the left.

pp. 525-
528

b. Side-to-side dribbling.	b. Group demonstration/discussion, then each student dribbling with a puck in general space.	b. Move the puck with a series of light taps to the left and right. Keep puck out in front of the body. Whats happening to your hands, wrists and elbows?	p. 529
c. Push pass: stationary passing with a partner.	c. Group demonstration/discussion, then in general space with a partner 10-'15' away.	c. Right hand 6" below left. Feet in forward/backward stride position. Stick on puck. Step forward onto right foot as stick sweeps forward. Control force so pass can be easily controlled.	pp. 529-531
d. Receiving.	d. Practice with push pass.	d. Watch puck onto stick. "Give" with the stick to absorb force.	pp. 531-534
III. Culminating Activity a. Hockey dodge. Each student dribbles through general space. If a player's puck comes into contact with anything, that player has to stop in that spot and dribble in place with the side-to-side dribble.	a. Scattered in general space with a stick and a puck. Each game lasts 45-60 seconds; play several games with a brief discussion between each.	a. How did your speed change during the game and why? How did you control the puck/ball to avoid contact or collisions?	p. 539

SPECIFIC OBJECTIVES/EVALUATIVE CRITERIA	EQUIPMENT

To move a puck with control in the side-to-side dribble, tapping puck lightly to keep it within width of the body.

To push pass in a forehand manner to a teammate with accuracy and proper force, sweeping the puck with the stick and following through slightly ahead of receiver.

To receive a pass with control, lining up with pass, reaching out with stick on contact and giving with stick to absorb force.

To move to an open space to receive pass.

Hockey sticks
Plastic pucks/balls
Traffic cones

ACTIVITY	PROCEDURES/ORGANIZATION	POINTS OF EMPHASIS	REFERENCES

I. Opening Activity
  a. Partner passing.

a. Partners passing and receiving back and forth from various distances.

a. Keep the stick low for the push pass. Push to the partner's stick. "Give" with the stick to control the ball when receiving.

II. Motor Skills/Movement
  Concepts
  a. Side-to-side dribble: review skills/ practice.
    1. Dribble in general space.

a. Seated in group for demonstration/discussion, scattered in general space.

a. Keep puck close for control.

1. Control puck and look up to avoid others.   p. 529

2. Alternately dribbling in self space and then in general space.

2. In general space, responding to teacher's signals to dribble in place and in general space.

2. Control puck in self space. Now in general space.

b. Passing/receiving: review/practice.

b. Group demonstration/discussion, then partners in general space.

b. "Lead" the person's stick with the puck. Keep stick low, "sweeping" it forward. "Give" with the stick when receiving to absorb the force of the puck.

pp. 535, 541-542

c. Moving to an open space to receive a pass. Players move to an open space, passing to each other, avoiding others and the cones.

c. A number of cones are scattered in the playing area. Students in groups of 2 or 3.

c. Look up to see open spaces? Were you able to accurately pass to your partner?

p. 474

III. Culminating Activity
a. Floor hockey challenge. Players, one at a time, come out, pass to each player in line and then take one shot for a goal. After 2 minutes, count goals made. Repeat, with each team trying to increase the number of goals they made.

a. In groups of 4-6 players in a line, with one goal at one end of the playing area. A restraining line in front of the goal may be needed to challenge goal shooting.

a. Pass softly so that puck is easy to control. Push puck slightly ahead of moving receiver. Shoot quickly with control.

SPECIFIC OBJECTIVES/EVALUATIVE CRITERIA	EQUIPMENT

To dribble with control and speed, keeping puck close
  to stick.

To pass in a forehand or backhand manner accurately to
  a teammate with proper force so that it can be easily
  received.

To shoot accurately at the goal, following through in the
  direction of the corner of the goal.

To move to open spaces to receive a pass and looking for
  teammates to pass to in game play.

To stay between offense and goal when playing defense.

Hockey sticks
Plastic pucks/balls

ACTIVITY	PROCEDURES/ORGANIZATION	POINTS OF EMPHASIS	REFERENCES

I. Opening Activity

  a. Open dribbling. (*FC)

a. Each student with a puck, dribbling in general space within the playing area.

a. Always move into the open spaces, avoiding collisions and contact with other players. Keep the ball near the stick.

  b. Stretches. (*FF)

b. Self space; each student following the lead of the teacher or student leader.

b. Slow, static stretching of several muscle groups, including lower back.

II. Motor Skills/Movement
   Concepts
   a. Dribble/pass/shoot: review/practice. Partners dribble, pass and shoot at various goals scattered around the playing area.

   a. Seated for group demonstration/discussion, then in partners that each has a chance to use forehand and backhand passes. Change relationship with partner after 1 minute.

   a. Keep puck close when dribbling. Pass softly so teammate can control the pass. "Give" with the stick when receiving a pass to gain control. Follow through to corner of goal when shooting.

   p. 536

   b. Staying between offense and goal when on defense. Player with puck dribbles and tries to move puck to end line. Defense moves with player, staying between the player with the puck and the goal line.

   b. Players arranged in small areas marked off with cones.

   b. Did you move quickly to the defense if you lost the puck? How did you keep the puck from crossing the line?

   p. 542

III. Culminating Activity
   a. Sideline hockey.

   a. Two games may be played simultaneously on smaller, adjacent areas. Call 1 or 2 numbers depending on ability of the players.

   a. Players should move to an open space to receive pass. What should you do as soon as you gain control of the puck? Keep stick down to be ready to intercept a pass. Control of the ball and sticks is major emphasis. Move to goal side of puck when playing defense.

   p. 543

| SPECIFIC OBJECTIVES/EVALUATIVE CRITERIA | EQUIPMENT |

To dodge quickly to tag or avoid being tagged.

To throw a forward pass, gripping ball with 2 or 3 fingers on laces, snapping wrist on release and following through in direction of throw.

To catch a thrown ball with the fingers and hands, watching ball into hands, reaching out and pulling it in.

To carry a football close to the body and on the side opposite the defenders while running.

To move the ball toward a goal by running and dodging.

Flag football belts and flags
Junior footballs or foam footballs

| ACTIVITY | PROCEDURES/ORGANIZATION | POINTS OF EMPHASIS   REFERENCES |

I. Opening Activity
  a. Tear tag

| 1. Partner game: each player tries to tear off the flags of partner. When one player loses two flags, the flags are replaced and game is repeated. | 1. Partners in self space. Demonstration of use of belts and flags. | 1. Players must stay in small self space area. Contact may not be made. Can you dodge quickly to keep your flags? |
| 2. Group game: Everyone is "it" and tries to pull off everyone else's flags. All players remains in the game even if both their flags are pulled off. (*FC) | 2. Duration of the game should be 30-60 seconds and can be repeated 2-3 times. | 2. Move into open spaces to avoid being tagged. Move discretely into position to steal a flag. Twist and turn to avoid losing flag. |

b. Stretches. (*FF)

b. Self space. Student leaders.

b. Slow, static stretching. Use this time as a cool-down and rest from tear flag.

II. Motor Skills/Movement Concepts

a. Carrying the ball.

a. Group demonstration/discussion, then scattered in general space.

a. Carry the ball close to the body and on the side opposite the defenders.

p. 559

1. Ball tag: those with balls move in general space. Those without attempt to take flags of ball carriers.

1. In general space, all but 3 or 4 have a ball.

1. Keep the ball on side away from defender. Hold ball firmly when running. Move to an open space.

b. Passing: forward pass/demonstration and practice.

b. Seated for demonstration/ discussion, then with a partner general space.

b. Hold ball slightly behind middle, with two or three fingers on the laces. Bring arm straight back past ear. Step when throwing, snap wrist and follow through in direction of flight. Watch ball into hands. Catch with fingers and palms; pull ball into body.

pp. 555-556

III. Culminating Activity

a. Catch and run: the ball is thrown from the goal area. The receiving partner catches and runs to the goal. If the ball carrier's flag is torn off, players change places. If the receiver touches the goal, he gets to receive again.

a. Facing a partner, 10'-20' apart, with a cone (the goal) behind the partner who has the ball.

a. The thrower should throw as far as possible, but may not begin the chase until the receiver touches the ball. The receiver should try to catch the ball in the air, to get the best possible start toward the goal. The receiver should carry the ball firmly against the body. How can you get past the person to get to the goal?

| SPECIFIC OBJECTIVES/EVALUATIVE CRITERIA | EQUIPMENT |

| To dodge quickly to tag or avoid being tagged. | Flag football belts and flags |

To dodge quickly to tag or avoid being tagged.

To throw a forward pass accurately and with proper force by gripping ball on laces, snapping wrist and following through in direction of throw.

To pass laterally with an underhand motion, releasing ball at waist height, index finger pointing in direction of flight.

To center the ball to a quarterback from a stride position, ball held in two hands, arms extending back between legs and controlling release of ball from finger tips.

To catch a pass, watching ball into hands, reaching out with hands and fingers and pulling the ball in to the body.

To anticipate the path of a receiver by placing the ball in front of the receiver for an easy reception.

Flag football belts and flags
Junior footballs or foam balls
Traffic cones

ACTIVITY	PROCEDURES/ORGANIZATION	POINTS OF EMPHASIS	REFERENCES
I. Opening Activity			
a. Group tear tag: on a signal each player tries to tear off as many flags as possible. When both flags are gone, the player becomes a stationary tagger, pivoting in a spot, pulling flags off those running past. (*FC)	a. Players scattered in general space.	a. Move into open spaces. Avoid contact when pulling flags. Twist and turn to protect flags.	
b. Stretches. (*FF)	b. Self space with student leader.	b. Slow, static stretching.	

c. Football fitness jumps: partners alternating turns, each jumps sideways back and forth over the ball as fast as possible for 15 seconds (2 turns each). (*FS)

c. In general space with a partner.

c. Jump lightly. Encourage your partner to go very fast. How many can you do in 15 seconds? Can you break your record on the second turn?

II. Motor Skills/Movement Concepts
a. Passing/catching: review and practice.
    1. Stationary.

    1. In general space, partners playing catch 8'-12' apart.

    1. Grip ball on laces. Bring arm straight back and forward past ear. Step forward and follow through in direction of the throw. Catch with fingers and hands. Watch ball into hands. Reach out and pull it in toward the body.

pp. 555-556

    2. Pass pattern. One partner runs down 10'-15', then turns sharply to the right or left. Passer throws a forward pass as soon as the partner makes the turn.

    2. In general space, partners in an area way from others.

    2. Receiver must turn sharply and continue running. Passer must anticipate path of receiver and throw the ball in front of the receiver so that he/she runs into the pathway of the ball. Watch ball into hands. Give with the ball.

p. 556

b. Lateral Toss. Teach skills and practice: partners begin side by side, 4' apart. Passer gives verbal signal to indicate

b. Seated with partner for group demonstration/discussion, then with a partner, beginning side by side 4' apart.

b. Step toward the receiver. Underhand toss with fingers, releasing at waist height, index finger pointing in direction of flight.

p. 556

when receiver should begin moving. Receiver begins moving away from passer to receive pass, then runs forward up field.

c. Centering. Teach skills and practice.
    1. Partner hiking. Partners, one as the center, the other as the quarterback. Each hikes 3 times, then they change places. On third hike, the center may go out for a pass.

c. Seated with partner for group demonstration/discussion, then practicing in general space.

c. "Shot gun" skill is used (quarterback several feet behind center). Use 2 hands, feet spread. Control release of ball from finger tips. Quarterback uses verbal signals.

p. 559

III. Culminating Activity
    a. Hike. On the signal "go" the center hikes to the quarterback. Immediately the quarterback turns and moves into a centering position and the center turns, moving into a quarterbacking position. The ball is hiked again. This process is continued until the teacher gives the signal to stop after 1 minute. Count number of snaps. Repeat several times.

a. Partners 6' apart, one as center, the other as a quarterback.

a. The ball must touch the ground before it is hiked. The center should hike directly to the quarterback's hands. Accurate snaps are faster in the long run than hurried ones. Can you increase the number of snaps from what you did last time?

| SPECIFIC OBJECTIVES/EVALUATIVE CRITERIA | EQUIPMENT |

To anticipate the path of the ball carrier to intercept
that path.

To dodge to tag or to avoid being tagged.

To center the ball with two hands, extending arms back
between legs and controlling force in release from
finger tips.

To pass forward to a receiver, anticipating his pathway,
placing the ball slightly ahead of receiver, and following through in direction of flight.

To catch a pass while running, lining up with ball, reaching
out with both hands, watching it into hands, and pulling
it in toward the body.

To punt a ball, holding ball in front of body, dropping it
parallel to the ground, contacting ball on instep, toes
pointed, and kicking leg continuing to follow through in
direction of flight.

Equipment:

Flag football belts and flags
Junior footballs or foam balls
Cones

| ACTIVITY | PROCEDURES/ORGANIZATION | POINTS OF EMPHASIS | REFERENCES |

I. Opening Activity

a. Color flag. On the signal, half the class (offense) tries to take the flags of the other half (defense). At 30 seconds, the game ends on a loud whistle or signal; the number of

a. Students scattered in general space, each half of the class with different colored flags.

a. Avoid contact with other players, particularly when reaching for flags. Twist and turn to protect flags. Move into open spaces. Offense may want to use two players to cut off pathways and trap defensive players.

flags taken is scored for
the offense. Roles are
reversed, and the second
half of the game is played
The team with the most
flags wins.   (*FC)

II. Motor Skills/Movement
    Concepts
    a. Passing/catching/
    centering. Review
    skills/practice. Center
    hikes the ball, receiver
    runs a pass pattern,
    quarterback passes.

a. Seated for group demon-
stration/discussion, then
in groups of 3: a center, a
quarterback and a receiver.
Players change positions
so that each has a turn
at each position.

a. Center uses 2 hands to snap
the ball and should follow
through toward quarterback's
hands, controlling force and
releasing ball off fingers.
Can you anticipate the path of
the receiver? Quarterback
passes in front of receiver,
stepping and following through
in the direction of the receiver.
Receiver must watch ball into
hands.   Reach for ball and pull
it in.

b. Punting.   Teach
skills/practice: part-
ner punting and receiv-
ing back and forth.

b. Seated for group demon-
stration/discussion, then
in partners 20'-40' apart.

b. Hold ball in front of and away pp. 559-
from body. Drop ball parallel to   560
ground. Contact on instep of
foot, toes pointed, follow through
in the desired direction of flight.

III. Culminating Activity
   a. Punt return. One
   partner punts from in
   front of a goal (traffic
   cones). The receiver
   catches the ball and runs
   for the goal. The punter
   tries to tag (pull off
   the flags) of the receiver
   before he gets to the goal.
   A player is tagged when
   one flag is pulled off.
   Players exchange places
   after each turn.

a. Partners 20'-40' apart.

a. The punter must wait until
the receiver catches the ball
before he begins chase. How
can the chaser best anticipate
and intercept the pathway of
the receiver? What can the
receiver do to get to the goal
untagged?

SPECIFIC OBJECTIVES/EVALUATIVE CRITERIA	EQUIPMENT

To explore striking a variety of objects with the hand.
To develop an underhand hit, dropping the ball in front
and to one side of the body, contacting ball on the
fleshy part of the hand and fingers and following
through in direction of hit.

A variety of foam and playground balls
table tennis and tennis balls, etc.
Several hand ball tennis courts (2-square
courts)

ACTIVITY	PROCEDURES/ORGANIZATION	POINTS OF EMPHASIS	REFERENCES

I. Opening Activity

a. Controlling a ball in general space. Students move in general space with a variety of balls, controlling them as they move, changing balls and activities on teacher's signal. (*FC)

a. In general space, each student with a ball. On signal, students exchange balls with one another.

a. How many different ways can you move and control the ball?

II. Motor Skills/Movement Concepts

a. Explore striking with a variety of balls and in many different ways. Students try different ways to strike a ball.

a. With a ball in general space. Change objects after 1 minute. Repeat several times. After a little exploration, students suggest ways for others to try.

a. How many different ways can you strike the ball with control? Do some ways work better with some objects?

pp. 216-217

b. Strike the ball so that it hits the wall and comes back to you.

b. Students select a ball to use and find a wall space.

b. What ways were easiest to control?

pp. 216-217

c. Strike the ball so
it hits the wall
at the high level.
Medium. Low level.

d. Strike the ball so
it hits the wall
and then the floor be-
fore coming back to you.

e. Strike the ball so
it hits the wall,
bounces and comes back
to you 3 times in suc-
cession. 5 times.

f. Underhand hit. Stu-
dents hit to wall after
bounce so ball returns
to them to hit again.

III. Culminating Activity
a. Hand ball Tennis.

c. Students may change
objects if they wish.

d. Students may change
objects if they wish.

e. Students may change
objects if they wish.

f. Seated for demonstration/
discussion. Then working
individually at a wall space.

a. With a partner 12'-15'
apart in general space, a
line or rope between them,
1 ball.

c. Did you use different techniques for each level? Can
you adjust one type of hit
for each level?

d. How can you control the
force to accomplish this task?

e. How did you hit the ball to
control it? Control its force
and path to come back to you?

f. Drop ball slightly in front
of and to the hitting side of
the body. Use an underhand
motion, contact with fleshy part
of the hand and fingers. Follow
through in direction of hit. Try
to control ball so that it hits
at your medium level.

a. Control hits so ball   p. 577
crosses line to land in opposite court. Can you hit the
ball 5 times in succession?
10 times?

258

| SPECIFIC OBJECTIVES/EVALUATIVE CRITERIA | EQUIPMENT |

To strike a moving ball with an underhand hit, moving
   in relation to the ball, contacting the ball off the
   fleshy part of the hand and fingers and following
   through in the direction of the ball.
To vary the underhand hit from very soft to very hard.
To successfully play 4-square, controlling and varying
   the amount of force of the ball.
To anticipate receiving the ball in your square.

Variety of playground balls
Several 4-square courts

| ACTIVITY | PROCEDURES/ORGANIZATION | POINTS OF EMPHASIS | REFERENCES |

I. Opening Activity a. Striking ball back and forth to a wall, trying to achieve 10 consecutive hits.	a. In general space with a ball and wall space.	a. Control force. Line up with ball. Follow through in direction of flight.	p. 575
II. Motor Skills/Movement Concepts a. Hitting ball back and forth with a partner. Start with a drop and hit and then try to keep it going.	a-d. In general space with a ball and a partner, within a loosely-defined court.	a. Control force. Follow through where you want ball to go. Contact ball with fleshy part of hand and fingers.	
b. Hitting with a partner, only very soft hits.		b. Hit softly, directing ball with fingers.	pp. 216-217
c. Hitting hard shots.		c. Control force so ball lands in bounds.	pp. 216-217

d. Alternate hard and soft shots with a partner.

III. Culminating Activity

a. Varying force game: each student establishes a pattern of 3 hits, varying from soft to hard, which is repeated. Partner tries to guess what pattern is; i.e., (soft-hard-soft; hard-hard-soft, etc.)

b. 4-square.

a. With a partner in a 2-square court with 1 ball.

b. Divided into groups of 4 on 4-square courts.

d. Vary hit from soft to hard. Can you control force to hit softly sometimes and with more force other times?

a. Can you control force to perform and repeat the sequence? Can you disguise your hits so that partner isn't sure if it will be hard or soft?

b. Try to vary the force of your hits. Control force to keep the ball in bounds.

p. 576

SPECIFIC OBJECTIVES/EVALUATIVE CRITERIA	EQUIPMENT

To hit a ball with an overhand motion by lining up with ball, contacting ball with fleshy part of hand and fingers and following through in a downward motion in the desired direction of the hit.

To vary the path of the ball hit with an underhand and overhand motion by following through in path.

To play 4-square, varying path and force of the ball.

Variety of playground or 4-square balls
Cards to record consecutive hits

ACTIVITY	PROCEDURES/ORGANIZATION	POINTS OF EMPHASIS	REFERENCES

I. Opening Activity
  a. Consecutive hits with a partner: partners hit back and forth, counting consecutive hits and recording best scores after 1 minute.

a. In general space with a partner and a ball. Repeat activity 3 times. Record scores on cards.

a. Can you control your hits to keep it going many times? Can you direct your hits so that the ball is easily returned? Did you improve your scores from last time?

II. Motor Skills/Movement Concepts
  a. Overhand hit.
    1. Against the wall. Begin with a throw so that ball bounces for an overhand hit. After hit, catch rebound and repeat.

a. In general space with a ball and wall space.

a. Line up with ball. Contact with hand high with an overhand motion. Follow through down and in desired direction of hit. Control force of hit.

2. Striking with a part-
ner: bounce ball to
partner who strikes
the ball.

2. In general space with
a partner.

3. Hit ball back and
forth with a partner.

b. Varying path of the
ball: varying pathway by
hitting to the right and
then left of partner.
   1. Use underhand hits
   only.

b. In general space with a
partner.

b. Follow through in desired
path.

2. Use overhand hits
only.

3. Vary hit with level
of ball.

III. Culminating Activity
   a. 4-square

a. In groups of 4 on
4-square courts.

a. Vary hits and force used.   p. 576
Place ball to left and right
of other players.

SPECIFIC OBJECTIVES/EVALUATIVE CRITERIA   EQUIPMENT

SPECIFIC OBJECTIVES/EVALUATIVE CRITERIA	EQUIPMENT
To dribble with head up, tapping ball with inside of the feet to keep the ball within playing distance.	Soccer, foam and rubber playground balls
To pass accurately to a partner with the inside of the foot, placing supporting foot next to ball, body and head over ball, and following through in direction of pass.	
To receive and control (or trap) a pass, lining up with the ball, and giving with the ball on contact.	
To keep spread out on offense to make space for passers.	
To intercept the path of the ball on defense.	

ACTIVITY	PROCEDURES/ORGANIZATION	POINTS OF EMPHASIS	REFERENCES
I. Opening Activity			
a. Open dribbling. (*FC)	a. Every student with a ball, (not necessarily a soccer ball) dribbling throughout general space.	a. Keep the ball near the feet as you move. Keep head up, look for open spaces to move into. Run at an even pace to be able to continue for 1-2 minutes.	p. 514
b. Soccer jumps. (*FS)	b. Students in self space with their own balls on the ground. On a sign, each jumps sideways back and forth over the ball for 15 seconds. Repeat 3 times. (Some students may need to jump behing their ball first time through)	b. How fast can you jump? Keep the jumping continuous.	
II. Motor Skills/Movement Concepts			
a. Passing skills			
1. Pass the ball many	1. Partners in self space.	1. Which part of the foot	pp. 590-592

times, each time with
a different part of
your foot.

      gave you the most control?
The most power?

    2. Teach the inside-of-the-foot pass; demonstration/practice.

    2. Seated in a group for demonstration, then with a partner 10'-20' apart.

    2. Support foot even with the ball, body and head over the ball. Foot follows through in direction of the pass.

p. 590

  b. Controlling the ball.
    1. How many ways can you stop and control the ball when it is passed to you?

    1. Partners 10'-20' apart.

    1. Which ways kept the ball near your feet? Could you collect and quickly return the pass?

p. 595

    2. Teach collecting (or trapping) the ball and practice collecting the pass, using the inside of the foot and inside of the thigh.

    2. Seated with partner for demonstration, then practicing with partner 10'-20' apart.

    2. Move to meet the ball. Relax the foot or leg as the ball touches it to lessen the impact.

p. 595

III. Culminating Activity
  a. Keep Away: 2 on 1. Two players attempt to control the ball by passing, dribbling and juggling so that the third player cannot touch it. When the third player touches it, he/she changes places with one of the others.

  a. Groups of 3, spread out in general space.

  a. Passes must be direct and quick. Defensive player should be ready to quickly anticipate and intercept the pathway of the ball. Spread out to make space for passes on offense.

p. 603

SPECIFIC OBJECTIVES/EVALUATIVE CRITERIA	EQUIPMENT

To pass accurately to a teammate while moving, kicking the ball with the inside or outside of the foot to a space ahead of the receiver.

To dribble to avoid an opponent, keeping the ball close and under control and shielding the ball by keeping body between ball and opponent.

To control an incoming pass, lining up with ball and giving with foot on contact.

To tackle an opponent to gain control of the ball, using the inside of the foot to lift ball over opponent's feet, keeping ankle firm.

To defend the goal, assuming a ready position, moving to ball, getting down on one knee and gathering ball in the arms and hands.

Soccer, foam and rubber balls

ACTIVITY	PROCEDURES/ORGANIZATION	POINTS OF EMPHASIS	REFERENCES

| I. Opening Activity
  a. Partner passing and dribbling. (*FC) | a. Partners moving throughout general space, 8'-12' apart, dribbling and passing the ball back and forth. | a. Passer should "lead" the receiver so that he controls it without stopping. Use both the inside and outside of the foot when passing. Line up with ball and give with foot on contact to receive ball. | p. 590 |

b. Ball control: drib-
bling 1 on 1. One
dribbles, the other
attempts to take it
away when it is off
the dribble foot. (*FC)

b. Partners playing in a
small area (20'x20').

b. Use both feet and all   p. 589
parts of the foot to con-
trol the ball. How did you
protect the ball from your
partner?

II. Motor Skills/Movement Concepts

a. Tackling:

1. Review the block
tackle.

1. Group demonstration
using 2 students.

1. Defensive player   p. 598
(tackler) must be persist-
ent. Use the inside of the
foot to lift ball over opponent's foot; keep ankle firm.
Nobody contact.

2. Practice the block
tackle. One partner
attempts to tackle the
other, who controls the
ball within the area.

2. Partners walking in small
area 20'x20'.

2. Same as above.

b. Goalkeeping:

1. Teach the skills
of goaltending.

1. Group demonstration, students in semicircle around
goal area.

1. Where should the goalie   p. 600
be positioned before the
shot is taken? What posi-
tion should the goalie be
in when anticipating a shot?

2. Goalie play. One
partner rolls or throws
the ball into the goal;
the other defends the
goal.

2-3. Goal areas designated
for each 2 students. Partners, 1 in the goal, the
other 20' in front of the
goal.

2. Same as above. If the ball
is rolling, get down on one
knee to prevent it from rolling through. Keep eyes on the
ball.

3. Goal shooting. Part-
ner begins 25'-35' from
goal, dribbles in and
shoots. Goalkeeper de-
fends.

III. Culminating Activity
   a. Advanced line soccer.
     fends.

3. Where do you want to shoot
for goal? How can you position
yourself to defend the entire
goal?

a. In teams of 6-8 players.
Several games may be
organized.

a. Pass ahead of receiver.   p. 604
Shield ball from would-be
tacklers. Be ready on goal
line to defend against shots
on goal.

SPECIFIC OBJECTIVES/EVALUATIVE CRITERIA   EQUIPMENT

To dribble with control with the inside of the foot, tapping ball, and keeping it within playing distance.
To pass to a teammate, looking up and kicking the ball to
  a space ahead of the receiver with appropriate force so
  that ball can be easily received.
To move to an open space to receive a pass from a teammate.
To shield the ball while dribbling by placing the body
  between opponent and the ball.
To use team work to move the ball toward the opponents' goal.
To position oneself in line with the ball and be ready to
  move on defense.

Soccer balls
Rubber balls
Nerf or foam balls.

| ACTIVITY | PROCEDURES/ORGANIZATION | POINTS OF EMPHASIS | REFERENCES |

ACTIVITY	PROCEDURES/ORGANIZATION	POINTS OF EMPHASIS

I. Opening Activity
  a. Soccer fitness
  stations.
    1. Soccer jumps.
	a. Four groups rotating to 4 stations (1 minute at each station).	1. Land lightly on balls of feet.

2. Modified situps and pullups.	2. As many situps as possible in 30 seconds. As many pullups as possible (partner may assist by lifting on hips).	2. Work with a partner; help and encourage each other.
3. Stretches.	3. Charts, signs or group leaders to indicate which stretches to do.	3. Slow stretching, emphasizing the quadriceps and hamstring groups.

4. Standing broad jump.
(*FC) (*FF)

4. Taped lines on floor can be quickly prepared and used many times.

4. Swing arms forcefully; jump high for more distance.

II. Motor Skills/Movement
Concepts
a. Passing in general space with a partner. Receiver moves to an open space to receive a pass from dribbler.

a. Seated for demonstration, then in partners in general space.

a. Keep ball close and controlled on dribble. Look up to see where to pass. Pass ahead of receiver. Move to an open space to receive a pass.

p. 590

III. Culminating Activity
a. Advanced line soccer.

a. In teams of 6-8. Several games may be played side-by-side.

a. Short, quick passes should be primary means of moving the the ball. Goal line guards should be in position ready to move to ball and quickly clear the area of the ball. Players spread out to create spaces for a pass. What types of passes worked best?

p. 604

SPECIFIC OBJECTIVES/EVALUATIVE CRITERIA	EQUIPMENT

To throw overhand to another player, turning side to
receiver, transferring weight back to front foot,
leading with elbow, and following through in direction
of receiver.

To catch a thrown ball, lining up with ball, reaching out
with gloved hand, giving on contact, and covering ball
with other hand.

To catch a rolling or bouncing ball, bending legs, hips
down, watching ball into glove and fingers pointing down.

To catch a fly ball, fingers pointing up, watching ball
into glove.

To run to first base, touching base with foot and sprinting
past base in a straight line.

Softball gloves (students should
be encouraged to bring their own)
1 ball for each 2 students
Bicycle inner tube
Bases

ACTIVITY	PROCEDURES/ORGANIZATION	POINTS OF EMPHASIS	REFERENCES

I. Opening Activity

a. Jog and toss. (*FC)

a. Partners jogging in
general space, tossing a
softball back and forth.

a. Toss the ball so that your
partner can catch it. Toss
underhand. Cover all the
spaces in the field.

b. Softball fitness
stations.
　1. Throwing strength:
one student holds a
bicycle inner tube,
the other stretches
the tube out using an
overhand throwing
technique.

b. Students divided into 2
equal groups rotate to
each of the 2 stations.
Teacher should demonstrate
each and explain that new
stations will be added as
unit progresses.

1. Position feet and body as
if throwing. Pretend the
tube is the ball. Move
through the throwing range
of motion in slow motion,
stretching the tube slowly.

2. Base sprinting: student starts at home plate and sprints to first base, overrunning the base, then jogs back. (*FS)

2. Sprint past the base, not just to it. Look straight ahead at the base.

II. Motor Skills/Movement Concepts

a. Teach/review the overhand throw: students catching with a partner.

a. Seated in group. Demonstration by teacher and student. Then in partners 15'-20' apart. Gradually increase to 30'-40' if students are able. Everyone should be throwing in the same direction.

a. Turn side to teacher, transfer weight from back to forward foot. Lead with elbow on throw. Follow through in direction of receiver.

pp. 214, 613

b. Teach/review the 2-hand catch. Practice with overhand throw.

b. With demonstration of throw.

b. Give with the hands as the ball enters the glove. Position body in the pathway of the ball. Watch the ball all the way into the mitt. Cover ball in glove with other hand.

pp. 214, 615

c. Teach fielding a fly ball. Students throw and field with a partner.

c. Seated for demonstration, then in partners.

c. Judge the pathway and flight of the ball; position body under it. Have glove up in position fingers up, and ready.

p. 616

d. Teach fielding a ground ball. Students throw and field with a partner.

d. Seated with partner for demonstration, then in partners.

d. Move the body into the pathway of the ball. Bend legs, hips down. Get hands down as low to the ground as possible, fingers pointing downward.

p. 616

III. Culminating Activity

a. Flies and grounders. One partner throws fly balls, ground balls and straight throws. The other tries to field each throw without error. Play continues until the fielder has fielded 5 balls.

a. Partners 20'-30' apart. Groups far apart from each other. Thrower may use any combination of types of throws. Receiver throws straight back to the thrower.

a. Have knees bent and hands ready. As soon as the ball is thrown, line up with the pathway. An error is committed when a player misses, drops or bobbles the ball.

SPECIFIC OBJECTIVES/EVALUATIVE CRITERIA	EQUIPMENT

To throw overhand accurately, gripping ball in fingers, side turned in direction of throw, elbow leading arm action forward, following through to receiver and controlling force so that the ball may be easily received.

To catch a thrown or hit ball with 2 hands, lining up with ball, fingers pointing up or down appropriately, reachout and pulling glove and ball in and covering ball in glove with other hand.

To pitch to a batter within the strike zone, gripping ball in fingers, stepping forward on opposite foot and pointing fingers on follow-through in direction of the pitch.

To bat a pitched ball, facing plate, bat off shoulder and with a smooth, level swing.

To cover the field in long base, each player sharing the space with teammates and assuming a ready position to move to meet the ball.

Softballs
Whiffle balls
Plastic bats
2 bases for each game

ACTIVITY	PROCEDURES/ORGANIZATION	POINTS OF EMPHASIS	REFERENCES

I., Opening Activity
  a. Softball fitness
  stations.
    1. Throwing strength.
    (See softball plan #1.)

    2. Base sprinting.
    (See softball plan #1.)

    3. Partner situps:
    legs intertwined, one

a. Students are divided into 4 groups and rotate to each station. Review the previously taught station; teach the new station.

a. Each of these muscle groups is used in softball. Stronger, more flexible muscles will improve softball skills.

partner goes up while
the other goes down.
(*FS)

4. Stretches. (*FF)

II. Motor Skills/Movement
   Concepts

a. Review overhand throw.	a. Group demonstration, then practice with partners, all throwing in same direction.	a. Side turned, ball held in fingers, elbow leads, transfer from back to forward foot. Follow through toward partner.	pp. 214, 613
b. Review catching.	b. With throwing demonstration.	b. Position body in pathway of the ball. Watch the ball into mitt. Cover ball in glove with other hand.	pp. 215, 615
c. Teach the underhand throw (pitch).	c. Seated with partner for demonstration, then in general space, pitching in same direction.	c. Grip ball in fingers, step forward on opposite foot. Follow through to catcher's mitt.	p. 613
d. Teach batting skills. Demonstration and practice, using plastic bat and ball. Each batter gets 4 hits, then change places. Pitcher throws so that batter can hit the ball, then attempts to field the hit ball.	d. Seated in groups of 3 in semicircle near the home plate area. Each group has a home plate with 1 partner pitching, one catching and the other batting.	d. Face the plate, close enough to touch the far side with the bat, knees bent, bat back off shoulder. Swing level, smooth and with moderate force. Pitch easily so that the batter can hit the ball.	p. 617- 618

III. Culminating Activity
    a. Long base.

a. In teams of 6 players. Several games may be set up, all moving and throwing in the same direction.

a. Position yourself to cover all the space. Look for open spaces for your throws.

p. 621

SPECIFIC OBJECTIVES/EVALUATIVE CRITERIA   EQUIPMENT

To catch fly balls, ground balls and straight throws,   Softball bats
    lining up with all, watching it into glove and cover-   Softballs
    ing ball and glove with other hand.   Bases (2 sets)
To run the bases safely, controlling movement, overrun-
    ning 1st base and touching base on inside corner for
    2nd and 3rd.
To throw accurately to teammates, controlling force of
    throw and following through to teammate.
To identify and play the various positions in the field.
To bat a ball, facing home plate, feet in easy side stride
    position, bat back off shoulder and a smooth, level swing.

ACTIVITY   PROCEDURES/ORGANIZATION   POINTS OF EMPHASIS   REFERENCES

I. Opening Activity
    a. Pop-ups.   a. Partners playing catch,   a. How many can you catch with-
                            throwing only pop-up fly   out a miss? Line the body up
                            balls to each other.   with the flight of the ball,
                                                              fingers up to catch flies.

    b. Grounders.   b. Partners playing catch,   b. Line up with ball. Get
                            throwing only grounders to   hands down to the ground
                            each other.   before the ball arrives,
                                                              fingers pointed downward.
                                                              Watch ball into glove. Cover
                                                              glove and ball with other hand.

II. Motor Skills/Movement
    Concepts
    a. Base running: demon- a. Seated in group in the   a. Touch the inside corner   p. 618
       stration and practice.   infield where they can see   of the base. Run a straight
       Several students at   each base.   line to the base; have knees,

each base; on signal,
first runner at each
base takes off, runs
bases, touches next per-
son in the group, who
runs, etc. until all
have run. Time running.
Repeat. (*FC)

hips and ankles flexed when
preparing to leave the base.
Can you improve your time?

b. Batting: brief review
of batting skills, then
group batting and field-
ing. Change batter after
5 hits.

b. Seated for group demonstration and discussion.
Students in groups of 4:
batter, pitcher, catcher,
fielder.

b. Feet spread, knees flexed,
facing home plate. Swing
level and smoothly. Watch
the ball hit the bat. Fielders
be ready at every pitch. Pitch
so that the batter can hit the
ball.

pp. 617-
618

c. Position play: ex-
planation of positions
in softball and areas
covered by each player.

c. Students in group.
Teacher may use a diagram
or preferably players in
the field to explain positioning.

c. What areas does each player
cover?

pp. 619-
620

III. Culminating Activity
   a. Beatball.

a. Team of 6 players. Two
games may be played at the
same time.

a. No player may strike out.
Controlled pitching will keep
the game moving and exciting.
Fielders will make more accurate
throws if they take their time
and throw correctly. Be ready
in covering positions. Throw
softly so that teammates can
control the ball. Overrun 1st
base. Touch bases on inside
corner when running more than
one base.

p. 624

| SPECIFIC OBJECTIVES/EVALUATIVE CRITERIA | EQUIPMENT |

To learn the history of volleyball.

To assume a ready position with legs bent and in a comfortable stride position to be able to move into
position to play the ball.

To move in relation to the ball, under it and catching it
above the forehead.

To hit an overhand volley, tossing the ball up, moving
under the ball, legs and arms flexed and extending
legs and arms to create force as the ball is hit with
fingers.

To direct the ball into an open space across the net.

EQUIPMENT

2 volleyball nets
Elementary size volleyballs
Foam balls

| ACTIVITY | PROCEDURES/ORGANIZATION | POINTS OF EMPHASIS | REFERENCES |

I. Opening Activity
    a. Catch over the net.

a. Partners facing each other
on opposite sides of the net,
playing catch across the net.
The net should be fingertip
height.

a. How many in a row can you
throw and catch? How far
back can you get and still
throw and catch? How high
can you throw it over the net?

II. Motor Skills/Movement
    Concepts
    a. Introduction to
    volleyball.

a. Group discussion.

a. History of sport.

b. Overhead volley.
   1. Moving in relation to ball. Partner throws ball so that it can be caught above the forehead.

   1. Group demonstration/discussion, then in partners.

   1. Be in ready position to receive the ball, knees bent, comfortable stride position. Move under ball, catch it above your forehead.

   pp. 633-634

   2. Practice the skill. Each partner tosses the ball vertically, then passes it to partner using the overhand volley.

   2. Partners facing each other 4'-6' apart.

   2. Toss ball straight up. Move under ball, legs and arms flexed. Hit ball with fingers, extending legs and arms in direction of the hit.

   3. Volley over the net. Volley back and forth.

   3. In partners, one on each side of the net.

   3. What must you do to clear the net? Be ready to receive the ball?

III. Culminating Activity
   a. Catch and volley: a 2-on-2 form of volleyball with play started by tossing the ball over the net with 2 hands.

   a. Groups of 4, partners on same side of net facing 2 other partners. Game is played by tossing and hitting the ball back and forth across the net. When it hits the floor, the throwing team scores a point.

   a. Aim the ball into the empty spaces on the opponent's court. If the ball is caught in the back court, pass to the partner near the net.

SPECIFIC OBJECTIVES/EVALUATIVE CRITERIA   EQUIPMENT

To perform an overhead volley, moving in line with and
   under the ball, flexing arms and legs, contacting ball
   with fingers and extending arms and legs to create force.
To pass to a partner with the overhead volley, controlling
   the ball and hitting to a space above the receiver.
To place the ball in an empty space in the opponent's court.

2 volleyball nets
Elementary size volleyballs
Foam balls
Plastic balls

| ACTIVITY | PROCEDURES/ORGANIZATION | POINTS OF EMPHASIS | REFERENCES |

I. Opening Activity
   a. Catch over the net.

a. Partners tossing (ver-
   tically, overhand) over the
   net to each other.

a. No competition, just the
enjoyment of trying to catch
every throw. How high can
you throw over the net? How
many in a row can you catch?

II. Motor Skills/Movement
Concepts
   a. Overhand volley.
      1. Review/practice.
      Toss ball vertically,
      pass to partner with
      overhead volley.

1. Seated for group demon-
stration/discussion, then in
partners facing each other
4'-5' apart.

1. What body parts create
the force for a good
volley? What should you
look like as the ball
approaches? Toss the ball
high enough to get set
underneath it. Pass the ball
to a space above your partner so that your partner can
get under it for the catch.

pp. 633-
634

2. Overhead volley without the catch.

2. In partners, but partner will try to return the pass without catching the ball. Students may choose from a variety of balls best suited for their ability.

2. How must you pass the ball so that your partner can return it? How many times can you pass back and forth without missing?

3. Partner passing over the next. Back court player tosses ball and hits it to teammate who may catch and hit it or just hit it over the net.

3. In groups of 4, 2 on each side of the net, lined up as net and back court players.

3. Where did you want to receive the ball to play it best? Did you control force so that the ball was easy for teammate to handle?

b. Building strength for the overhead volley with partner pushes. Sitting partner places fingers on the ball held directly overhead (1" from forehead) by standing partner. Standing partner presses gently on ball, while sitting partner extends arms completely, slowly. Repeat 4 times, then reverse places.

b. Partners, 1 sitting on the floor, the other standing behind with the ball.

b. Standing partner creates enough downward force so that sitting partner reaches extension very slowly. Sitting partner: head back, look at ball; contact ball with finger pads.

III. Culminating Activity
a. Advanced Newcomb. Students individually selecting skills for use in game (modified or regular overhead volleys.

a. In teams of 4 players.

a. Players in back line should   p. 641
pass to players in front line. Make passes very high to help teammates handle the ball more easily. Vary the force and path of the volley to keep opponents off guard. Look for empty spaces to place ball in opponent's court.

| SPECIFIC OBJECTIVES/EVALUATIVE CRITERIA | EQUIPMENT |

| To pass with an overhead volley, placing ball in the space above a teammate.
 To vary the force of the overhead volley.
 To place the ball in an empty space in the opponent's court. | 2 volleyball nets
 Elementary size volleyballs
 Foam balls
 Plastic balls |

| ACTIVITY | PROCEDURES/ORGANIZATION | POINTS OF EMPHASIS | REFERENCES |

I. Opening Activity			
a. Volleying over the net. Students may catch and hit or just hit it over the net.	a. Partners across the net from each other. Each pair selects the ball that works best for them (volleyball, foam or plastic).	a. How long can you continue a volley? Move quickly on each volley to intercept the pathway of the ball. Use the legs to help create force.	
b. Volleyball fitness. Partner pushes.	1. See previous volleyball lesson.	1. Slow release of force by standing partner.	
2. Net jumps. Partners jump vertically, touching hands. Two sets of 3 repetitions.	2. Partners facing each other across the net. Net at fingertip height.	2. Create force for jumping by springing off legs. Touch hands lightly at apex of jump.	
3. Fingertip inchworm. Each student does the inchworm on the fingertips. (*FS)	3. Self space.	3. How far out can you walk your hands?	

II. Motor Skills/Movement Concepts

a. To vary force in the overhead volley. Review skills/practice. Lone player alternately hits ball over the net, first to the net player, then to the back court player.

a. Seated for group demonstration/discussion. Then in groups of 3, 2 on one side of net, 1 on the other.

a. Get under ball. Use legs to create force. What did you do to vary force to hit just across net and then deep into back court?

pp. 635-636

b. To place the ball in an empty space. One team begins play. Try to hit ball so that it lands in an empty space (hits to floor untouched) in opponent's court. Play continues until an empty space is hit (1 point for each space hit). Begin play again with team not scoring putting ball in play with an overhead volley.

b. In teams of 3 players.

b. How did you find the empty spaces? How did you direct the ball to get it to the space?

p. 640

III. Culminating Activity

a. Advanced Newcomb.

a. In teams of 4.

a. Players may play any ball with either a catch or overhead volley. Back row must make high passes to front row. Look for empty spaces to place ball. Vary force to hit just over the net onto the back court.

p. 641

LEVEL IV

SPECIFIC OBJECTIVES/EVALUATIVE CRITERIA	EQUIPMENT

To review safety procedures emphasizing personal responsibility for the safety of self and others.

To perform shoulder, forward and backward rolls maintaining the tuck and pushing with hands in forward and backward rolls.

To perform a variety of balances emphasizing a stable base of support and weight evenly distributed over the base.

To smoothly combine skills with a change of direction, pathway and level.

EQUIPMENT

Mats
Music

ACTIVITY	PROCEDURES/ORGANIZATION	POINTS OF EMPHASIS	REFERENCES

I. Opening Activity

a. Aerobic/rhythmic warm-up to music.Student leaders lead class in locomotor movements and rhythmic stretching. (*FC) (*FF)

a. Self space on mats.

a. Work at a steady pace pace to best work cardio-respiratory system. Stretch slowly and gently through the range of motion. Review need for warm-up in gymnastics.

p. 250

b. Review safety for stunts and tumbling

b. Self space on mats. Make a poster of rules identified.

b. What are some important rules for working safely on the mats? How can we make tumbling safe for ourselves and others?

pp. 303-306

II. Motor Skills/Movement Concepts

a. Review roll variations.
   1. Shoulder roll

a. Seated on mats for review. Rolling the length of mats for practice. Students choose variations to practice.

1. Keep body curled and roll smoothly from knee to shoulder, to back and back to knee.

p. 312

2. Forward roll and
variations: pike, stag,
straddle.

2. Keep tuck, push with hands. p. 316
Maintain position throughout
roll.

3. Backward roll and
variations: pike, stag,
straddle, back extension.

3. Push with hands at   p. 316
shoulders. Maintain position
throughout roll.

4. Combining rolls:
Combine 2 rolls; 2 rolls
with a change in direction;
2 rolls with a change in
pathway.

4. Can you continuously
move from one roll to the
next? What adjustments did
you need to make to change
direction or pathway?

b. Review individual
balances: v-sit, arabesque,
knee scale, tripod, head-
stand, tip-up, handstand.

b. Seated for demonstration.
Work on mats with partners as
spotters where needed.

c. What base of support aids   pp. 321-323
the balance? How do you distri-
bute your weight over the base?
Can you hold the balance for a
count of 5?

III. Culminating Activity
a. Stunt combinations:
Combine 3 of the skills
from the lesson including
a change of level, and
direction or pathway.

a. Seated for discussion of
possible combinations, then
working individually on mats.

a. Can you move smoothly from
one skill to another? Hold your
balance?

| | SPECIFIC OBJECTIVES/EVALUATIVE CRITERIA | EQUIPMENT |

To work with others in performing partner stunts.

To experience balancing at various levels, on various body parts, while stationary and moving.

To support the body on a variety of body parts.

To safely build and dismantle pyramids.

Mats

ACTIVITY	PROCEDURES/ORGANIZATION	POINTS OF EMPHASIS	REFERENCES

I. Opening Activity
  a. Partner stunts:
    1. Elephant walk.

a. Partners sharing space on mats. Establish one direction for all to move and boundaries for groups to avoid collisions.

1. Walk slowly keeping legs wrapped at the waist.

p. 311

    2. Camel walk.

2. Move forward as top child moves hands and feet, supporting the other child.

p. 260

  b. Partner stretches: Partners work together to stretch one another. Hold stretches for 8 counts, then gently release and change places.

b. Partners using space on mats.

b. Only stretch partner as far as is comfortable for him/her.

II. Motor Skills/Movement Concepts
  a. Review safety procedures for building

a. Seated on mats for discussion.

a. Bases must be strong enough to support others. Weight bear-

p. 326

pyramids. Demonstrate
safe weight bearing,
mounting and dismount-
ing.

ing only on those body parts
firmly supported. Do not use back
for weight bearing. Get on and
off base gently. Use mats.

b. Review designs for
pyramids. Discussion.

b. Seated on mats.

b. Problem solving approach.   p. 320
Encourage creativity in choosing
a design.

c. Review possible indi-
vidual and partner bal-
ances which may be used
in building designs.

c. Seated on mats. Student
and teacher suggestions.

c. Discuss shapes balances   p. 321-327
create.

d. Build pyramids in
stages. Discuss organ-
ization needed.

d. Seated on mats.

d. Plan a good beginning and   p. 326
ending. One leader should be
chosen to signal addition of
each stage of the pyramid and
to dismantle it after formation.

III. Culminating Activity
a. Creating pyramids.

a. Divided into groups of
6 to 8 students. Mats may
need to be rearranged to
provide a safe space. Students
volunteer to present pyramids
to the class.

a. Can you smoothly build and   p. 326
dismantle your pyramid? Balances
are added in what sequence? Can
some be held longer than others?

SPECIFIC OBJECTIVES/EVALUATIVE CRITERIA	EQUIPMENT

To perform tumbles, inversions, locomotor, and dance movements
  with good body control moving smoothly from one skill to the
  next.

To perform a floor exercise evaluated for form, continuity,
  creativity and content.

To perform the above with variations in level, direction, tempo
  and force.

Mats
Music
Paper and pencils to write
down floor exercises

ACTIVITY	PROCEDURES/ORGANIZATION	POINTS OF EMPHASIS	REFERENCES

I. Opening Activity
   a. Three stations set up
   as follows: one with activities for strength development, one for flexibility,
   and one for cardiorespiratory endurance. Students
   choose one activity at each
   station. (*FS) (*FF) (*FC)

a. Students rotate to each
station working at own pace,
until all tasks are completed.

a. Challenge yourself in
choosing activities that
meet your personal needs.

II. Motor Skills/<Movement
    Concepts
    a. Practice tumbling
    skills of individual's
    choosing.

a. Separate mats for rolls and
balances established. Moving
skills performed the length of
the mat. Spot students as needed. Group students working on
the same skills. Keep all students in view.

a. Try to perform with the
best technique that you can.
Have a good beginning and
ending.

b. Review criteria for
a floor exercise from
previous lessons.

b. Seated on mats. A poster
with criteria is helpful with
examples of possible moves.

b. Criteria: 10 points, one   p. 328
point from each of the following:
1. Two or more tumbling moves
2. Balances
3. Locomotor movements
4. Nonlocomotor movements
5. Variation in level
6. Changes in direction
7. Changes in tempo
8. Interesting floor pattern
9. Dynamic beginning, definite
ending
10. Smooth, flowing connection
of movements and creativity.

III. Culminating Activity
a. Evaluation of floor
   exercises.

a. Students perform when
ready. Others continue to
practice their routines.

a. Evaluated on above criteria.
Are skills put together smoothly?
Are each of the criteria met?

| SPECIFIC OBJECTIVES/EVALUATIVE CRITERIA | EQUIPMENT |

To perform a pullover to the high bar pushing from bar with foot, kicking straight leg over the bar and pulling with arms to bring the upper body close to the high bar.
To work independently combining skills on apparatus.
To begin planning final routines for 2 pieces of apparatus and listing possible skills.

Parallel bars, uneven bars, vaulting box, balance beam, horizontal bar, paper and pencils, criteria for routines posted, mats under equipment.

| ACTIVITY | PROCEDURES/ORGANIZATION | POINTS OF EMPHASIS | REFERENCES |

I. Opening Activity
   a. Strength exercises.
   (*FS)

a. Self spaces with one or two student leaders, who choose and lead exercises.

a. Try to perform exercises in good form. What muscles are working?

   b. Stretches.(*FF)

b. Self space. Students individually choose stretches to warm-up for apparatus of their choice.

b. What muscles need stretching?

II. Motor Skills/Movement Concepts
   a. Pullover to high bar Explanation/demonstration.

a. Seated where all can see demonstration.

a. Push with foot on bar; kick straight leg over bar; pull with arms to bring upper body to the high bar.

p. 342

   b. Practice on all apparatus.

b. Students wishing to try pullover go to unevens, others to apparatus of their choice. After a period of time rotate to other equipment (2 times).

b. What skills can you put together to make an interesting combination? Make the movements flow from one skill to the next.

III. Culminating Activity
a. Planning for final
routines on 2 pieces of
apparatus. Check posted
criteria.

a. Sitting for explanation.

a. Choose two pieces of apparatus.
List skills you can do for possible
inclusion in a routine. Look at
criteria. Where do they fit?

| SPECIFIC OBJECTIVES/EVALUATIVE CRITERIA | EQUIPMENT |

To choose skills for a routine and practice skill combinations.
To smoothly combine skills with transitional moves where
  needed.

Parallel bars, uneven bars, vaulting
bench, balance beam, horizontal bar,
mats under all apparatus, students'
project sheets and pencils

| ACTIVITY | PROCEDURES/ORGANIZATION | POINTS OF EMPHASIS | REFERENCES |

I. Opening Activity
  a. Strength exercises.
   (*FS)

a. Self space with 2 student
leaders who choose and lead
exercises.

a. What muscles are working?

  b. Stretches. (*FF)

b. Self space. Individuals
choose stretches to do to
warm-up for apparatus use.

b. What muscles need stretching
for your work today?

**II. Motor Skills/Movement
Concepts**
  a. Individual work on
  routines: Students work
  with lists developed in
  last class, working on
  individual skills and
  combinations.

a. Teacher spots vaulting.
Set times for teacher to
work with students at each
piece of apparatus.

a. Be sure to have a spotter
where needed. Which skills make
good combinations? Meet routine
criteria? Can you combine skills
smoothly? Do you need to plan some
transitional moves for some combinations to work smoothly?

III. Culminating Activity
  a. Student demonstrations
  of some skill combina-
  tions and transitional
  moves.

a. Seated where all can see.

a. Did the movements flow from one
skill to the next? What concepts
were included (change of level,
direction, pathway, tempo)?

SPECIFIC OBJECTIVES/EVALUATIVE CRITERIA	EQUIPMENT
To practice skill combinations and transitional moves. To develop a gymnastic routine including a change of level, direction, pathway, and tempo.	Blank list to list order of skills Parallel bars, uneven bars, vaulting bench, balance beam, horizontal bar, mats under all apparatus.

ACTIVITY	PROCEDURES/ORGANIZATION	POINTS OF EMPHASIS	REFERENCES
I. Opening Activity a. Strength exercises. (*FS)	a. Self space. Student leaders choose and lead exercises.	a. What muscles are working?	
b. Stretching. (*FF)	b. Students choose own stretches for warm-up.	b. What muscles need stretching for today's activities?	
II. Motor Skills/Movement Concepts a. Practice skill combinations: Students practice skill combinations and transitional moves.	a. Students work at apparatus of their choice.	a. Emphasize good technique. Do movements flow smoothly? Be sure to have a spotter where needed.	
b. Movement concepts: Discussion/practice Teacher/student examples of concept application. Students check lists of skills and propose use of concepts. Practice combinations with concept use.	b. Seated for discussion, then in groups to practice.	b. What skills lend themselves to practice with which concepts? How does the inclusion of these concepts make the routine more interesting?	

III. Culminating Activity
  a. Student demonstrations
  of concept applications
  in routines.

a. Seated so all can see.

a. How well did skills lend them-
selves to the concepts applied? Any
suggestions? Do the movements flow?

| SPECIFIC OBJECTIVES/EVALUATIVE CRITERIA | EQUIPMENT |

To run comfortably for 200 yards at an even pace, landing on
  the balls of the feet, and swinging arms forward and backward.
To review hurdling, leading with the same foot and opposite arm
  each time.
To review a bunch start, fingers and thumbs behind starting line,
  hips down, knee next to foot, raising hips, eyes looking
  forward, legs extending and arms driving on signal to go.
To review the 50 yard dash, driving with arms for speed, and running at full speed well beyond the finish line.
To review the long jump, determining steps to take-off board,
  extending legs, raising arms for height and distance, and
  landing on two feet in a balanced position.
To review the soccer throw for distance, taking several steps behind
  the line, using an overhand throw, and following through in the
  direction of the throw.
To participate in a mini meet choosing two events and attempt to
  better your previous record.

EQUIPMENT:
  Stop watch
  Hurdles or cones with plastic tubes
  Long jump landing area
  Soccer balls
  Measuring tape

| ACTIVITY | PROCEDURES/ORGANIZATION | POINTS OF EMPHASIS | REFERENCES |

I. Opening Activity
  a. Distance run. (*FC)

a. A 200 yard oval or cross
country course.

a. Run at a steady pace.
Arms swing comfortably
at sides. Land on balls of
the feet.

  b. Stretches. (*FF)

b. Self space. Discuss
distance run while stretching.

b. Slow static stretches of
hamstrings, quadriceps, and
calf muscle groups.

II. Motor Skills/Movement
   Concepts
   a. Stations
      1. Hurdles.

a. Seated for demonstration, then divide into groups for practice.

1. Determine power leg and   p. 353
lead leg. Use the same over
each hurdle. Opposite arm
leads. Run low over hurdle.

      2. Bunch start and
      50 yard dash.

2. Fingers and thumbs behind   p. 349
starting line, knee next to
foot. Raise hips and eyes looking straight ahead. Extend legs,
drive with arms on "Go". Run at
full speed past finish line.

      3. Long Jump.

3. Determine steps to take-   p. 356
off board, take-off, extending legs, and swinging arms
forward for distance; land in
a balanced position.

      4. Soccer throw.

4. Take several steps to   p.357
build momentum. Use an overhand throw, follow through in
direction of throw.

III. Culminating Activity
   a. Mini-meet:
      1. Hurdles
      2. 50 yard dash
      3. Long jump
      4. Soccer throw.

a. Students pick 2 events to try to better their own previous records.

a. Try to perform in your best best form. Help each other to measure and record scores.

SPECIFIC OBJECTIVES/EVALUATIVE CRITERIA	EQUIPMENT

To run a distance of 300 yards at an even pace, and record times.

To high jump with a scissors jump, taking off on foot away from
 bar, forcefully swinging free leg and arms up to clear bar,
 and landing softly.

To long jump for distance, lifting arms and legs on take-off for
 added height.

To sprint for 50 yards maintaining own lane.

To perform a pursuit relay , passing baton in passing lane,
 swinging arm up to place baton in receiver's hand between
 the thumb and index finger.

To increase distance in the soccer throw with a 3-4 step approach
 and a forceful arm swing.

EQUIPMENT

Long jump landing area
High jump standards and landing pit
50 yard dash area with lanes marked
4 batons
Soccer balls,
Measuring tape and stop watch

ACTIVITY	PROCEDURES/ORGANIZATION	POINTS OF EMPHASIS	REFERENCES

I. Opening Activity
 a. Distance run. (*FC)

a. A 300 yard oval or cross
country course. Students set
own pace. Record times for
monitoring improvement.

a. Begin at a comfortable pace.
Increase speed gradually. Swing
arms comfortably at your sides.

 b. Stretches. (*FF)

b. Self space. Discuss
run while stretching.

b. Slow static stretching of running, throwing, and jumping
muscle groups/

II. Motor Skills/Movement
 Concepts
 a. Pursuit relay.

a. Seated for demonstration
and explanation. Then divided
into groups of 4 to practice.

a. Must pass baton in passing   p. 351
area. Passer extends arm as
both run, swinging baton upward

to place it in the hand of the receiver between thumb and index finger.

III. Culminating Activity
  a. Stations:
    1. High jump.

    2. Bunch start and 50 yard dash.

    3. Long jump.

    4. Soccer ball throw.

a. Divided into groups to practice events. Rotate to next station on teacher's signal.

a. Work on good technique.
1. Forcefully extend leg and swing arms and free leg up to clear bar in high jump.   p. 354

2. Stay in own lane throughout the run.   pp. 349-350

3. Forceful take-off raising arms and legs for greater distance.   p. 356

4. Take 3-4 steps behind line to add force to the throw.   p. 353

SPECIFIC OBJECTIVES/EVALUATIVE CRITERIA	EQUIPMENT

To compete in track and field events trying to achieve a personal best performance. To time and measure accurately several track and field events.	High jump standards and landing area Long jump landing area Measuring tape and 2 stop watches 4 pound shot Hurdles or cones and plastic tubes Batons

---

ACTIVITY	PROCEDURES/ORGANIZATION	POINTS OF EMPHASIS	REFERENCES

ACTIVITY	PROCEDURES/ORGANIZATION	POINTS OF EMPHASIS
I. Opening Activity a. Light jogging. (*FC)	a. Each student runs a 200 yard jog for warm up.	a. Set an easy pace to warm up for the events.
b. Stretching. (*FF)	b. Individual stretching.	b. Slow static stretches of muscle groups used in events.
II. Culminating Activity a. A three-person track meet. 1. Organization of competing groups.	1. Students form their own groups of 3. Each group decides how many events they will compete in and in what order.	1. Groups will need to decide which events each will try. Some compromise may be needed. Groups will probably be formed according to ability which will provide challenging competition.
2. Review scoring.	2. Each team has a score sheet to record scores.	2. Students compete within their own group. In each event three points are awarded for personal best.

3. Organization for competition:

High jump
Long jump
Shot put
50-yard-dash
50-yard-hurdles
300-yard run
Pursuit relay.

3. Each group moves from event to event, waiting for their turn to compete. While waiting they officiate for other groups, timing and measuring and recording scores. The pursuit relay will be held during lesson 8 at the end of the meet.

3. Support and encourage each competitor. Helping with the events will make the meet go more smoothly.

4. Duration of meet.

4. Competition lasts for 2 classes to allow maximum participation in the events.

4. Encourage each student's efforts in achieving personal bests.

5. Culmination of the competition.

5. Group recognition for all scorers in achieving personal bests.

5. Recognize the efforts and cooperation of all in conducting and participating in the events.

UNIT: Creative Dance   LEVEL: IV   LESSON:1st of 8

SPECIFIC OBJECTIVES/EVALUATIVE CRITERIA   EQUIPMENT

To move in response to an underlying beat and musical phrasing.   Music
To vary the range of movements from big to small.   Drum
To use time, force and flow in creating movements.
To perform in front of a partner.

ACTIVITY	PROCEDURES/ORGANIZATION	POINTS OF EMPHASIS	REFERENCES
I. Opening Activity			
a. Moving to music. Change locomotor movement to suit the music playing.	a. General space. Music playing in which tempo, beat, loudness and rhythm vary.	a. Listen to the underlying beat. Change types of movement speed, force, time and flow with a smooth transition.	
b. Moving to the drum beat. Students take turns beating the drum using different rhythms, loudness, and tempo.	b. General space.	b. How can you move to variations in rhythm? Tempo? Loudness?	
II. Motor Skills/Movement Concepts.			
a. Moving to musical phrasing.	a. Self and general space.	a. Students match their body rhythm to the rhythm of the musical phrase.	p. 382
1. Clap the phrases of a piece of music.			
2. Move in general space on one phrase and then in self space on the next.			

3. Take big movements on one phrase and small movements on the next.

III. Culminating Activity
a. Using imagery to create movement sequences. Ask students to think about their favorite sport or activity. Close their eyes and imagine yourself doing it.

   1. Develop a series of movements for one phrase of music depicting the movements of your activity.

   2. Perform for your partner.

a. Students work with partners in general space. Each creates a series of movements and then performs it for their partner. Music playing.

3. Can you vary the size of your movements and still move to the phrase?

a. Use movements and facial expressions to help the image. Use range, force and time to give the locomotor and nonlocomotor movements clarity. The movements should last at least one phrase of the music.

   1. How can you depict the movements? Refine your movements for added clarity.

   2. Can your partner determine in detail what is taking place?

pp. 373, 381

| SPECIFIC OBJECTIVES/EVALUATIVE CRITERIA | EQUIPMENT |

To move to the beat and rhythm of the drum and music.

To perform a variety of locomotor movement combinations to the beat.

To move in sequence with others.

To explore ways to use time and flow in their movements.

To create a dance to a round using a variety of movement skills.

To work with a partner or group to combine movements.

Music
Drum
List of rounds
Pencils and paper

| ACTIVITY | PROCEDURES/ORGANIZATION | POINTS OF EMPHASIS | REFERENCES |

I. Opening Activity

a. Creative partner fitness activities:
   1. Do the following in unusual positions, in rhythm with a partner:
      a. Pushups.
      b. Situps.
      c. Jumping jacks.

a. Self space. Select some of the most unusual to show the class. Music playing.

a. Create unusual ways to do these exercises. As the movements change different muscle groups may be used.

2. Do the above in sequence with a partner. One begins on the first beat, the other on beat 2 or 3.

2. Can you do the same movements but not at the same time time as your partner?

II. Motor Skills/Movement Concepts

a. Locomotor combinations: run, run, walk, walk, repeat; skip, skip, walk,

a. Students divided into three groups, one in each of three corners of the space.

a. Can you move to the beat of the music and the rhythmic pattern of the drum?

walk; hop, hop, walk, walk; gallop, gallop, slide, slide; step, together, step, walk, walk; etc.

One group moves at a time, with 2-4 students in the group beginning on the signal, the others in similar size groups moving after those ahead have completed one sequence. Each group moves to the empty corner of the space. Music is playing with the teacher also beating the rhythmic pattern of the movements on the drum.

III. Culminating Activity
a. Developing a movement sequence to a round.
   1. Select a round from choices listed or another that you know.

   2. Develop a series of locomotor movements to perform while singing the round.

   3. Move with a partner or group as a round one beginning to move, the others coming in appropriately.

a. Students work with a partner or in groups of 3 or 4. The dance will be developed over 2 classes with a performance at the end of the next class. The dance will involve a variety of movements and concepts. Students will write down their movement sequences at the end of this lesson.

a. Select movements from the combinations explored earlier in the lesson or their own. Move to the beat and/or rhythmic pattern and the musical phrasing. Make the movements flow. Can you sequence your movements with your partner or group?

p. 376

305

| SPECIFIC OBJECTIVES/EVALUATIVE CRITERIA | EQUIPMENT |

To review a locomotor movement sequence from lesson #5.
To add a change of direction or level to the movement
  sequence.
To add nonlocomotor movements to the movement sequence.
To blend a series of movements into a total movement with
  flow.
To work and create in a cooperative, group effort.
To perform in front of peers.

Music
Student combination lists from lesson #5

ACTIVITY	PROCEDURES/ORGANIZATION	POINTS OF EMPHASIS	REFERENCES

I. Opening Activity
  a. Review locomotor
  sequence from lesson #5.
	a. In general space with
	partner or group.
		a. Move on the beat. Make
		the movements flow.	

II. Motor Skills/ Movement
  Concepts
  a. Nonlocomotor Movements.
	a. With same partners or
	groups from lesson #5.
		a. Move smoothly from
		one movement to the next.
			p. 376

1. Move in self space giving the appearance that you are traveling.		1. Can you move your body parts so you appear to be traveling?	
2. Move as though your body was covered with chewing gum.		2. Imagine the gum is stuck to everyone. Move several body parts at the same time.	
3. Move as though some- one replaced your joints with rubber bands.		3. Look at all the joints. Begin moving the small joints,	

306

b. Changing level:
Move in general space
changing level on each
change of movement.
measure, or phrase.

b. General space moving
individually, with movement
sequence.

b. Can you change level and still pp. 376, 379
make the movements flow?

c. Changing direction:
Move in general space
changing direction with
change in movement,
beat, or phrase.

c. Can you anticipate the change
in direction so you move in a new
direction smoothly?

III. Culminating Activity
  a. Putting dance together.
    1. Review movement
    sequence.

a. With same partner or
groups from lesson #5.

a. Move in time to round. Move
smoothly from one movement to
another.

    2. Explore possible
    nonlocomotor movements
    to add.

    3. Explore possible
    level changes.

    4. Explore possible
    direction changes.

    5. Put dance together,
    with at least 2 of the
    3 (#2 - 4) added.

  b. Perform the dance.

b. One group at a time.
   All sing round.

b. Which movements matched
the beat and round best?
Did the group move as a round?

| SPECIFIC OBJECTIVES/EVALUATIVE CRITERIA | EQUIPMENT |

To review and use the step-hop to the beat and phrasing of the Crested Hen.

To move to the beat and phrasing of folk dances.

To control force and adjust size of steps to move with others.

Records: Crested Hen, and dances from previous lessons

| ACTIVITY | PROCEDURES/ORGANIZATION | POINTS OF EMPHASIS | REFERENCES |

I. Opening Activity

a. Review new dance from previous lesson.

a. In dance formation.

a. Move to the beat. Anticipate ending of phrases to be ready for change of movements etc. on beginning of next phrase.

b. Stretches. (*FF)

b. Self space. Led by students, stretches selected by teacher. Music playing.

a. Slow, steady stretches. Comfortable breathing.

II. Motor Skill/Movement Concept

a. Review the step-hop.

a. General space. Review and practice to Crested Hen music.

a. Keep a steady beat. Small steps make it easier to stay with the music.

p. 389

b. Review circling clockwise and counterclockwise. Use step-hop.

b. Sets of three, in a large circle.

b. Keep the small circle tight. Adjust steps to move with your group.

c. Teach Crested Hen.

c. Sets of three, in a large circle.

c. Accentuate the stamp on the first beat. Continue the step-hop

p. 413

on part B. Circle smoothly and under control.

III. Culminating Activity
   a. Students' choice of dances previously learned.

a. Appropriate dance formation.

a. Move to the beat, phrasing, and style of the dance. Adjust steps to stay with partner and keep formation.

| SPECIFIC OBJECTIVES/EVALUATIVE CRITERIA | EQUIPMENT |

| To review the promenade, ladies chain, swing, and allemande left and right.
To combine movements in time to the music.
To learn the dance "Coming Round the Mountain".
To move with a partner smoothly, controlling force, and adjusting size of steps. | Records: dances previously taught; Coming Round the Mountain |

ACTIVITY	PROCEDURES/ORGANIZATION	POINTS OF EMPHASIS	REFERENCES

I. Opening Activity a. Students choice of previously learned dance for cardiorespiratory warm-up.	a. In dance formation.	a. Listening carefully, adjust movements to stay with partner and music. Did you get your heart rate up? Was it a good cardiorespiratory activity?	
b. Fitness fun: 1. Partner challenge. One partner selects a previously learned fitness skill; the other must match the skill and repetitions. (*FS)	1. With a partner in general space.	1. Encourage your partner to do well. Work at least 3 major muscle groups.	
2. Stretches. (*FF)	2. Students create partner stretches for muscle groups used in partner challenge.	2. Can you stretch those muscle groups you were just working to strengthen?	

II. Motor Skills/Movement
Concepts

a. Review square dance formations:
1. Sets.
2. Side and head couples.

a. Demonstration and participation with one set, the other children in sets nearby.

a. Maintain formation throughout the dance. Use space to keep couples appropriately spaced.

b. Review square dance skills:
1. Swing.

b. In sets, one group demonstrates, then others try it.

p. 390

1. Control movements to swing easily with partner.

2. Allemande left and right.

2. Left to corner, move all the way around to face partner. Repeat with right to partner.

3. Promenade.

3. Adjust steps to move with partner remembering person on the outside must take bigger steps.

4. Ladies chain.

4. Reach with hand to meet the person. Boys, bring girls around smoothly.

III. Culminating Activity
a. Coming Round the Mountain.
1. Walk through the dance without music.

a. Square dance formation.

a. Listen for the verbal calls preceding each skill. Promenade with a new partner to the boy's home position. Move to the beat and phrasing of the music.

p. 424

2. Perform with music.

| SPECIFIC OBJECTIVES/EVALUATIVE CRITERIA | EQUIPMENT |

To enjoy an "old time hoedown".
To use previously learned square dance skills with students and
  adults.
To move to the beat and phrasing and in good square dance style.
To adjust steps to move with a partner.

Records of previously learned
square dances.
Bandana, hats, overalls, hay bales

| ACTIVITY | PROCEDURES/ORGANIZATION | POINTS OF EMPHASIS | REFERENCES |

I. Square Dance Festival
  a. Introduction
  This activity was introduced during lessons 5-7.
  In this lesson the teacher
  welcomes the students and
  guests to the dance hall
  for a class of "foot
  stomping and leg slapping"
  good time.

a. Students dressed in jeans,
overalls, bandanas, flannel
shirts, etc. Teacher dressed
as a square dance caller.

  b. Selection and performance of dances. Students
  choose from list of all
  dances learned in previous
  lessons.

b. With partners, students
move into groups and square
dance sets. Other adults,
have been invited including
parents, school nurse, prin-
cipal, etc. who participate
with students as partners.

b. Keep set formation.
Move smoothly to calls
and phrasing. Adjust
steps to move with part-
ner.

| SPECIFIC OBJECTIVES/EVALUATIVE CRITERIA | EQUIPMENT |

To move a ball rhythmically in a variety of ways in self and
   general space.
To move a ball on and off the beat.
To move the ball as an extension of body movement.
To perform rhythmic ball skills with control.
To smoothly combine ball skills so movement flows from one to another.

Balls of various kinds and sizes
Music

| ACTIVITY | PROCEDURES/ORGANIZATION | POINTS OF EMPHASIS | REFERENCES |

I. Opening Activity			
a. Warm ups: Strengthening and stretching exercises. (*FS) (*FF)	a. Students choose and lead exercises.	a. Exercises are important for maintaining fitness and to prepare the body for activity.	
II. Motor Skills/Movement Concepts			
a. Review/warm up with balls.	a. Seated for discussion, then in general space with a ball of their choice. Music playing for activities.		pp. 436-437
1. Students describe rhythmic ball skills from previous lessons.		1. What skills do you remember from last year's unit?	
2. Movement with balls in self space: Move the ball on the beat and off the beat.		2. Try bouncing, rolling, and tossing at various levels, etc. Think of the ball as an extension of the body's movement.	

3. Movement with balls in general space: Use many different ways to move the ball on and off the beat.

3. Keep the ball under control. Try moving at different levels, in various directions and pathways with many different locomotor movements, while performing ball skills. Think of the ball as a continuation of the body's movement.

p. 436-438

b. New skills:
1. Bounce ball between legs while moving forward.

b. Scattered in general space, music playing.

1. Bounce ball at wide angle. Control its force.

2. Toss ball behind back and catch.

2. Use a straight, controlled toss.

3. Toss ball vertically, sit down on floor, then stand up to catch it.

3. Use A high, but controlled toss.

4. Bounce ball in front of body from left to right hand while sliding to the side.

4. Control force and use a wide angle for bounce.

5. Roll the ball up one arm, across the shoulders, and down the other arm and catch it.

5. Steady torso, anticipating the roll.

III. Culminating Activity
a. Free practice: Students work on skills of their choice or to share skills with others.

a. In general space. Music playing.

a. Work for control of body and ball movements. Can you move yourself and the ball to the beat?

b. Building skill combin-
ations: put 2 different
skills together. Try
other combinations.

b. Students working alone or
with others in general space.
Music playing.

b. Work for a smooth transition
from one skill to the next and
moving with the music. Make the
combinations flow smoothly.

SPECIFIC OBJECTIVES/EVALUATIVE CRITERIA	EQUIPMENT

To perform ball skills to music with control.

To work cooperatively in a small group, choosing four ball skills, ordering the skills into a sequence, and choosing a formation in which to work.

To combine skills smoothly and in time to the music and other members of the group.

To perform a rhythmic ball sequence for classmates.

Balls of various kinds and sizes

Music

ACTIVITY	PROCEDURES/ORGANIZATION	POINTS OF EMPHASIS	REFERENCES

I. Opening Activity			
a. Locomotor warm up: Students move to the beat of the music keeping the beat with feet and upper body. (*FC)	a. Moving in general space, music playing.	a. Move at a comfortable pace. Check pulse rates at conclusion of the activity.	
b. Stretches. (FF)	a. Students choose stretches and work individually. Music playing.	b. All have different degrees of flexibility. All need to work on their own to improve.	
II. Motor Skills/Movement Concepts			
a. Review/warm up of skills previously learned.	a. In general space, music playing.	a. Work for control and moving to the beat.	pp. 436-438
b. Creation of movement sequence including at least 4 ball skills.	b. Seated for explanation, then in small groups working in general space. Music play-	b. Work to synchronize movements with the group. Make the ball an extension of the body's	

ing. Each member of the group must contribute at least one skill.

movement. Skills should flow smoothly and with the music.

III. Culminating Activity
  a. Groups perform skill sequences.

a. Seated where all can see. Music playing.

a. Reinforce creativity, cooperation, ball control and rhythm. What combinations were most interesting? Which would you like to try?

  b. Teaching others.

a. Students work with others who would like to try their combinations.

a. Go through it slowly, helping those who are learning. Then put put it together with music.

UNIT: Rhythmic Activities - Balls   LEVEL: IV   LESSON: 8th of 8

SPECIFIC OBJECTIVES/EVALUATIVE CRITERIA	EQUIPMENT
To perform a rhythmic ball routine with a definite beginning and ending and smooth transitions in movements. To combine skills, using them in good form, as an extension of the body's movement, and flowing smoothly from one to the next.	Variety of balls varying in kind and size Music in 2/4 and 4/4

ACTIVITY	PROCEDURES/ORGANIZATION	POINTS OF EMPHASIS	REFERENCES
I. Opening Activity a. Warm-up: Students lead strengthening and stretching exercises. (*FS) (*FF)	a. Self space. Two or three student leaders in front of the group.	a. What muscles are being strengthened? stretched?	
II. Motor Skills/Movement Concepts a. Individual and group practice of final routines, meeting the the following criteria: definite beginning and ending; movements are to the beat and phrasing of the music; changes in level and direction are included; routine lasts 45- 60 seconds.	a. Students practice alone or in groups they have chosen to music they have selected.	a. Begin work on parts which are most difficult for you. Put movements together smoothly. Work for control of ball and body movements. Remember the ball is an extension of the body's movement.	pp. 436-438

III. Culminating Activity
   a. Performance of final routines.

a. Performers in front of seated audience. Groups and individuals perform one at a time.

a. Did they move to the beat and phrasing? Were the movements executed in unison with other members of the group? Which movements were most unusual? Which would you like to try?

| SPECIFIC OBJECTIVES/EVALUATIVE CRITERIA | EQUIPMENT |

To practice basic rope jumping skills, maintaining the rhythm of jumping.

To turn a rope smoothly from the wrists.

To work cooperatively with others, monitoring performance and sharing skills.

To combine rope jumping skills smoothly.

Individual jump ropes
Music in 2/4 and 4/4 time
Poster of jumping skills

| ACTIVITY | PROCEDURES/ORGANIZATION | POINTS OF EMPHASIS | REFERENCES |

I. Opening Activity

a. Individual rope jumping. Students practice skills learned previously. (*FC)

a. In self space, music playing.

a. Remember the rope increases your self space. What rope jumping skills can you do? Can you repeat them several times in a row without losing the jumping rhythm? Turn the rope from your wrists, arms down at your sides.

b. Stretches. (*FF)

b. Self space, ropes on the floor. Students individually stretch muscles for the day's activities.

b. Slow, static stretches. What muscles need a warm up today?

II. Motor Skills/Movement Concepts

a. Review individual rope jumping skills.

a. Seated for discussion. Students demonstrate skills they learned in previous lessons.

a. Which skills can you do easily? Which need more practice?

p. 290

b. Introduce new skills.

b. Seated in a group in front of rope skills poster. Student or teacher demonstrate new skills.

b. Which of these skills can be done to the beat of the music?

p. 291

c. Skills practice.

c. Stations for various skills are scattered in the space. Children randomly move from skill to skill. Teacher circulates helping children at each station. Music playing.

c. Can you maintain the jumping rhythm as you jump in various ways? Can you repeat the skill 5 times without missing? Which can you do to the beat of the music?

pp. 291, 441

d. Rope jumping clubs: Students work on their own to perfect skills. When they feel they are ready they may join the skill club by performing the skill 5 times in a row for another student to watch.

d. Large pieces of paper, on the walls with pencils. Each sheet names a skill. Consecutive jump clubs are also included. Successful jumpers add their names to the club list. Each students tries to complete a minimum number of clubs.

d. Which skills can you do 5 times without missing?

III. Culminating Activity
a. Rope jumping skill combinations: Combine 2 skills. Try 2 others, etc.

a. Working with a partner in general space. Partners take turns suggesting combinations. Music playing.

a. Can you combine 2 skills smoothly? What other skills can you combine? Can you jump to the beat as you combine 2 skills?

p. 441

| SPECIFIC OBJECTIVES/EVALUATIVE CRITERIA | EQUIPMENT |

To turn the rope to the beat of the accompaniment.	Individual jump ropes
To smoothly and rhythmically combine rope jumping skills.	Long ropes - one per 3-4 students
To perform a variety of long rope jumping skills to a beat.	Music in 2/4 and 4/4 time
To coordinate jumping skills and rhythm with a partner or small group.	

| ACTIVITY | PROCEDURES/ORGANIZATION | POINTS OF EMPHASIS | REFERENCES |

ACTIVITY	PROCEDURES/ORGANIZATION	POINTS OF EMPHASIS	REFERENCES
I. Opening Activity			
a. Individual rope jumping practicing skills learned previously. (*FC)	a. Self space. Music playing.	a. Jump to the beat of the music. Take pulse at end of activity. Did you get your heart rate up?	pp. 291-292
b. Partner stretches. (*FF)	b. Partners assist each other to achieve maximum stretches.	b. Stretches should be comfortable, slow, and static. Pain means one has stretched too far.	
II. Motor Skills/Movement Concepts			
a. Review/practice turning rope to the beat.	a. In groups of 4 with a long rope.	a. Rope should touch floor on the beat. Hold the rhythm steady.	p. 290
b. Review long rope jumping skills.	b. Students seated as students describe and demonstrate skills they have previously learned.	b. What skills can you do in the long rope? Which might be good skills for rhythmic rope jumping?	p. 291
c. Introduce/practice new skills:	c. Practice in groups of 3 or 4 taking turns jumping and		

1. Partner jumps:
back to back;
holding hands;
turning together;
entering together;
exiting together.

turning the rope. Music playing.

1. Coordinate jump with the   p. 291
rhythm of the rope and your
partner.

2. Jumping combin-
ations using a
variety of foot
placements, turns,
and levels.

2. Can you smoothly change
skills without losing the
rhythm ?

3. Follow the leader.
Partners jumping
together. One initi-
ates a skill, the other
joins in after 4 beats.

3. Take turns being the
leader.

3. Can you maintain the
rhythm? Begin on the next
measure?

III. Culminating Activity
a. Rope skill combinations:
Combine 2-4 skills in 8
beats. Repeat sequence 3
more times.

a. Students work individually
or in small groups with short
or long ropes. Volunteers
share some combinations
throughout the practice. 4/4
music playing.

a. What combinations can you   pp. 441-
do? What skills are easiest to   442
combine? More difficult?

SPECIFIC OBJECTIVES/EVALUATIVE CRITERIA	EQUIPMENT

To smoothly combine short and long rope skills alone or with others.

To use a change in level or direction in jumping rope.

To practice twirling the rope, moving rope smoothly and to the rhythm of jumping.

To write a twirling and rhythmic jumping combination.

To perform dance steps rhythmically while jumping rope.

Individual jump ropes
Long ropes
Music
Pencils and paper

ACTIVITY	PROCEDURES/ORGANIZATION	POINTS OF EMPHASIS	REFERENCES

I. Opening Activity			
a. Stretches. (*FF)	a. Self space. Students stretch individually.	a. What muscles will need stretching today?	
II. Motor Skills/Movement Concepts			
a. Skill combinations: 1. Combine rope twirling and jumping: combine single or double side swings, front and horizontal swings with basic jumping skills;	a. In general space with a short rope. Music playing.	1. Control rope. Twirl in time to the music.	p. 291
b. Introduce twirl and toss.	b. In general space with a short rope. Music playing.	b. Begin with single side or front swing. Toss with control, fingers pointing in desired direction of toss.	p. 291

c. Dance steps: Perform a step-hop, bleking, step-swing, grapevine, or schottische in rhythm while jumping.

c. In general space with a short rope. Music playing.

c. Establish the rhythm of jumping first. Take small steps to maintain the rhythm of the rope.

p. 442

III. Culminating Activity
   a. Discuss and begin work on final project. Develop a rhythmic rope skills sequence for 2 phrases of music with 1 repeat, including a variety of jumping and twirling skills; one dance step; a change of direction or level.

a. Seated for discussion and then working in general space, alone or with a partner or small group. 4/4 music playing. Share some combinations at the end of the class.

a. Combine skills smoothly, maintaining the rhythm of jumping. Jump to the beat of the music.

p. 442

   b. Explore possible twirling and jumping combinations.

b. Write down possible combinations, then those you will use.

b. What skills, twirls, and dance steps can you combine smoothly without losing the rhythm of jumping? Can you do them to the beat of the music?

   c. Add a dance step; a change of level or direction.

c. If time permits add these additional elements. Write them down where they occur in the movement sequence.

c. Where can you add a dance step? A change or level or direction?

        SPECIFIC OBJECTIVES/EVALUATIVE CRITERIA   EQUIPMENT

To pass quickly and accurately with the chest and bounce passes,   A junior basketball or utility ball for
    gripping ball in fingers, stepping forward on release and   each student
    snapping wrists to increase force.   Pinnies or vests
To pass to a space in front of a partner.   8 foot baskets
To move quickly to an open space to receive a pass.
To shoot a set shot using legs and wrists to create force.
To dribble in the medium level, pushing the ball with the fingers,
    and changing direction, pathway, and speed.
To close paths open to the ball while playing defense by position-
    ing oneself between the ball and the opponents.

    ACTIVITY   PROCEDURES/ORGANIZATION   POINTS OF EMPHASIS   REFERENCES

I. Opening Activity
   a. Free shooting.   a. Students divided into small   a. Create force with legs and
                             groups and shooting freely at   wrists. Shoot from a variety of
                             all available baskets.   spots and distances.

   b. Partner passing.   b. With a partner in general   b. Grip ball in fingers. Step
   Use the chest and   space 6 - 10 feet apart.   forward and snap wrists for
   bounce passes.   added force. Pass to partners
                                                               hands.

   c. Partner push.   c. With a partner in general   c. Create even pressure for
   Each partner places   space.   partner. Stand in a forward
   hands on the ball, one   stride position. Push with
   with arms flexed, the   fingers also.
   other with arms extend-
   ed. Take turns pushing
   ball, while the other

creates resistance by
pushing back. (*FS)

d. Stretches. (*FF)

d. Self space. Individual
stretching of muscles used
in basketball.

d. Slow , static stretches.
What muscles need warming up
for basketball?

II. Motor Skills/Movement
   Concepts
   a. Introduction to basketball. Review skills
   learned in previous units
   and basic rules.

a. Students seated for discussion. Use a question/answer
approach i.e. "Who can tell
me........?

a. A brief outline of what
will happen in the unit is
important to get them off to
a good start.

b. Dribbling skills.
Review/demonstration/
practice. Students move
in general space respond-
to the teacher's signal
to change hands, level,
direction, pathway, and
speed. (*FC)

b. Seated for review and student demonstration, then with
a ball in general space.

b. Push ball with fingers.
Stay low, look up. Can you
dribble in the medium level?
Low? Change direction?
Pathway? Speed? Can you keep
dribbling without stopping?

p. 501

c. Passing.
Review/demonstration/
practice of chest and
bounce passes. Station-
ary passer passes ball
to moving partner who
calls "yes" when open to
receive a pass.

c. Seated for review and student demonstration, then with
a partner and ball in general
space.

c. Snap wrists. Step forward.
Control force so ball is easily
received. Pass to a space in
front of receiver. Receiver
moves to an open space to
receive ball.

pp. 503-
506

327

III. Culminating Activity
  a. "Galloping Lizzie".

a. In groups of 4 or 5 in a circle with 1 ball.

a. Pass quickly and accurately.   p. 507
Control force for an easy pass.
Defense: Where should you posi-
tion yourself to tag a receiver?

b. "Keep Away".
Team in possession of
ball attempts to com-
plete 5 consecutive
passes without an inter-
ception. Each member of

the team must handle the
ball during each series
of passes. One point is
scored for each set of 5
passes completed.

b. In groups of 6, 3 on each
team, in a small court with 1
ball.

b. Pass quickly, controlling
force of pass. Move to an open
space to receive the ball. Defense:
Where should you position yourselves to intercept? Where are your
hands? Do you have a balanced defensive
stance?

        SPECIFIC OBJECTIVES/EVALUATIVE CRITERIA   EQUIPMENT

To dribble changing hands, direction, pathway, and speed.   4 Medicine balls
To develop skill in guarding by positioning oneself between   Junior basketball or utility balls - one
  an opponent and the basket and closing space to opponents.   per student
To protect the ball while dribbling by keeping the body be-   Pinnies or vests
  tween the ball and an opponent.   8 foot baskets
To move to an open space while dribbling or to receive a pass.
To control force in passing so the ball can be easily received
  at chest height.
To move around opponents to receive a pass.

    ACTIVITY   PROCEDURES/ORGANIZATION   POINTS OF EMPHASIS   REFERENCES

I. Opening Activity
  a.Basketball fitness:
    1. Dribbling in general   1. In general space with a   1. Look up, move ball in the
    space changing hands,   ball.   new direction or path before
    direction, pathway, and   moving the body. Control the
    speed on the signal.   ball and keep dribbling through-
    (*FC)   out the activity.

    2. Medicine ball pass.   2. In groups of 4-6, with 1   2. Step and snap when passing.
    Throw the ball to each   medicine ball.   Can you control the force as
    other.   you throw to each other?

    3. Super jumps.   3. Randomly moving to sta-   3. Jump with arm swing. Jump
                              tions along the wall, with   straight up focusing on power
                              varying height markers.   in the legs.

  b. Stretches. (*FF)   b. In self space, stretching b. Slow, static stretching. par-
                              individually.   ticularly the quadriceps and
                                                            triceps.

II. Motor Skills/Movement Concepts

a. Free shooting: Practice a variety of shots, stationary and moving, from various spots and distances.

a. Divided into small groups at each basket.

a. Adjust force for various positions on the court. When using the backboard, try to have the ball touch it softly. (Remember relaxed shot and follow through to the basket).

pp. 508-509

b. Dribbling in general space in relation to others:

b. In general space, 2/3 of the students with balls.

p. 502

1. Dribble dodge. Stationary players attempt to knock the ball away from dribblers as they move in general space.

1. Dribble and move low. Keep body between ball and others.

2. Whirl dribble.

2. Keep the dribble going. Change hands to "whirl".

p. 503

c. Passing and moving to an open space.

c. Four players spaced along the foul shooting lane.

c. Pass and move immediately. Move away from the ball. Look up to see where the empty space is. Pass with control.

p. 513

d. Moving around an opponent to receive a pass: One stationary player attempts to pass to a partner as if throwing the ball in from out of bounds. The receiver attempts to move away from the defender to receive the pass.

d. Groups of 3 in general space.

d. Control pass. Move to an open space to receive the pass. How can you move to get away from the defender? How do you position yourself on defense to stay with the receiver?

p. 513

III. Culminating Activity
   a. Advanced Alley
   Basketball.

a. Students divided into teams of 5 players. Two games on 2 courts.

a. Stay between your opponent and the basket while on defense. Close spaces to the offense. Look for open spaces on offense and move quickly to receive a pass.

p. 520

SPECIFIC OBJECTIVES/EVALUATIVE CRITERIA	EQUIPMENT

To dribble with control, avoiding an opponent, keeping head up, and protecting the ball.

To shoot a lay-up, using the correct take-off foot and touching the ball softly to the backboard.

To pivot to protect the ball, keeping the pivot foot stationary.

To create open spaces to move oneself and the ball to the basket.

To play a two-on-two game with knowledge and respect for the rules.

Junior basketballs or utility balls - 1 per student
Pinnies or vests
8 foot baskets

ACTIVITY	PROCEDURES/ORGANIZATION	POINTS OF EMPHASIS	REFERENCES

I. Opening Activity			
a. Lay-up shooting.	a. Divided into small groups at each basket. Two lines, 1 shooting and 1 rebounding; after each turn go to the end of the opposite line.	a. Dribble with control looking at the basket. Last step is foot opposite shooting side. Use the backboard, with the ball touching it softly.	p. 509
b. Dribble tag: students dribble, while attempting to tag the other players' balls. (*FC)	b. In general space, each student has a ball.	b. Dribble low. Watch for others, protecting the ball by changing hands, and moving the body between the ball and the opponent. Tag the ball, not the other players.	p. 512
c. Stretches. (*FF)	c. In self space, with a student leader leading stretches.	c. Slow, static stretching.	

II. Motor Skills/Movement Concepts

a. Creating open spaces to move the ball to the basket: Two players guard the goal area. Three offensive players attempt to pass into the goal area for a shot at close range. No dribbling is allowed.	a. Groups of 5 at a basket.	a. Defensive players work together to protect the goal area. Offense keeps spread out and tries to find an open space to move to receive a pass. Pass quickly, using a bounce pass when possible. p. 513
b. Pivoting. Review/practice. Pivot tag: One partner has the ball and pivots to protect it, while the other attempts to tag it.	b. Seated for demonstration, then in partners in general space.	b. The pivot foot must remain stationary and may not slide on the floor or be lifted. Pivot in many directions, and move the ball up and down to protect it. Tagger may only tag the ball. p. 510

III. Culminating Activity

a. Discussion of game strategy and rules needing review.	a. Seated for review.	a. What must the defense do to be successful? The offense?
b. Two-on-two game.	b. Groups of 6 at each basket. 4 play and 2 referee. Rotate positions after each basket.	b. Remember the referee has the final word. Pass quickly, dribbling only when a pass is not possible. Guard your opposing player on defense. Use all your space. Move to open spaces to receive a pass.
c. Three-on-three game.	c. Add a 3-on-3 game for those who are ready.	c. Game emphasis the same as b. above.

SPECIFIC OBJECTIVES/EVALUATIVE CRITERIA   EQUIPMENT

SPECIFIC OBJECTIVES/EVALUATIVE CRITERIA	EQUIPMENT
To dribble a ball with gentle taps, keeping the ball close to the stick.	Hockey sticks
To push pass beginning with the stick touching the ball, and sweeping the stick forward and close to the ground throughout the movement.	Hockey, plastic, tennis balls Cones or markers
To receive a pass, lining up with ball, reaching with stick, and giving with stick on contact.	
To tackle by lining up with the dribbler and contacting the ball when it is off the dribbler's stick.	
To dodge with a stick-side dodge, pulling the ball and stepping first to the left and then around the defense player.	
To pass to a partner, pushing the ball with control to a space in front of the receiver.	
To move in general space in relation to an opponent and the ball.	

ACTIVITY	PROCEDURES/ORGANIZATION	POINTS OF EMPHASIS	REFERENCES
I. Opening Activity a. Open field dribbling: Students dribble in general space. Begin with a large area and reduce the size several times. (*FC)	a. With a ball in general space.	a. Control the ball with gentle taps. Move to open spaces. Keep the ball in front of the body. How did your dribbling change as the space changed in size?	p. 525
b. Hockey fitness: 1. Side straddle jumps: Alternate jumps with feet going out to the side and back with stick raised over head.	b. In self space all activities, but 3, done while holding a stick.	1. Keep an even rhythm. Stay on toes.	

2. Front/back straddle
jumps: Alternate jumps
with legs moving for-
ward and backward.

2. Jump with an even rhythm.

3. Stick jumps: Jump
sideways back and
forth over the stick.
(*FS)

3. Stick is on the ground.

3. Keep a steady rhythm.

4. Stretches. (*FF)

4. Reach with stick. Emphasize
stretches for lower back and
hamstrings.

II. Motor Skills/Movement
Concepts

a. Push pass and receiving:
Review/practice. Partner
passing beginning in a
stationary position and
then moving.

a. Seated for group demonstration, then in partners 10-20'
apart. Finally movingside
by side, 8-12 ' a part, in
general space.

a. Feet in forward/backward
stride position. Shift weight
onto forward foot as stick is
swept forward. Keep stick low
throughout the movement. Move
toward the ball to receive it.
Receive the ball with the flat
side of the stick, giving as
the ball contacts the stick.

pp. 528-534

b. Straight tackle: Intro-
duce/practice. Partner
tackle. One dribbles toward
the other who executes a
straight tackle.

b. Seated for demonstration,
then with a partner and ball
in general space. Dribbler
should offer little resistance at first.

b. Tackler lines up with dribbler. Contact ball as it comes
off dribbler's stick. There
should be no contact with the
the dribbler's stick.

p. 540

c. Stick-side(forehand)dodge:
Introduce/practice.

c. Seated for demonstration,
then with a partner in general

c. Pull the ball to the left
with just enough force to get

p. 537

335

Partner dodge: Dribbler dodges partner.

III. Culminating Activity

a. One-on-one: Using the dribble, dodge, and tackle, players try to score goals against their partners by dribbling the ball past a goal line. The defensive player tries to tackle to gain possession of the ball to move it to the opposite goal line.

space. Tackler should offer little resistance at first.

a. Partners in areas marked off with cones or markers. Begin play with one player in possession of the ball 30 - 40' from the goal line, and the defensive player between the ball and the goal.

it by the defense but not enough to lose control. Step to the left as the ball is moved to the left.

a. Keep the stick low and under control at all times. Dribbler should keep the ball close and under control. Move to an open space. Close space to offense and attempt to tackle on defense.

p. 543

336

SPECIFIC OBJECTIVES/EVALUATIVE CRITERIA	EQUIPMENT

To pass accurately to teammates, sweeping stick forward and low
   to the ground, controlling force, and pushing ball to a space
   ahead of the receiver.

To receive a pass, moving to ball, and giving with stick on
   contact.

To dribble and dodge an opponent, keeping ball close and under
   control.

To shoot on goal, avoiding defenders, and aiming for the corners
   of the goal.

To mark an opponent while on defense by staying on the goal side
   and ball side of the player.

To tackle an opponent, contacting the ball when it is off the stick
   of the dribbler.

To avoid obstructing another player by keeping the ball between the
   player and the opponent.

To move to an open space and toward the goal on offense.

Equipment:
Hockey sticks
Hockey balls
Cones or markers
Pinnies or vests

ACTIVITY	PROCEDURES/ORGANIZATION	POINTS OF EMPHASIS	REFERENCES
I. Opening Activity			
a. Partner passing: Partners move and pass the ball with control. (*FC)	a. With a partner in general space.	a. Lead your partner with the pass. Control force so the ball can be easily received.	pp. 529, 534
b. Partner keep away: One dribbles and controls the ball, keeping it from the other.	b. With a partner in a small area (20 by 20'). When the ball is stolen, the players change roles.	b. Keep your head up. Keep ball close to stick, moving in a small area. Tackle only when ball is off the stick. Avoid obstruction.	p. 529

II. Motor Skills/Movement Concepts

a. Moving to an open space to receive a pass: Ball is passed to open corner with player moving to that corner to receive the pass.

a. Three players are arranged as 3 corners of a square, with one empty corner. Each player is numbered, with player #1 passing to player #2, etc.

a. Look up to see where the empty space is. Move quickly to receive the pass, with stick down.

p. 542

b. Passing/receiving. Give and Go: Partner A dribbles, then passes diagonally to player B and continues to move to the goal. Player B returns the pass quickly to A who to shoots. Both rush the goal.

b. Partners working at a goal. Cones or other obstacles are placed in the goal so only the corners are open. Players reverse roles after each shot on goal.

b. Player B should control the ball before passing back to A. Pass ahead of receiver. Partner A continues to move toward goal and to an open space to receive the pass. Aim for the corner of the goal when shooting.

p. 534

c. Marking. Review/ practice. Offensive player moves in various pathways toward a marker. Defensive player moves with him/her, staying between the player and the goal.

c. With a partner, one on defense, the other on offense. Offense should move slowly at first until defensive player becomes skilled at marking.

c. Stay between the player and and goal. Keep stick down. Stay on ball side of player.

p. 539

III. Culminating Activity

a. Advanced alley field hockey

a. In teams of 6 players. Two games played simultaneously.

a. Play in the open spaces, not near the alley lines or other players. Work to control the ball at all times. Look up to see teammates and opponents.

p. 549

SPECIFIC OBJECTIVES/EVALUATIVE CRITERIA	EQUIPMENT

To dribble with control, keeping the ball close to stick and
dodging opponents when necessary.

To pass ahead of a receiver, controlling force so the ball is
easily controlled.

To move to a open space to receive a pass.

To tackle an opponent, contacting the ball when it is off the stick.

To mark a player, by staying on the goal side and ball side of an
opponent.

To create spaces for teammates and the ball while playing offense.

To close spaces to the offense while playing defense.

Hockey sticks
Hockey balls
Cones or markers
Pinnies or vests

ACTIVITY	PROCEDURES/ORGANIZATION	POINTS OF EMPHASIS	REFERENCES

I. Opening Activity			
a. Partner passing: Moving in general space, partners pass back and forth as they move. (*FC)	a. With a partner and ball in general space. Change sides occasionally so both players are on the right and left sides.	a. Move to open spaces to avoid collisions with others. Pass to space in front of partner so he/she can continue moving as they receive the ball. Control ball on receiving it, dribble a short distance and pass back.	pp. 529, 541
b. Stretches. (*FF)	b. In self space, students lead stretches.	b. Slow, static stretches of the lower back, hamstring, and quadriceps muscle groups.	
II. Motor Skills/Movement Concepts			
a. Creating an open space for self, teammates and	a. Seated for demonstration, then in groups of 3, 2 players	a. Move quickly to open spaces to avoid being marked by the	p. 541

the ball: Offensive play-
ers dribble, pass, and
shoot while the defensive
player attempts to tackle.

on offense, 1 on defense.
Rotate positions frequently.

defense. Use all the space on
offense to make the job of the
defense more difficult. Pass with
control.

b. Game strategy and
rules.

b. Seated for discussion.

b. All players must play their
positions. Keep spread out. Use
all the space. Move to open spaces.
Play with control, using appropriate
force and keeping stick low.

III. Culminating Activity
a. Modified field hockey

a. In teams of 6 players, 2
games played simultaneously.

a. Attack should move toward   p. 550
goal when a teammate has the
ball. No more than 2 players
should attempt to play the ball
at a time. On defense mark only
your player. Keep spread out to
create spaces on offense.

340

SPECIFIC OBJECTIVES/EVALUATIVE CRITERIA	EQUIPMENT

To pass forward and laterally to a moving receiver, control-
  ling force.
To catch a pass while moving, reaching out, watching ball
  into hands, and pulling it in toward the body.
To place kick a ball, contacting ball with instep, and follow-
  ing through in desired path of the kick.
To hold a ball steadily for a place kick, holding ball with
  fingers on same side as kicking foot.
To run with a ball inbounds, and carrying it close to
  the body.
To move within the boundaries of the playing area.
To close spaces to the ball carrier on defense.
To move to an open space on offense.

Flag football belts and flags
Junior footballs or foam balls

ACTIVITY	PROCEDURES/ORGANIZATION	POINTS OF EMPHASIS	REFERENCES

I. Opening Activity

a. Pass and catch. Part-
ners forward passing and
catching 10'-20' apart.
Partners lateral passing
and catching.

a. With a partner and ball
in general space. Increase
distance as you become warmed
up.

a. Follow through to target.
Lead receiver with the pass.
Watch ball into hands. Reach
out and pull it in.

p. 555

b. Football fitness:
  1. Football jumps:
Students jump side-
ways, back and forth
over the ball, as fast
as possible for 15
seconds. (*FC)

b. Four stations. Students
rotate to each.

1. Use hands for balance.
Stay on balls of feet.

341

2. Football inchworm:
Hands on the ball in
pushup position, stu-
dents walk feet as far
away as possible, then
back in.

3. Modified situps:
traditional or 2 students
playing catch with a football as they do situps.

4. Stretches. (*FS) (*FF)

4. Self space. Using
stretches taught and practiced in previous classes.

2. Use arms and shoulders to
support weight. Focus on
their strength to keep you up.
Move feet back in small steps.

3. Throw and catch in the "up"
position, both players going
up simultaneously.

4. Slow, static stretches.

II. Motor Skills/Movement
Concepts
a. Center/quarterbacking:
review skills/practice.
Hiking relay: 1 partner
hikes to the other. Each
turns around. The receiver
now becomes the hiker and
the hiker, the receiver.
The first team to complete
10 successful hikes is the
winner.

a. Seated for group demon-
stration/discussion; then
with a partner 6' away.

a. Quarterback calls out signals. How can the center make
sure the ball is hiked into
the quarterback's hands?
Quarterback should have hands
extended and ready. A missed
hike takes time. Accuracy is
the most critical factor.

pp. 559-561

342

b. Place kicking: intro-
duce/practice. Kicking
practice.

b. Seated for group demon-
stration/discussion; then
in groups of 3, 1 kicker,
1 holder, 1 receiver. After
each turn, players rotate
to different positions.

b. Ball holder uses index
finger, faces in direction of
the kick and is on the same
side as the kicking foot.
Ball is contacted on the instep. Leg follows through in
direction of the kick.

pp. 559-561

c. Ball carrying: ball
carriers run through
playing area, "tacklers"
try to tag them by tak-
ing flags. If you are
tagged or run out of
bounds, change places
with the "tackler". (*FC)

c. In general space, half
the students with balls.
Change roles after 1 minute.

c. Carry ball close to body.
Twist and turn to avoid
"tacklers". Use all the space,
but stay within boundaries.

p. 559

III. Culminating Activity
a. Kick return. Receiver
tries to score a touch-
down by running over a
goal line formed by 2
markers. Both the kicker
and the holder try to tag
the runner. Several small
fields can be made with
markers so that everyone
may play at one time.

a. Groups of 3, 1 kicker,
1 receiver, 1 holder.

a. How can the kicker and the
holder work together to cut
off the runner's pathway to
the goal? The runner will
need to fake the chasers to
elude them.

SPECIFIC OBJECTIVES/EVALUATIVE CRITERIA	EQUIPMENT

To use as much space as possible on offense.

To block an opponent from a forward/backward stride position, head up, arms down and in close to body, holding shirt at shoulders.

To defend an opponent, preventing him from catching a pass.

To play within boundaries, aware of available space.

To run a pass pattern quick enough and short enough to catch a pass.

To center the ball accurately to the quarterback.

Flag football belts and flags
Junior footballs or foam balls
Traffic cones or markers

ACTIVITY	PROCEDURES/ORGANIZATION	POINTS OF EMPHASIS	REFERENCES

I. Opening Activity

a. Tear tag. Each player tries to pull off as many flags ask possible. When a player loses two flags, he steps out of the playing area. This penalty is minimized because the game lasts only 30-60 seconds. (*FC)

a. Scattered in general space.

a. If a player steps on or over a boundary line, he must take off one flag. Always be aware of the boundary lines as well as the open spaces. Twist and turn to protect flags.

b. Stretches. (*FF)

b. Self space. Individual stretching. A good time to discuss space concepts regarding the game.

b. Slow, static stretching.

II. Motor Skills/Movement
Concepts

a. Blocking. Review/ practice: on a signal by the teacher, the 1 defensive player tries to move through the 2 offensive players to touch a ball 6' behind them.

a. Seated for group demonstration/discussion, then groups of 3, 1 on defense, 2 on offense.

a. Feet apart, knees flexed. Hold shirt at shoulders. Head up, elbows down. Contact is light, and involves moving into the pathway of the opponent.

pp. 560-562

b. Defending the pass.
   1. Defensive skills.

   1. Seated for group demonstration/discussion.

   1. Defensive player should stay behind the receiver and move quickly to intercept the pathway of the ball when the player turns.

   2. Pass patterns.

   2. Seated for group demonstration/discussion.

   2. The pass pattern should be quick and short for greater accuracy. Keep running once the turn is made.

p. 556

   3. Passer, receiver and interceptor: the center hikes the ball and runs a short pass pattern. The defender attempts to block or intercept the pass from the quarterback. Rotate positions after each turn.

   3. Groups of 3, 1 defensive player, a center, a quarterback.

   3. Change speed to get away from defender. At what distance were you most effective as a passer?

III. Culminating Activity
    a. One-down football.

a. Organized in teams of 5, 3 line players and 2 backs. Several games going on simultaneously.

a. Offensive players should spread out to create open spaces for running and passing. Strongly encourage (or make a rule) that each player gets to be a back and carries or passes the ball. Defending team needs to work together to close space to the offense.

p. 567

SPECIFIC OBJECTIVES/EVALUATIVE CRITERIA	EQUIPMENT

To twist and turn to avoid being tagged. To lateral pass, bringing ball across body in an underhand motion, releasing ball with control at waist height. To play a variety of positions in a game situation, understanding the skills and responsibilities of each. To anticipate the path of the ball and opponents to intercept.	Flag football belts and flags Junior footballs or foam balls

---

ACTIVITY	PROCEDURES/ORGANIZATION	POINTS OF EMPHASIS	REFERENCES

ACTIVITY	PROCEDURES/ORGANIZATION	POINTS OF EMPHASIS	REFERENCES
I. Opening Activity a. Moving lateral pass. As they jog, the player on the right passes to the next player on his left, then moves to the end of the line.	a. Groups of 4 in a line, jogging forward. Players are 4'-6' apart, each slightly behind the person on his right.	a. Bring ball across body in preparation for the pass. Throw with an underhand motion from both hands, releasing ball about waist height. How far can you go without dropping a pass? Can you get to the end of the line quickly enough to receive the ball? What can you do to make this a team effort?	p. 556
II. Motor Skills/Movement Concepts a. Anticipating the path of the ball and opponents to intercept. Quarterback passes to moving receiver while defender tries to intercept.	a. In groups of 3, 1 quarterback, 1 receiver and 1 defensive player.	a. Where should you position yourself to be able to move for an interception? Offense: how can you disguise your intentions?	p. 563

III. Culminating Activity
    a. Modified flag foot-
       ball game.

a. Game may also be modified
to 4 players on a team, with
several games taking place if
facilities and supervision
allow. Change positions
periodically.

a. Use a variety of plays,
passes, pitchouts, hand-
offs, etc.

p. 567

| SPECIFIC OBJECTIVES/EVALUATIVE CRITERIA | EQUIPMENT |

To use a paddle and ball in a variety of ways.
To perform a serve, shaking hands with the paddle, turning the opposite side in the direction of the hit, dropping the ball in the front and to the side of the body, and swinging with a smooth level swing.
To record your best performance.

Nerf tennis balls
Paddles
Skill cards and pencils

ACTIVITY	PROCEDURES/ORGANIZATION	POINTS OF EMPHASIS	REFERENCES
I. Opening Activity			
a. Moving the ball with the paddle: Moving in general space. steer the the ball on the floor with a paddle. Move in a variety of ways.	a-b. In general space, with a paddle and ball.	a. Shake hands with the paddle. Keep the ball close to you as you move. What ways can you move and maintain control of the ball?	
b. Roll the ball around on the paddle face. Repeat standing on one foot.		b. Watch the ball. Move the paddle carefully to keep the the ball from rolling off. Was it more difficult to control the ball when you were trying to balance?	
II. Motor Skills/Movement Concepts			
a. Bouncing the ball with a paddle:	a-c. In self space with a paddle and ball.		p. 570-571
1. Count the number of consecutive bounces.		1. Contact the ball with the center of the paddle.	

2. Bounce the ball
tracing your shadow
(or following a line
on the floor.

3. Bounce the ball
turning the paddle
over to hit with
the opposite surface
on each hit.

4. Bounce the ball
changing the level
of the bounce.

b. Hit the ball in the
air:
1. Repeat as many times
as possible without
losing control.

2. Turn the paddle over
alternately hitting with
the opposite surface.

c. Alternately hit the ball
up and then down to bounce
on the floor.

2. Push the ball a little
ahead of you. as if you were
dribbling. Control the force.

3. Control the paddle to
contact the ball in the
center of the paddle.

4. Vary the force to control
the level of the ball? Was it
more difficult to control a high
or low bounce?

1. Control the force, only   pp. 570-571
hitting the ball as high as
you can control it for repeated
hits.

2. Control movement of paddle
to time paddle and ball.

3. Control the force to keep
the ball going.

d. Serving. Introduction/
practice.

  1. Drop the ball in
front of the body and
catch it.

  2. Drop the ball, bring
hand back, come through
and catch ball slightly
in front of the body.

  3. Drop ball and strike
it with the hand. After
a few tries, use a
paddle to hit the ball.

  4. Serve to a wall target.

III. Culminating Activity
  a. Paddle challenges:
Repeat any of the activ-
ities above and record
personal bests on skill
cards.

d. With a ball and a wall
space. Place the paddle on
the floor for activities 1-3.

  4. Hit to a large wall
target.

a. In self space with a ball
and paddle.

p. 572

  1. Control ball drop to land
in front of the body on the
serving side.

  2. Catch the ball where you
would make contact if you
were to hit it.

  3. Coordinate ball drop and
swing. Swing through the ball.
Now do the same thing with a
paddle. Grip the paddle as if
shaking hands with it. p. 575

  4. Can you control the serve to
hit the target. Where did you
follow through?

a. Work for control of the paddle
and ball. Create just enough force
to accomplish the task.

SPECIFIC OBJECTIVES/EVALUATIVE CRITERIA	EQUIPMENT

To vary the force and pathway of the serve.

To review the forehand stroke with side facing forward, legs flexed, paddle brought back and then forward with a level swing, contacting ball to the side and slightly ahead of the forward foot, and following through to the target.

To review the backhand stroke, turning hand over on paddle, side facing direction of hit, swinging through with a level swing, and contacting the ball to the side and slightly ahead of the forward foot.

To assume a ready position with legs flexed and a comfortable distance apart, and paddle up in front of the body.

To control paddle and ball in paddle challenges.

To play a game varying the force of hits.

To record your personal best scores.

Equipment:

Nerf tennis balls

Paddles

Skill cards and pencils

ACTIVITY	PROCEDURES/ORGANIZATION	POINTS OF EMPHASIS	REFERENCES

ACTIVITY	PROCEDURES/ORGANIZATION	POINTS OF EMPHASIS	REFERENCES

I. Opening Activity
  a. Paddle Challenges:
    1. Pick-ups: Place ball on the floor to the outside of the foot. Squeeze the ball between the paddle and foot and lift it up.
	a. With a paddle and ball in self space. Some challenges require a wall space.	1. Can you do this with the inside of the foot? Your heel?	pp. 570-571

2. Repeat challenges from previous lessons. Record personal best scores.		2. Work for control of paddle and ball.	

b. Stretches. (*FF)

b. In self space. Individual stretching.

b. What muscles need stretching for today's activities?

II. Motor Skills/Movement Concepts

a. Serve placement: Partner calls placement to the wall targets. Serve 3 balls to each placement called.

a. With a partner and a wall space. Each student has a paddle and ball. Several targets on the wall.

a. How did you direct the ball to the target called? Have your partner check the follow through of your hit. Did you control the force of your hit?   p. 575

b. Forehand: review/ practice. Partners alternate hits to the wall.

b. Seated with partner for review, then working at a wall.

b. Assume a good ready position. Side is turned in the direction hit. Bring paddle back and then forward with a level swing. Follow through in desired direction of hit.   p. 575

c. Backhand: review/ practice. Partners alternate hits to the wall.

c. Seated with partner for review, then working at a wall.

c. Assume a ready position. Turn hand over on paddle. Bring paddle back and then forward with a level swing. Follow through to target.   p. 575

III. Culminating Activity

a. Wall paddle tennis

a. 2 or 4 players in a small court.

a. Work to control hits. Can you vary the force and placement of your serve? Be ready to move for a forehand or backhand hit.   p. 583

SPECIFIC OBJECTIVES/EVALUATIVE CRITERIA   EQUIPMENT

To perform backhand and forehand strokes with appropriate   Paddles
  grip, a level swing, and follow through in the intended   Nerf tennis balls
  direction of hit.   Skill cards and pencils
To vary the placement of serves.
To hit the ball so it rebounds into an open space.
To change the expected path of the ball.
To work for control of paddle and ball in paddle challenges.
To record your personal best score.

| ACTIVITY | PROCEDURES/ORGANIZATION | POINTS OF EMPHASIS | REFERENCES |

I. Opening Activity
  a. Paddle challenges: | a. With a paddle and ball in | a. Work for control of paddle | pp. 570-571
Work on challenges from | self space. Some require a | and ball. Note improvements
previous lessons, record- | wall space. | over the 6 lessons.
ing personal best scores.

  b. Paddle stretches. (*FF) | b. In self space, students | b. Slow, static stretching.
| lead stretches with paddles. | Where do you feel the stretch?

II. Motor Skills/Movement
  Concepts
  a. Individual practice: | a. In self space with a ball | a. Work for control of the ball.
Students work on skills | and paddle. | Use appropriate grip, turn body
needing more work. | | so side faces direction of hit.
| | Swing should be level and control-
| | led. Follow through. Vary force and
| | placement.

b. Hitting to an open space: Partner moves to various parts of the court. Hitter tries to place ball away from them.

b. In groups of 3, with a wall space. Each with a paddle and ball. One hits, one moves, one retrieves.

b. Check follow through on each hit. Did the ball go where you intended? Did you hit the ball to the open space?

pp. 575-576

c. Changing the expected path of the ball: Hit the ball so it hits the wall to the left and right of the court.

c. In partners with a wall space.

c. Vary the placement of your hits. Plan where the ball will go. If it does not go where you want it to go, check your position on the hit and follow through.

pp. 575-576

III. Culminating Activity
a. Wall paddle ball

a. 2 or 4 players on each court.

a. Try to control your hits varying force and placement. Try to hit to open spaces.

p. 583

SPECIFIC OBJECTIVES/EVALUATIVE CRITERIA	EQUIPMENT

SPECIFIC OBJECTIVES/EVALUATIVE CRITERIA	EQUIPMENT
To dribble a soccer ball, tapping the ball with the inside of the foot.	Soccer balls or rubber balls Pinnies or vests
To juggle the ball 2-3 consecutive times, alternately absorbing and creating force.	
To pass the ball ahead of the receiver with the inside or outside of the foot, controlling force so the ball may be easily controlled.	
To head the ball from a forward/backward stride position, upper body and head back to watch ball coming to forehead, and projecting the head through the ball.	
To contact a ball with various body parts, lining up with ball and giving on contact.	
To mark an opponent, staying with him/her on the goal side of the ball.	
To move to an open space on offense.	

ACTIVITY	PROCEDURES/ORGANIZATION	POINTS OF EMPHASIS	REFERENCES

ACTIVITY	PROCEDURES/ORGANIZATION	POINTS OF EMPHASIS	REFERENCES
I. Opening Activity a. Soccer dodge: each student dribbles, avoiding contact with anything. If a player's ball touches anything, he does 10 soccer jumps over the ball, then returns to play.	a. General space.	a. Keep head up, watch for other players and balls moving nearby. Move into open spaces. Keep ball near feet and under control at all times.	
b. Stretches. (*FF)	b. Self space. Stretches led by a student leader.	b. Work slowly and smoothly on quadriceps and hamstring muscle groups.	

II. Motor Skills/Movement
Concepts

a. Juggling.

a. Students in self space, each with a ball.

a. Repeat, giving with the ball and then creating a little force to juggle the ball. Small, light movements will help keep ball close and under control. Patience. This skill requires practice. Try to improve the number of consecutive contacts with the ball.

pp. 593-594

b. Team passing: review inside and outside of the foot passing/practice. Three-person passing: one person from each line moves down the field passing from center to wings and back.

b. Seated for group demonstration/discussion, then divided into 3 lines.

b. Lead teammate with the pass. Pass quickly and directly. When receiving the pass, control the ball, dribble briefly, then pass.

p. 593

c. Heading: one partner tosses 5 times, while the other heads the ball back. If this skill is accomplished, players may head the ball back and forth consecutively.

c. Seated for group demonstration/discussion, then in partners 3'-8' apart.

c. Feet spread in forward/ backward stride position. Upper body and head bent back in anticipation of the ball. Watch ball come to head - project head through ball.

p. 598

d. Creating open spaces by drawing an opponent: two attempt to pass, while a third attempts to intercept. If intercepted, the defender becomes a passer and the person making an errant pass, the defender.

d. In groups of 3.

d. Passers use as much space as possible. Do not pass until defense commits to person with the ball.

pp. 602-603

III. Culminating Activity

a. Team keep away: review marking and play the game: 2 partners use dribbling, passing, and ball control to keep the ball from the other players.

a. Seated for discussion, then in groups of 4, with pinnies or vests.

a. Offense: move to an open space when you do not have the ball. Keep head up when handling the ball; watch for your partner and the opposing players. Defense: mark by staying with opponent between ball and other offensive players.

SPECIFIC OBJECTIVES/EVALUATIVE CRITERIA	EQUIPMENT

To juggle a ball using many body parts, alternately absorbing and creating force.
To pass to a space in front of a teammate, controlling force
   so ball is easily controlled.
To throw-in to a teammate with 2 hands, feet in contact with
   ground behind sideline, and leading the receiver.
To head the ball, moving to meet ball, watching ball coming to
   forehead, and projecting head through ball.
To move to an open space to receive a pass.

Soccer and rubber balls
Pinnies or vests

ACTIVITY	PROCEDURES/ORGANIZATION	POINTS OF EMPHASIS	REFERENCES

| I. Opening Activity
a. Team juggling: count number of consecutive contacts with the ball. | a. Partners in self space. Repeat several times. | a. Small, light movements. Keep ball moving vertically. Call, "I've got it," when the ball is between players. Try to gradually increase your score. | p. 593 |
| b. Partner soccer dodge: partners dribble and pass throughout playing area. If the ball touches anything, they must each do 15 soccer jumps over the ball, then resume play. | b. Partners in general space. | b. Always look for and move into open space. Keep head up to see all people and objects in the immediate area. Pass in front of receiver, controlling force so ball is easily controlled. | p. 589 |

II. Motor Skills/Movement Concepts.

a. The throw-in.

1. Introduce/practice. One partner throws the ball to the other; change places and repeat several times.

a. Seated for demonstration, then with a partner in general space.

1. Throw from behind the head, with feet in contact with the ground. Look for an open teammate, then lead him/her with the throw-in.

pp. 600-601

2. Throw-in, pass back: the person who throws in moves down the field to receive a pass.

2. After throwing in, move toward the goal to receive pass. On receiving the throw-in, control the ball and pass quickly to partner moving toward the goal.

b. Heading. Head-control pass: one partner tosses, the other heads it back. First partner then controls the ball and passes it back to the header. The header controls the ball and begins the process with a new toss.

b. Seated for group demonstration/discussion, then in partners in small area.

b. Move to meet the ball. Watch the ball. Project head through ball.

p. 598

III. Culminating Activity

a. Advanced alley soccer. Review/play. The offensive team brings the ball from midfield and attempts to score. Play ends when a goal is scored.

a. Students divided into teams of 6, 3 on defense: 1 goalie and 2 fullbacks; the other 3 on offense with a center and 2 wings. Rotate positions after each goal.

a. Each player must be responsible for playing his/her position. Stay in your alley. Quick passes will beat the defense. Move to an open space to receive pass. Defense: be in position between marked player and goal.

p. 608

SPECIFIC OBJECTIVES/EVALUATIVE CRITERIA	EQUIPMENT

To close space to the offense near the goal.   Soccer and/or rubber balls
To pass with control to a space ahead of receiver.
To identify and play various positions in a game situation.
To use as much space as possible on offense to keep defense
   spread out.
To dribble, shielding ball from opponent.

ACTIVITY	PROCEDURES/ORGANIZATION	POINTS OF EMPHASIS	REFERENCES
I. Opening Activity			
a. Partner passing.	a. In general space with a partner and a ball.	a. Move to an open space. Control pass to partner. Lead your partner with the pass.	p. 593
b. Dribbling and shielding: one partner ner attempts to dribble and control the ball, keeping it from partner. When the ball is stolen, the other person becomes offense and the roles are switched.	b. Partners in a small area (20'x20').	b. Keep head up, watch your partner. Keep ball close to feet, moving in a small area. Move body between ball and partner to shield it from partner.	pp. 589, 602

II. Motor Skills/Movement
Concepts

a. Using as much space as possible on offense to keep defense spread out: one team attempts to complete 5 consecutive passes, while the other team tries to intercept. Score 1 point each time 5 passes are completed.

a. Teams of 2 players in limited space. Repeat, gradually increasing the space.

a. Move to an open space. How did the increased space help you complete your passes?

p. 602

b. Closing spaces near the goal on defense: on signal, both run out to get to the ball. The first one to the ball tries to dribble it to the end line. The player not getting the ball plays defense, trying to force the other player over the sideline or away from the goal.

b. With a partner and a ball in a limited area.

b. On offense use as much space as possible, dribbling while shielding the ball. On defense try to position self on goal side and to the inside of players to keep them from goal and force them out-of-bounds.

p. 602

III. Culminating Activity
a. Introduce modified soccer: review position play, rules and strategy. Play the game.

a. Seated for discussion, then organized into teams of 7 players.

a. Each player must play his/her position and avoid chasing the ball. What do we do when hand ball occurs? An out-of-bounds? A foul? On offense move to an open space toward the goal for a pass. Keep spread out to create space for teammates and the ball. On defense position yourself on goal side of player you are marking.

p. 609

SPECIFIC OBJECTIVES/EVALUATIVE CRITERIA

EQUIPMENT

To run the bases in the fastest way, stepping on the inside
   corner and running in a straight line between bases.
To overrun first base, running past the base at full speed.
To bunt, facing pitcher, focusing on ball, knees flexed,
   hands apart, bat parallel to the ground.
To field a batted ball, moving in line with ball, getting
   low, giving with ball on contact, and covering ball in
   glove with other hand.
To identify and play each position in the field.
To recognize the area to be covered by each position in the field.

Softball bats and balls
8 bases
Gloves
Batting tees (optional)

ACTIVITY	PROCEDURES/ORGANIZATION	POINTS OF EMPHASIS	REFERENCES

I. Opening Activity			
a. Running the bases: one after the other, students run the bases 2 times around. (*FC)	a. Two sets of bases, students divided into groups one positioned behind each of the bases.	a. Step on the inside of the base. Run a straight line between the bases. Run fast!	p. 619
b. Running to first: first persons in line run, trying to beat other runners to first base.	b. Four sets of 2 bases, home and first base. Students divided into 4 groups, 1 behind each home plate. Runners will run against those of comparable ability.	b. Overrun first base to ensure top speed in getting there.	

II. Motor Skills/Movement
Concepts
a. Bunting.

1. Demonstration/
practice. Each part-
ner does the bunt posi-
tion and motion while
the other watches and
and helps.

1. Students in a semicircle
around home plate for demonstration and explanation,
then divided into partners
sharing a bat.

1. Move to a position facing
the pitcher. Knees flexed,
eyes focused on ball. Slide
top hand up bat toward trade-
mark, fingers and thumb behind
the bat, bat parallel to ground.

p. 618

2. Bunting a ball.

2. One partner pitches, the
other bunts. They stand
10'-15' apart.

2. Pitch to bat. Watch ball
carefully. Turn, slide hands
to position. Control bat
parallel to ground to meet ball.

b. Fielding and throwing
to a base. Review/prac-
tice fielding. The
batter throws a grounder
into the infield. The
appropriate fielder fields
the ball and throws to
the base player called
by the batter.

b. Groups of 4, with a home
plate, 1st and 2nd bases for
each group. Players rotate
positions after every 10
throws.

b. Batter must throw grounders
within field of play. The
fielder must line up with ball,
get down low with hands and body
to prevent the ball from rolling
through. Give on contact and
cover ball in glove with other
hand. How did you cover the
space with other infielders?

pp. 616, 620

III. Culminating Activity
a. Workup.

a. Two games going on simultaneously, with modification
of positions for number of
players in each game.

a. No strikeouts are allowed.
Players must know every position and think of their re-
sponsibilities as they change
to each new position. Work
with other players to cover
all the space.

p. 627

<table>
<tr><td>SPECIFIC OBJECTIVES/EVALUATIVE CRITERIA</td><td>EQUIPMENT</td></tr>
</table>

SPECIFIC OBJECTIVES/EVALUATIVE CRITERIA	EQUIPMENT
To hit a pitched ball into specific areas, turning the body in direction of intended hit. To pitch with control, stepping forward and releasing the ball toward the strike zone. To recognize the area covered by infields and outfielders. To play various positions in the field, covering all areas in that position. To cover a base without interfering with the runner.	Traffic cones or bases Softball bats, gloves and balls Batting Tees (or large traffic cones)

ACTIVITY	PROCEDURES/ORGANIZATION	POINTS OF EMPHASIS	REFERENCES
I. Opening Activity			
a. Jog, toss and catch: partners jog throughout the field area tossing a ball back and forth. (*FC)	a. In general space with a partner.	a. No gloves are used. Use only the right hand; left hand; 2 hands. How many different ways can you toss and catch?	
b. Grounders: students roll ball back and forth to each other, quickly fielding and rolling it back.	b. Students in 2 lines facing each other.	b. Use 1 hand to pick up and immediately roll the ball. Get down low in the pathway of the rolling ball.	
c. Stretches. (*FF)	c. Self space, individual stretching.	c. Slow, static stretching. Spend time on the shoulders and triceps group and discuss their use in throwing.	
II. Motor Skills/Movement Concepts			

a. Batting skills. Review/practice. Hitting into a designated area.

a. Seated for demonstration, then in groups of 4, a batter, a pitcher and 2 fielders.

a. A slower, controlled swing will allow the hitter to place the ball better. Smooth, level swing. Turn body to line up with intended placement.

pp. 617-618

b. Pitching skills. Review/practice. Pitching to a batter.

b. Seated for demonstration, then practicing with batting in a.

b. Pitcher must release pitch and place ball over the plate between batter's armpits and knees.

pp. 614-615

c. Position play.
1. Outfield positions.

1. Group demonstration using students in those positions. Brief demonstration, as this concept is most easily taught during the game situation.

1. Fielders must be in ready position (knees flexed, feet spread) to cover a large area when ball is hit.

pp. 613, 620

2. Infield positions.

2. Group, brief demonstration.

2. Base players are fielders first, then base players. Cover your part of the infield, moving to the base before the ball is thrown. The base player must touch the side of the base so as not to interfere with the runner.

III. Culminating Activity
a. Three-on-three softball game: a team gets 1 out, then sides change. No walks or strikeouts. A batter stays up until a hit is made hitting off a tee (or large traffic cone) after 5 pitches.

a. Students in groups of 3 playing a modified game against 3 other players. Team at bat furnishes a catcher. Each game has a home plate, 1st and 3rd bases. (Traffic cones make good bases.)

a. Players must move to the positions that will cover the most territory. (Usually a team will have 2 fielders and a pitcher.) Decide and agree on how you will cover the bases and field areas.

SPECIFIC OBJECTIVES/EVALUATIVE CRITERIA	EQUIPMENT

To play various positions in the infield and outfield.	Bats, balls, gloves
To run the bases safely, stepping on the inside corner and moving in a straight pathway between bases.	8 bases, Batting tees (or large traffic cones)

ACTIVITY	PROCEDURES/ORGANIZATION	POINTS OF EMPHASIS	REFERENCES

ACTIVITY	PROCEDURES/ORGANIZATION	POINTS OF EMPHASIS	REFERENCES
I. Opening Activity			
a. Run the bases: one after the other the players run the bases twice around.	a. Two sets of bases with players divided into groups, 1 group behind each base.	a. Step on the inside of each base. Run the straightest line to each base.	
b. Stretches. (*FF)	b. Self space.	b. Slow, static stretching.	
II. Motor Skills/Movement Concepts			
a. Throw and catch.	a. In partners, using a variety of flies, grounders, and straight throws.	a. Throw at a variety of levels and forces. Throw quickly. Be ready to move to the ball.	
III. Culminating Activity			
a. Modified softball mini-tournament.	a. Class is divided into 4 teams (players placed on a team ahead of time by the teacher). Each team plays the other one time. Two playing diamonds are used. Infielders and outfielders change each inning. No strikeouts. Use tee after 5 pitches.	a. With fewer players on a team, covering all areas of of your position is important. Be ready. Think ahead where best play might be made on next hit.	p. 627

| SPECIFIC OBJECTIVES/EVALUATIVE CRITERIA | EQUIPMENT |

To develop strength for the overhead volley (fingers and
   wrists).

To pass with an overhead volley, getting under ball, using
   arms and legs, and hitting ball with finger pads to a
   space above a teammate.

To pass with a forearm pass, getting under ball, keeping
   forearms level, and extending legs to project ball gently
   to a space above a teammate.

To serve, stepping on opposite foot, contacting ball at
   waist height, and following through in desired direction.

To vary force in the overhead volley.

EQUIPMENT

2 volleyball nets
Elementary size volleyballs
Foam balls
Plastic balls
Hoops

| ACTIVITY | PROCEDURES/ORGANIZATION | POINTS OF EMPHASIS | REFERENCES |

I. Opening Activity

  a. Group volley.

a. Group of 3 volleying across the net to another group of 3. Only the overhead pass may be used. No scoring; no serving. Each group of 3 plays a triangle with 1 person at the net and 2 people in back.

a. Volley for fun! How many consecutive volleys can you make? Strike the ball with the pads of the fingers. Get under the ball. Keep the ball high. Use your legs as well as your hands and arms.

  b. Warmup stations.

b. A warmup session with several stations. Students move from one to the other with a partner. Students may not complete the circuit each lesson and should pick

up where they left off the
previous lesson.

1. Partner overhead volley. Volley with the overhead pass.

1. Partners in self space.

1. Get under ball. Control force. Gently pass to space above partner.

2. Partner forearm pass. Volley with the forearm pass.

2. Partners in self space.

2. Flex knees to get under the ball. Keep forearms level. Control force to put ball into space above partner.

3. Partner push. One partner sits on the floor, the other stands behind with the ball. Sitting partner places fingers on ball held directly overhead (close to forehead) by standing partner. Standing partner presses gently on ball while sitting partner extends arms completely, slowly. Repeat 4 times. Reverse roles.

3. Partners, 1 sitting and 1 standing.

3. Standing partner creates enough downward force so sitting partner reaches extension slowly.

4. Bleachers or bench sets. One partner hits an overhead volley by hitting the ball out of the partner's hands.

4. Partners, 1 standing on a bench or bleacher holding the ball with arms extended. Second partner is positioned directly under the ball.

4. It is easier to hit a stationary target, so concentrate on creating force with legs and strong fingers.

5. Individual wall volleys. Students try to see how many consecutive wall volleys they can make. Catch balls not in high level and begin again.

5. Individual volleying against the wall.

5. Control force so ball comes back the same each time. Use legs. Stay under ball. Contact ball with finger pads.

6. Fingertip inchworm. Each student does the inchworm on the fingertips, 3 repetitions.

6. Self space.

6. This will strengthen the fingers and wrists for the overhead volley.

7. Wall serves. Each serves into a hoop (taped to the wall 8' high) or similar target - 3 repetitions.

7. Partners taking turns.

7. Smooth, easy serve. Step, contact, and follow through in the direction of the target.

II. Motor Skills/Movement Concepts
a. Serving underhand: review skills/practice. Serve to hoops scattered in playing area. Get 1 point for hoops in center of court, 3 points for those just over the net or near boundary lines.

a. Group demonstration/discussion. Then in partners on opposite sides of the net. Hoops scattered in playing area.

a. Step with opposite foot. Hand should follow through in the direction of flight. Contact is made at waist level. Try to hit hoops just over net or near side of end lines.

p. 637

b. Varying force: A
volleys ball alternately
to B and C.

b. In groups of 3, 2 on
1 side of the net, 1 (B)
at the net, the other (C)
in the back court, the third
(A) on the opposite side of
the net.

b. How did you vary force
to get ball to B and then
to C?

p. 636

III. Culminating Activity
a. Modified volleyball I.

a. Equal teams of 4 on opposite side of the net.

a. Pass to space above teammates. Back row cannot send
ball over the net, but must
pass to net players. Try to
control force to place ball
just over the net or to the
back court.

p. 641

SPECIFIC OBJECTIVES/EVALUATIVE CRITERIA	EQUIPMENT

To pass to a teammate with the overhead volley, getting under ball, extending legs on contact, and placing ball in space above teammate.	2 volleyball nets Elementary size volleyballs Foam balls Plastic balls
To pass to a teammate with forearm volley, getting under ball, using legs to create force and keeping forearms level.	
To use an appropriate skill for the level at which the ball is received.	
To move on the court in relation to teammates.	

ACTIVITY	PROCEDURES/ORGANIZATION	POINTS OF EMPHASIS	REFERENCES

ACTIVITY	PROCEDURES/ORGANIZATION	POINTS OF EMPHASIS	REFERENCES
I. Opening Activity a. Warmup stations: partner overhead volley. Partner forearm pass. Partner push. Bleacher or bench sets. Wall volleys. Fingertip inchworm. Wall serves. (*FS)	a. See volleyball Lesson 2. Students should begin where they left off during previous lesson.	a. More emphasis is now placed on working independently and striving to improve skills.	
II. Motor Skills/Movement Concepts a. Overhead volley: keep it up.	a-c. Groups of 4, keeping the ball alive with continuous volleys. Count each legal hit for a group score.	a. Call for a hit in your area. Pass high so the next player has a good play. Get under ball and control force.	pp. 635-636

b. Forearm volley: keep
it up.

c. Overhead/forearm com-
bination: keep it up.

d. Moving on court in
relation to teammates:
1 player throws ball up
with an underhand toss in
his/her position, as if not
controlling the ball. A
teammate moves into that
position and under the ball
to set it up to another
player who hits it over net.

III. Culminating Activity
  a. Modified volleyball II.

b. Get under ball. Use legs   pp. 634-635
to create force. Keep forearms
level.

c. Use the pass appropriate for
the level at which the ball is
hit.

d. In terms of 3 or 4 on   d. Player 1 must move away   p. 639
opposite sides of the net.   from the ball to allow team-
                                 mate to move to ball to hit
                                 it. Control force of set to
                                 net player.

a. Teams of 4 players on   a. Net players try to control   p. 646
opposite sides of the net.   ball without catching it.
                                 Control force in passing and
                                 setting to designated hitter.

373

SPECIFIC OBJECTIVES/EVALUATIVE CRITERIA	EQUIPMENT

To pass overhead or forearm to a space above a teammate.
To review the floater serve controlling ball toss, stepping
    forward on opposite foot, and contacting ball with open
    hand high and in front of the body.
To place the ball in an empty space in the opponent's court
    by varying force and path of the ball.
To work as a team, encouraging and supporting each other's
    efforts, and assuming responsibility for controlling force
    and placement in passing.

2 volleyball nets
Elementary size volleyballs
Foam balls
Plastic balls

ACTIVITY	PROCEDURES/ORGANIZATION	POINTS OF EMPHASIS	REFERENCES

I. Opening Activity
  a. Volleyball warmup
  stations. (*FS)

a. See Volleyball Lesson 2.
Students should now be able
to work independently so that
the teacher can assist those
who need special help.

a. See Volleyball Lesson 2.

  b. Team keep it up.
Players in game posi-
tions pass the ball as
many times as possible.
Ball is never hit across
the net. Try to increase
the number of consecutive
hits each time.

b. Four teams in their own
court area.

b. This activity builds team-
work and teammate support.
Call for every shot. Pass
ball high to make it easier
for teammates to get into position and control the ball.

II. Motor Skills/Movement Concepts

a. Review floater serve: servers serve ball over net, receivers roll it back. Change roles every 5 serves.

a. With a partner on opposite sides of the net. Server on 1 side, receivers on the other.

a. Control ball toss, transfer weight forward on contact with open hand high and in front of body.

p. 637

b. To place the ball in an empty space in opponent's court: players using overhead and forearm volleys. Play singles, score only when ball hits floor untouched by opponent.

b. With a partner on opposite sides of the net, using a small court area. When point is scored, play resumes with player losing the point.

b. Vary force and path of ball. Always look for empty space.

p. 638

III. Culminating Activity

a. Volleyball tournament: modified volleyball II.

a. Four teams playing round robin. Students select names for their teams. To maintain a schedule of games during a class period. A time limit for each game may be used in addition to the 15 point rule.

a. Pass with control Vary force and pathway in hitting ball across net. Look for the empty space in your opponent's court. Work as a team, supporting teammates.

p. 646